Leitrim Observed

A Biography of John McGahern

Aubrey Malone

Aureus Publishing

First Published 2023
Digital Edition 2023
©2023   Aubrey Malone
©2023   Digital Edition Aubrey Malone
©2023   Aureus Publishing Limited

Aubrey Malone has asserted the Author's right under the Copyright, Designs and Patents Act 1988 to be identified as Author of this Work.

All rights reserved.

Front cover photograph of John McGahern: ©Eamonn Farrell/Photocall Ireland
Cover design: ©Meuryn Hughes

Hardback ISBN :   978-1-899750-60-3
Paperback ISBN :   978-1-899750-67-2
EPUB ISBN :   978-1-899750-61-0

Printed and bound by CPI Group (UK) Ltd, Croydon, CR0 4YY.
A catalogue record for this book is available from the British Library.
Aureus Publishing Limited
Tel: 00 44 (0) 1656 880033
E-mail: sales@aureus.co.uk
Web site: www.aureus.co.uk

Social Media
https://www.facebook.com/aureuspublishing/
https://www.instagram.com/aureuspublishing/
https://twitter.com/AureusPublish

Acknowledgements

I would like to thank all the newspaper and magazine editors and librarians and researchers who have helped me in the writing of this book. Sincere thanks also to Kenneth Allen, John Bredin, Daniela Campbell, Ken Clay, Mary Conefrey, Mary Costello, Patrick Donald, John Donohue, Margo Donohue, Andrew Isidoro, Ivan Keaney, Keith Nolan, Uinsin O'Donabháin, Cian O'Sullivan, Colleen Quinn and Derek and Debbie Savage.

Aubrey Malone has written a number of novels and short story collections. His most recent books include Maureen O'Hara: The Biography (University of Kentucky Press) and Queer Cinema in America (Greenwood). He has also written biographies of Tony Curtis, The Defiant One (McFarland) and Charles Bukowski, Bukowski (JC Publications). In 2021 he published a study of the film Shane: Shane: Paramount's Classic Western (Bear Manor Media) and a fictional biography of Elvis Presley, The Elvis Diaries. Forthcoming are biographies of Marlon Brando (Propertius Books) and Ernest Hemingway (Fonthill Media).

A former teacher, he lives in Dublin.

Contents

Introduction	7
Early Years	11
Breaking Away From Home	19
Two Lives	32
First Strides in Publishing	43
On the Up and Up	50
Romantic Entanglements	57
Notoriety	69
Exile	84
Emerging from Writer's Block	91
Back to Leitrim	101
Change of Direction	112
New Decade	120
Farmer John	127
Moran and his World	133
From Page to Stage	149
Late Flowering	167
Devastation	173
The King is Dead	189
Aftermath	193
Notes	199
Bibliography	214
Index	217

Introduction

My life has mirrored that of John McGahern in many ways. My mother grew up in Roscommon as his did. Both of them were gentle people. Both had many children in a short time: nine in sixteen years in my mother's case and seven in nine years in his. Both were married to larger than life men who came from outside the county, though my father wasn't cruel like McGahern's was. And both of them died of cancer.

Like him I was pampered by my mother. Going from home to the often harsh discipline of school was a shock to the system as a result but such things are important in anyone's maturity. As Hemingway said, we become strong at the broken places.

I always felt my mother wanted me to be a priest like his did. In the end both of us settled for what McGahern called the "second priesthood" of teaching. It was a kind of substitute.

I also studied for this at St. Patrick's College in Drumcondra, like him. Though it was in a different decade to his time, a similar theocracy was in evidence. In many ways I felt I was in a seminary. There was even stained glass on the windows.

Like him I was drawn to teaching by the short days and long holidays. These gave me a lot of time to pursue my second avocation of writing. I eventually left the profession, as he did, to pursue this activity full time. Before I did so I read *The Leavetaking*, his masterly evocation of the end of that period of his life. Each time I turned a page I felt that, as well as reading his mind, he was reading mine.

There were other similarities between us. We both worked in England and America and travelled in Europe. We also both bought houses in the Stoneybatter area of Dublin in 1981, enjoying it for its bohemian atmosphere.

The first time I met him was in 1990 when he was promoting *Amongst Women*. I'd been trying to arrange an interview for months and it kept getting delayed. He wasn't the type of man to play hard to get. He was just busy. It had been a number of years since his last novel. There was a lot of heat around this one.

Portrait of the artist (Ivan Keaney)

I was painting the kitchen ceiling when he rang to firm up a date. He said he could meet me the following week at the North Star Hotel in Amiens Street. I had a set of questions for him. We'd gone through a few of these on phone calls. It meant I'd have less pressure at the meeting, and him too.

I got there before him on the night. He breezed in jauntily soon afterwards. He was wearing a suit and a tweed overcoat. I had expected something more rustic. Most of the photographs I'd seen of him had him in a woollen jumper. In some of them he was wearing a flat farmer's cap.

I ordered two pints of Smithwicks. He started talking about his brother who was working in London. He mentioned a figure he was earning per week. "What would you think of that?" he said, sounding suddenly like the farmer.

He knew I was from the west but not that I had connections in Roscommon. When I told him I had, he started mentioning the names of various people I might have known. Some of them I did. The so-called "six degrees of separation" count for little in Ireland.

I asked him about his life in teaching. I was about to leave my own teaching job at the time to become a journalist. That became another topic of conversation. Though I was a lot older than him when he'd left, he told me to be careful. "Writing is an uncertain profession," he said, "Just because it worked out for me doesn't mean it will for everyone." After various other detours we finally got around to the reason for our meeting: *Amongst Women*. (That was another thing we had in common – lots of sisters.)

I only met him once more afterwards but we talked many times over the phone. I could never say I became a friend of his but he spoke to me in the familiar tones I associated with friendship. I always felt he enjoyed talking to me as a fellow Connacht man. Maybe it was a tribal thing, both of us being "culchies".

Almost every young writer who knew McGahern at some stage asked him to look at their work. It was something to do with the aura he gave off, an aura of concern, of warmth. You got the feeling he'd find some diamond in the rough, some phrase or sentence that could impel any narrative towards greater heights with the proper direction. In school or out of it, he was still The Teacher.

He put many red marks through writings I showed him over the years but they were never inserted cruelly. He had a sense of how things should be done that was as true as his heart. There was no malice in it, no sense of one-upmanship. If something wasn't good it had to be thrown out. It was as simple as that. He kept the same strict standards for himself as he had for others. There could be no compromises.

A positive word from him was enough to make my day. Sometimes I found myself writing in the style he did, consciously imitating him so that he'd like what I wrote, overlooking the simple point that it was people's differentness from him that he looked for.

I passed close to his house many times in subsequent years in journeys west. My inclination was to drop in on him but I always resisted. Something held me back. It was as if the presence of The Master would have been too much, notwithstanding the welcome I knew I'd get, and the good wishes.

The last time I interviewed him was on the occasion of his seventieth birthday in 2004. I didn't know how ill he was with cancer at the time and he didn't mention it. Instead he talked about the things he'd always talked about – his books, his farm, the easygoing life of Leitrim where people didn't bother much about things like birthdays. It's easy to say it now but I didn't think he was himself on the call. I was aware of some zest having gone from him without knowing why.

He died in 2006. I was sitting in my car across the road from a school – perhaps fittingly – when the news came on the radio. I was stunned. It was as if a light went out of the world. As the tributes from people who knew him flowed in, I realised how little I really knew about him.

Years later I read his collected letters in the detailed compilation edited by Frank Shovlin. The last one he wrote – an email dictated to his wife Madeline - was to his solicitor, Tom Callan, in Boyle. In yet another dovetailing of our lives, I learned that a woman who worked in my house in Mayo for sixteen years, someone who came to us when I was only a few weeks old and was in many ways like a second mother to me, worked for this man for thirty years after she left us. It was as if the wheel had come full circle.

Early Years

A handsome young police sergeant called Frank McGahern started dating Susan McManus, a primary schoolteacher, in 1924 in the small Leitrim town of Ballinamore where she had her first job. Soon afterwards they became engaged. Eight years later, when Frank was still dragging his heels about bringing her to the altar, she gave him back his ring. Pressed into action at this, he proposed to her again. She said yes.

They were married in 1932, the year of the Eucharistic Congress. It seemed appropriate. McGahern often said that religion was "the weather" of his childhood. He was born two years later.

A pair of twins, Breege and Rosaleen, arrived soon afterwards. McGahern was so jealous of the twins he caused their pram to crash one day by unlocking the brakes. Then there was another girl, Margaret. Monica and Dympna followed before the last child. It was another boy. He was born in 1943. They called him Frankie.

Having so many children in so few years wasn't unusual in the Ireland of the time. There was little family planning to speak of and McGahern's father wasn't the type of man to abstain from sex. Men generally married for sex in those days. McGahern wrote in *Memoir*, "There was no other way to have it."[1]

His mother came from a poor family. She grew up on the side of a mountain. Pupils from the school she went to brought turf from their homes to light the classroom fire. She was clever at school and won a King's scholarship to a boarding school in Carrick-on-Shannon. She was the first person in her family to go to Secondary School. Afterwards she won another scholarship, to Trinity College in Dublin. She trained to be a teacher there.

She was a gentle teacher who refused to hit her pupils. That was expected from teachers at the time. Her casual attitude to discipline got her into some trouble with the authorities but made her very popular with the children she taught.[2]

Aughawillan School (Kenneth Allen)

Her job was never secure. She was placed on what was called "The Panel." It meant she wasn't guaranteed being kept in any of the schools in which she taught. It all depended on the numbers. If they fell below a certain quota she lost her job. It was a case of, "Last in, first out."

She worked in most of the schools in the area at one time or another. Each time she got a new job she had to move house as well. McGahern attended no less than seven schools by the time he was nine.

She and her husband lived apart for most of the year. That was because of a ruling of the time that a Garda sergeant wasn't allowed have a wife who worked. He wanted her to give up her job even though she was earning more than he was. She refused to do that. She lived in Leitrim. He lived – and worked – in a barracks in Cootehall. That was twenty miles away in Roscommon. The family went to the barracks during the school holidays. McGahern's father cycled to Leitrim on his days off.

She eventually got a permanent post at Aughawillan national school. The money she was earning enabled her to buy a house. She bought one that was attached to a farm. It was easier to do that than to find one on its own. It was a small bungalow outside the town of Ballinamore. She farmed as well as taught.

McGahern's paternal grandmother lived with them as he was growing up. She was a difficult woman to get on with. He spent the first two years of his life with her when his mother was teaching. When he was three, his mother decided to bring him to school with her. She led him by the hand through the lanes that surrounded their house. He stayed with her all day in the classroom to give his grandmother a break from him.

McGahern felt cut off from other children as a sergeant's son. "Because of the long history of oppression in Ireland," he said, "law was associated with the British. People never thought the police force belonged to them. It was seen as alien, a hostile force."[3]

His father tried to get him to stay with him in the barracks, telling him he was too much amongst women (or words to that effect) in Aughawillan. He saw their world as a female one, a haven that was far too cosy. In the barracks he told him he'd be able to grow up as a man. 'McGahern didn't want to go. He was afraid of his father because he beat him. He also beat his sisters. The police authorities knew about this and warned him to stop.

The beatings stopped for a while after he was warned but then they started again. His mother would also get hit if she tried to stop them. McGahern spent the whole of one day in a tree trying to stay out of his way.[4]

His belligerent nature had a legitimacy to it before he married. He'd been active in the War of Independence before Ireland became a Republic. McGahern listened to tales of violence told in hushed tones as he sat around the fire at night, tales of ambushes, "of men followed to Australia and murdered, tales of men dumped over the sides of boats."[5] His father was in his element relating these.

When he was applying to become a guard he was asked what his previous work experience was. He replied, "Three years in the IRA." This was said with great pride.

He resented the fact that he was never promoted beyond the rank of sergeant. The main reason was his temperament. He was regarded as a loose cannon. He may have been a hero to fellow republicans but once the War of Independence ended a different regime took over. People became fearful of his rages.

He wanted the police to be armed. There was a bank robbery one time in Ballinamore and the robbers got away without being caught. He was enraged. He told McGahern that if he had a gun on him that day, not one of them would have left the town alive.

McGahern was both fascinated and repulsed by him. He had so many sides to him he could never figure him out. His aggressiveness was tempered by a tendency towards hypochondria, his egotism by a deferential attitude he held towards members of the clergy and people of a higher class than him.

He had an obsessive terror of poverty, what McGahern would later refer to as "the racial fear of the poorhouse." He frequently told his children that they were eating too much and that one day they'd all end up there. Playing the martyr in terms of finance, he bored them by listing out all the food they'd eaten and what it cost. Such an inventory was generally followed by a recitation of the Rosary. This was exploited for every ounce of dramatic potential. As McGahern listened to him saying it he was more aware of an actor giving a performance than somebody getting in touch with their spiritual side.

His father embraced the theatrical aspect of religion; his mother its spiritual dimension. He sat at the front of the church and she at the back. McGahern got his emotional depth from her. From his father he inherited an attraction to splendour.

The Bible, he once said, was his first book and in many ways his most important one. When he was a young boy, heaven, hell and purgatory were more real to him than Canada or Australia.[6] He thought God was behind the clouds, that if he climbed up high enough in the sky he'd be able to see him.

Aughawillan Church (Kenneth Allen)

Religion was superimposed over nearly everything he did growing up. Not to attend Mass was to risk being seen as "mad or consorting with the devil." Life stopped every day when the Angelus bell rang. The Rosary was said nightly. The calendar was dominated by Lent, Easter, Advent and Christmas. On All Souls Night, "the dead rose and walked as shadows among the living."[7]

Religion gave succour to people suffering in the vale of tears, offering a reward to them in the next life if they managed to get through this one. The church was his introduction to "ceremony, colour and sacrament." Before the printed word, churches were "the Bibles of the poor."[8]

"The authority was paternalistic," he said, "God the father in heaven, the Pope in Rome, the father who said the Rosary each night in the house."[9] The "earthly" father was less than perfect, seeing life only in terms of what he could get out of it to benefit himself.

After Dympna was born, his doctor told him it would be highly inadvisable to impregnate his wife again. She'd already undergone an operation for breast cancer. The risk of recurrence was high. It would be reduced significantly if she didn't have any more children.

But there was one more child to come, somebody McGahern would refer to as "the cancer child." It was Frankie, the "baby" of the family. After he was born, as the doctor predicted, Susan's cancer returned.

McGahern's father wanted him to be called Jude after the patron saint of hopeless cases. This was because of her cancer. It was a morbid idea. He was christened Francis Jude but he continued to call him Jude as he grew up.

He also continued to have sex with her even after Frankie was born – and even after she developed another tumour.

The cancer was a direct result of what can only be called sexual abuse. The church colluded in such abuse, encouraging married women to submit to any kind of carnal demands from their spouses with the same determination as they told single women they would burn in hell for pre-marital sex.

McGahern's father didn't visit her when she went to hospital this time. He said it would be too upsetting for him. Just as he hijacked every other situation in life so that he could take charge of it, so he did with this one. When Susan's situation became hopeless he still didn't change, remaining virtually indifferent to the impending demise of the person who was supposedly closest to him in the world. Amazingly, she didn't blame him for that, her faith superseding any anger she might otherwise have felt.

This was bad enough but he had all her furniture removed from the house as she lay dying. Only her deathbed was left behind. It was the final ignominy. McGahern was the antithesis of this. He had to be pulled away from her bed. The thought of leaving her was too much to take. He was distraught at her funeral Mass, running out of the church after her name was read out.

Her death was unacceptable to him. He loved her too much. In fact he didn't just love her, he was "in love" with her. This was the expression he used right through his life. It was as if she was a wife rather than a mother.

She thought he was going to be a priest. He promised her he would, that he'd say his first Mass for her after he was ordained. Now he wouldn't be doing that. His promise was really made to keep her alive. Once she died, the deal was off. The dream became as dead as herself.

He wasn't sure if he was strong enough to deal with her passing. No longer would he be able to walk the grassy lanes of Ballinamore with her to the Aughawillan school. Instead he'd have to lead his sisters to other schools on concrete paths.

With the protective cocoon of his mother gone, he was left to the harsh regime of his father. He went to live with him in Cootehall. So did all his siblings. The farm was sold. They were sent from it to "the fortress of the enemy."[10]

Now his father would have him all to himself. He wouldn't have to share him with a woman who spoiled him, a woman he was too tied to. He thought McGahern was too effeminate, too much under her sway. On his own admission he had "a head of curls like a girl."[11] He could have been seen as a mother's boy.

The beatings started again after her death. One day he hit McGahern on the head with a shovel. Another time he gave Margaret such a beating she went into a cataleptic fit. He beat Breege so badly with a spade after she had an accident on her bicycle that she was limping for days afterwards. Some of the family, McGahern included, started walking in their sleep from shock as a result of the beatings.

Rosaleen did this even more frequently. As well as the shock from the beatings she suffered from delayed trauma over her mother's death. She eventually had to go to hospital in Roscommon for two months to recover. The guards heard many of the beatings at night time as they tried to sleep in the barracks. The family slept badly. They were too afraid he'd land in on them in the middle of the night. Asked how such a monster could have attracted a person like his mother, McGahern said it was probably physical. Either that or she was taken in by his charm.[12]

Nobody knew what to expect from him from one day to the next. His good moods, brief and all as they were, were treasured on that account. His daughters watched for them as they might watch for the sun to come out after a shower of rain.

McGahern thought he might have even been touched by madness. There was a strain of it in his family. Much of his violence, he thought, came from sexual frustration. "That was such a force in Ireland then, the battle between sex – or love of the world – and the love of God."[13]

He believed his happiest years were when he was in the IRA, "where his propensity for violence was tempered by cold calculation and a keen sense of self-preservation."[14]

He bullied people at work as well, enjoying throwing his weight around, pulling rank on people for minor infringements of the law. One day he lectured a man for fifteen minutes merely because he hadn't a light on his bike. Eventually the man had enough. He said, "For Christ's sake, Sergeant, lay off the sermon. Either let me off or give me a summons." He didn't like his tone so he summoned him.[15]

His daughters drew closer together in their distance from him, the shared fear of him acting like a kind of glue to bind them. That wasn't to say they never argued. Like all sisters they did, but divisions were never created from such exchanges. They made up soon afterwards. McGahern was outside their loop to an extent, both because of being a boy and because of his excessive devotion to his mother. This continued after her death, maybe even becoming intensified by it.

In time her absence strengthened him. Denied her love, he became hard. As the new head of the house – his father's authority being merely honorific now he grew closer to his sisters. Frankie was close to them in a different way. They enjoyed pampering him in the same way McGahern's mother had once pampered him.

He became more involved in the life of the barracks, watching his father going through the motions of policing with a mixture of amusement and boredom, becoming friendly with the other guards.

There wasn't much crime in the area. They struggled to think of things to do. Some days consisted of doing little but playing cards.

The guards had to write reports of patrols they took. These were often made up. They sat in the barracks or in their cars writing accounts of trip they never took. McGahern helped them with them sometimes. He referred to them as "patrols of the imagination." He said they were his first experience of writing fiction.

At home he tried to get on with his life. The house screamed at him with his mother's absence. Various maids were employed to do the housekeeping after she died. He found many of these cruel. Others were disturbed and eccentric. Some of them had crushes on his father because of his handsomeness. He wasn't very polite to them. One of them who wasn't very feminine developed the idea that she wanted to marry him. He said to her, "So you think you're the man for the job?"[16]

McGahern was often kept home from school to work on the bog or dig potatoes. In his leisure time he fished for eels on a boat they owned. In the summer he saved the hay.

One day his father found him using the potatoes to develop his footballing skills. He was trying to float them over a wall with the side of his foot, being trained in this by a friend of his who was in the local football team, Eddie McIniff.

When his father saw them he blew a fuse, telling McIniff to get lost. McGahern was ashamed of him. He hero-worshipped McIniff and thought the incident might affect his relationship with him. Thankfully it didn't. That relieved him. McIniff knew his father had a problem.

McGahern now drew further and further away from his father. He realised there was a world outside his home that he could belong to without him encroaching on it. This was an important moment for him. It gave him the confidence to tap into the social side of himself, to enter a world outside the jurisdiction of a freedom-hating demagogue.

Breaking Away From Home

There weren't many books in McGahern's house when he was growing up apart from the medical texts his mother had to read and some republican tomes his father owned. Reading was frowned on rather than encouraged: "It was thought to be dangerous, like laughter."[1]

His first real exposure to literature was in the home of their neighbours, the Moroneys. This was a family McGahern became almost more at home with than his own the more he got to know them. Remnants of the Protestant Ascendancy, they were as relaxed as his father was tense, as outward-looking as he was insular.

They had an air of faded grandeur about them, of "old money." McGahern was first sent to their house to sell apples. Willie Moroney was in his eighties at the time. His son Andy was about half that. Andy described himself as a "gentleman farmer." This was a phrase the people in Leitrim scoffed at. They said it was a contradiction in terms.

Willie kept bees. Andy did some amateur astronomy. McGahern thought he was in the wrong county for that. The skies tended to be very dark in Leitrim. Neither man cared much for domesticity, washing dishes when they felt like it and then letting them pile up for weeks until the mood took them again.

McGahern admired them for their easy attitude towards life. When he was talking to Willie one day he put some jam on a slice of bread he was eating and it got stuck on his beard. In no time at all the beard was beset with bees buzzing around it. Willie wasn't unduly bothered. He casually went out the door and hooshed them away.

The Moroney's had a vast library. They gave McGahern a free run of it, something he never failed to appreciate. He could only get at the top shelves by use of a ladder. They had books by everyone from Shakespeare to Zane Grey.

"At the time," he said, "I remember thinking Mr. Grey held the edge over Shakespeare."[2]. There were also a huge number of books about the Rocky Mountains. He never found out the reason for that. Somebody from the family must have gone there once – or wanted to. "I became an authority on the Rockies," he joked.

Every time he was leaving the house he'd bring about six books to Cootehall with him in an oilcloth bag on the carrier of his bicycle. He'd bring them back when he was finished with them and take six more. He read books, he said, in the same way a boy from a future generation might watch television or go to the cinema. He liked to quote Proust: "There are no days more full in childhood than those days that were not lived at all, the days lost in a favourite book."[3]

The broken gate of McGahern's childhood home
(Leitrim County Library Local Studies Collection)

To the young McGahern an author was like someone from Mars: "One didn't think of it as something that would happen to oneself." But he'd always had a feeling for words. Each one, he thought, had a colour and personality of its own.

He didn't think of books as being from particular writers. They were all like one big book. They opened up worlds. He read them for stories. It was only later that he thought about things like character, structure, style. That brought a different kind of excitement: "You could call it the shock of consciousness, where you realise these things are about your life."

From this point of view, reading was a more vivid experience than going to the cinema. It was more vivid because you had to imagine your own screen: "The reader's imagination is an artist in a way a filmgoer's can never be. The reader takes up where the writer leaves off."

The kindness of the Moroneys gave McGahern a very positive attitude towards Protestants and the Anglo-Irish. This class wasn't in favour with the community in which he grew up. It associated them with Ireland's ills in the past, not least the Great Famine. The distinct charms of the "Big House" culture would figure strongly in his work in years to come.

McGahern was surprised his father allowed him to spend so much time with the Moroneys. He concluded that, since they were Protestants, he took pity on them because they were "bound for hell in the next world." This was strange as he believed Protestants were purer in character than Catholics and much less mercenary. It didn't seem to strike him that these were hardly qualities designed to put people in hell. Religion apart, he liked them because they were posh. McGahern said he was so infatuated with them, his voice even changed when he spoke to them.

The Moroney's library helped McGahern develop his vocabulary and his general knowledge. Such things helped him when he went to secondary school. That was in Carrick-on-Shannon, the town where his mother was educated. He was happy there. The Presentation Brothers were good to him. Each day was "an anticipation of delights."[4] He studied hard. It didn't feel like work because he enjoyed it so much.

Sometimes his essays were read out in class. He didn't welcome this. It created a distance from the other pupils, as if he thought he was something special. Combined with being the son of the sergeant it made him feel even more alienated from them. He didn't want to be seen as a "teacher's pet" any more than he did a mother's boy.

He often recited poems out loud to himself as he cycled to school, the words of Shakespeare or Wordsworth or Tennyson etched into his brain. The roads were bad and he often got punctures. He spent many lunch breaks with his bicycle upside down in the corridor fixing it.

If he didn't have a puncture he played soccer at lunch time with a tennis ball. There was nothing else provided. Soccer was frowned upon in those days. It was the "foreign" game. Hurling and Gaelic football were all that were allowed.

He wondered what he'd do after he left school. He'd now decided not to become a priest. His mother's death had released him from that obligation. This was a relief to him. "The pull of life was too great."[5]

In later years he wrote about the moment he decided to be a writer rather than a teacher or priest: "Why take on any single life if a writer could create all these people far more vividly? In that one life of the mind the writer could live many lives, and all of life."

The John McGahern Museum in Leitrim (Keith Nolan)

He got top results in his Leaving Certificate. As a result he was given a scholarship to a teacher training college in Dublin. That was St. Patrick's ("Pat's") in Drumcondra. As soon as he'd done his exams he received "a call to training." That it was described as a call, he said, spoke volumes about the vocational origins of the profession.

Teaching wasn't McGahern's first choice of a career. He originally registered for Agricultural Science in Galway University.[6] This proved to be too expensive. As he said, "University was for the middle classes."[7]

He didn't have to pay for his accommodation or his tuition in "Pat's." It wouldn't have been feasible for him otherwise. "If I'd gone to university," He said, "I would have had to get first place in my class every year to keep the scholarship. Otherwise I wouldn't have been allowed to stay there."[8] He knew he wouldn't have been able to take that kind of pressure.

He kept his head down in Pat's, more so than he would have liked. He later felt he was too conformist there. The extent of his later rebellion against the church may have been a reaction against this.

Religion was the predominant influence rather than pedagogy. Daily Mass was mandatory. Absence from this led to automatic expulsion.

St. Patrick's Teacher raining College in Drumcondra

The atmosphere there was distinctly anti-intellectual. Any education he picked up, he said, was from the other students: "There wasn't a literary society, there wasn't a debating society, there wasn't a drama society." But there were lots of religious ones. "They weren't interested in education," he said, "What was under inspection was our characters. They wanted us to be obedient and conformist – cogs in a wheel of power."⁹ In many ways it was like a glorified secondary school.

He wasn't encouraged to read any experimental writers, only Catholic ones. Some racy French authors like Stendhal and Balzac slipped through the net because of the Catholic influence in France. Said McGahern, "I don't think they knew too much about these people." He later discovered Proust. He would become a favourite with him – indeed someone he would be compared to when he developed his own writing style.[10]

If students were seen reading any of the "progressive" writers like T.S. Eliot they were biffed on the back of the head.[11] He was too *outré*. Parochialism meant being against anything English – its literature, its mores, its culture. It was like, "D.H. Lawrence? Rubbish."[12] He was the "dirty" author of *Lady Chatterley's Lover*.

Behaviour patterns were laid down like laws. The way the students thought was also closely monitored. It was like a prison of the mind as well as the body, a theocracy that had the blessing of the state.

Nobody was allowed complain about anything. He saw a boy badly beaten one day when he complained to the authorities that his dinner had been taken away from him by some of the other students.[13]

As they ate they were waited on by boys in their early teens from a Catholic orphanage. "They had crew cuts," said McGahern, "and looked like young convicts. They wore little white tunics. We were like aristocrats by comparison."[14]

He didn't have to study much in St. Pat's. Getting in to the college was the hardest part. Once there, the standards dropped. "You needed 80 per cent in your exams to get in but only 40 per cent to graduate."[15]

He became friendly with a classmate called Éanna Ó hEithir, a nephew of Liam O'Flaherty. He introduced McGahern to the works of Joyce and Beckett, two writers he was yet to experience. They would become huge to him in time as they already were to most of his contemporaries. *Waiting for Godot* was playing in Pike Theatre at the time. He and Ó hEithir wrote a sketch based on it and produced it in the college. They were amazed they were allowed to.

Beckett was regarded as subversive at the time but they still got a full house. The people in the audience were so noisy they disturbed prayers that were being said in the college chapel at the time. The Dean stormed out in a rage. He was a strict disciplinarian whom they referred to as The Bat because he mainly came out at night. (He features in *That They May Face the Rising Sun* under that name.) McGahern thought he came within a whisker of being expelled from the college on account of the sketch.

He was only allowed out of it for three hours on Wednesday afternoons and four hours on Saturdays. Sundays were free days but he had to be in by ten o'clock at night. If anyone returned after that time they had to enter through the president's house and give an explanation.

McGahern heard of a student who got back late one night after leaving a girl home. He didn't want to have to present himself to the president so he decided to climb the wall that surrounded the college. He threw his trousers over first so he wouldn't tear them on the barbed wire that was on top of it. As soon as he got to the other side he saw The Bat standing in front of him with a flash lamp. "It won't happen again, Father," he said to him. The Bat smiled at him as if to say, "You're right." The next morning he was gone.[16]

Back in Leitrim McGahern's father was suffering. He hadn't taken well to widowhood, spending many years looking for someone to replace his dead wife.

Most of the women he met were unsuitable. The closest he came to marrying was the principal of a local school. He dropped her when he was given reason to think she might have had a heart problem. He was never good with any kind of sickness, either his own or anyone else's. He left McGahern to deliver a "Dear John" letter to her at a holiday resort where they were staying at the time.

He finally found a woman he liked enough to bring to the altar in 1954. Her name was Agnes McShera. He asked McGahern if he was in favour of him marrying her. He said he didn't mind one way or the other, that it was his own decision. Agnes took that to mean he didn't approve of her. There was always a distance between them afterwards. No woman could have replaced his mother for him but he would have tried harder to like her if he felt warmth coming from her. Instead of that he saw a darkness, the kind of darkness his father had. She said to him one day as she was smoking a cigarette, "I don't' think you'd be able to stand people if you didn't know they had to die."[17]

McGahern went to London for the summer of his twentieth year. He got the ferry to Holyhead and then the train to London. He was met at Heuston Station by men from a Catholic organisation who, he said, were monitoring youths like him who "might go wrong if let loose in London." They took him to a hostel run my Marist Brothers. There was a church on the grounds.

It doubled as a school. Every morning before he left for work he helped to put away the beds and replace them with desks. When he came home he was given a big meal. It was cooked by young Irish girls. Any flirting with them resulted in being sent home.

In the hostel he met a man who would become a good friend of his.

He was from Kilkeel in Northern Ireland. His name was Tony Whelan. McGahern was sitting on a bed putting on a pair of socks when Whelan walked in. He gave him a shy smile and held out his hand, introducing himself to him as "Sean." McGahern went by the name of Sean MacEachran in those days. The Gaelic language was the predominant one in his childhood years.

Whelan described the hostel as smelling of "male sweat and boiled cabbage." Most of the residents, he noted, were building site workers.[18]

He was working in a bookshop in the city at the time. This interested McGahern. They had a shared interest in literature. Whelan had ambitions of becoming a writer. McGahern hadn't developed such ambitions yet.

Whelan was more versed in the ways of the world than he was. One day McGahern said to him, "What do people do in restaurants?"[19] He must have felt like saying, "They eat!".

He got a job on the buildings. The work was hard but he didn't mind that. The people he met there provided him with fodder for some of his future work. Many of them were disgruntled emigrants. They carried bitterness with them about "the old sod."

McGahern liked telling the story of a man who, upon hearing that the rain was particularly bad in Ireland that year, said: "May it never stop. May it rise higher than it did for fukken Noah. May they all have to climb trees!"[20] Some accounts of McGahern's life suggest he worked on other building sites in later years because of the accounts of them in various stories. This is unlikely. His imagination was such that he was able to conjure up various scenarios from the rough diamonds he met here.

Breege and Rosaleen were living in a house near him that was owned by Tommy McShera. He was Agnes' brother. McGahern visited them at the weekends. His father was trying his best to contact him at this time. He was still seeking his approval of Agnes. Despite the way he'd treated McGahern in his youth – or possibly because of it – he wanted him back in his life. It became a pattern with all his children, driving them away by his cruelty and then seeking to re-capture their affections. His relationship with Agnes wasn't great. He seemed to need to bolster it by having his children around. As their numbers became depleted, such a need grew. He was delighted to have Breege and Rosaleen in his net because of the connection with Tommy.

McGahern didn't want to hear from him. He told them not to give him the address of the hostel. His father knew he was visiting them so he wrote to him care of Tommy's address.

McGahern read the letters but only replied to some of them, and even then half-heartedly. His father took this as further evidence of his disap-

McGahern worked on a building site for a time when he was in London. The experience gave him much material for his writing. (Pixabay)

proval of Agnes. McGahern was at pains to tell him he had nothing against her. He just needed to have his own life now.

He found it difficult to settle back in the college when he got home from London. His eyes had been opened to new kinds of experiences and he wanted more of them. He didn't have the bitter attitude of the emigrant he met on the buildings towards England. For him it was the land of Dickens, Shakespeare, Jane Austen. He loved all these writers. They opened up worlds he'd never have known about if it wasn't for the Moroneys. The city itself was exciting too.

The college became even more parochial to him when he returned to it. Nearly every effort he made to express himself was stifled. He attended the lectures in a daze, only half-listening to things that were being said to him. Not much of it meant anything. There were facts he had to take into his brain and regurgitate at exam time so he could move onto the next year. His ambition was to be anonymous, to fly under the radar.

His father visited him with Agnes. He found their deferential attitude to him annoying. Both of them fell over themselves trying to be friendly.

He was showing a new side to himself now, a softer one, but McGahern wasn't taken in by it. He knew how clever he could be. The second he dropped his defences, his addiction to control would emerge again.

McGahern didn't go to London at the end of his second year like he had at the end of his first. By now his father had bought a new house in the nearby village of Grevisk. He referred to it as his retirement home. McGahern spent the summer re-roofing it with Tommy McShera. His father was delighted to be getting the free labour. Agnes brightened it up inside. McGahern felt his approval of her was still being solicited.

He was still "courting" McGahern, still lavishing attention on him. Agnes spoiled him with lavish meals. She gave him the kind of attention his mother had bestowed on him when she was alive. He couldn't respond to this for obvious reasons. For him it was a form of manipulation organised by his father to try and bring him back to the boy he'd been growing up, i.e. someone he could mould to his wishes.

He tried to be away from them as much as he could. The absence of his mother still weighed heavily on him. It put a wall between himself and Agnes. He felt sorry for Dympna and Frankie. They may have been free of the worst of his father's rages but they'd also been deprived of his mother's love.

McGahern was more confident in himself now. He was starting to become interested in girls.

He went dancing at the local Ivy Leaf Ballroom. At the end of the night, couples leaped over walls and into fields to do their courting. As he wrote in *Memoir*, "There wasn't a haycock safe for a mile around in the month of July."[21]

His third year in Pat's was stressful. The lectures were still stifling and the general atmosphere still oppressive. Why, he wondered, had the church so much power over the place? It was almost as if a sense of servility was hardwired into the Irish DNA. Once it sloughed off the influence of the

The Ivy Leaf Ballroom where McGahern went dancing in his teenage years. Years later he would later buy a house near it.

colonial enemy it transferred it to members of the cloth.

As the year went on he started to think of practical things. He'd have to get a job soon. Some of the students were licking up to the priests with this in mind. It was well known that they had influence with school managers. He refused to do that. He didn't care if he had to wait a while to get employment.

It was annoying to him that religion impacted on jobs as well as thoughts. "We were being groomed," he said, "as non-commissioned officers to priests in the running of the different parishes throughout the country."[22]

The most shocking aspect of all was the lecture delivered to the students shortly before they graduated. The lecturer said that as teachers who were well paid they would be "an enormous source of sexual excitement" to girls. Such girls, as a result, might be tempted to do "certain things" with them. It was their duty to restrain them.[23]

McGahern thought the church's over-emphasis on sex made it more exciting than it was: "It elevated a normal human appetite into an importance that distorted the reality of almost the whole of life. It was a very dangerous and a very twisted thing."[24]

He was relieved to leave the college. He made some good friends there and read some interesting books but the reason he was there – to learn about education – wasn't served well. "I learned buck all from the lectures," he said, "but a lot from my friends. On the whole I think I knew more entering the institution than leaving it. I consider this rather a positive achievement."[25]

His father retired in 1958. He was described as having an exemplary record. The beatings weren't mentioned in the final report of his service. Everyone knew about them but they were brushed under the carpet.

He didn't take any better to retirement than he did to being a widower. After the importance of being a sergeant he felt depressed. Agnes minded him well but he took her for granted. His priority always seemed to be his children. There were less of these around as the years went on.

Breege and Rosaleen, as mentioned, were now living in London. Breege had been apprenticed to a dressmaker after she left school. Rosaleen became an assistant to a draper. This was a distressful experience for her as he made sexual advances on her.

The decision to become nurses led to their emigration. If they trained in Ireland they would have had to pay for it. In England, on the contrary, they themselves would be paid during their training. Much as they hated to leave home, there was no option but to go "across the pond."

Margaret and Monica moved to Dublin in 1959. That meant there was only Dympna and Frankie left at home. McGahern had a paternal attitude to Dympna. He wrote her many letters in which he advised her about life. She was bright academically, receiving a scholarship to go to secondary school.

Dympna and Frankie couldn't relate to Agnes as they had to their birth mother. Breege and Rosaleen had been able to minister to them when they were in the house. Afterwards they were left to their own devices. Frankie started to go off the rails as well.

Breege was the first of McGahern's sisters to marry. It was to a Cork man, Con O'Brien. He was the son of a baker from Kanturk. She met him at a dance. He was handsome and flamboyant. She was besotted with him. He worked on the buildings and drank heavily.

Margaret got a job in the Eastern Health Board. Monica worked for the Department of Industry and Commerce on Kildare Street. They lived in a house on the South Circular Road. McGahern's father felt they were drifting away from him. He turned on his charm to try and keep them sweet. They didn't hold grudges so it usually worked. They still loved "Daddy," regardless of when he'd done to them growing up. "When Daddy is nice," they'd say, "there's no one better." His sons were different.

He kept asking McGahern if he'd be interested in teaching locally. That

McGahern having a conversation with local librarian
Sean O'Suilleabháin on one of his visits home
(Leitrim County Library Local Studies collection)

prospect grew dimmer as the years went on. Part of the reason was that his Catholicism had started to lapse. He only went to Mass occasionally now. That would have been noticed more in a rural area than in the city if he was teaching there. He also refused to say the nightly Rosary when he was home. That created tensions with his father. He was reprimanded for giving bad example to Dympna and Frankie.

Once his father realised he wouldn't be able to persuade his daughters to come home he hatched a plan to move to Dublin. If the mountain wouldn't come to Muhammad, Muhammad would go to the mountain. McGahern thought this was a disastrous idea. He envisaged his father getting a new kind of power in the city. Once he installed himself there he would continue to treat his family as children. He would be the figurehead again. He wanted to buy a house and have them all as his tenants. It would be like the past all over again - with one change. Cootehall Daddy would turn into Dublin Daddy.

Margaret and Monica wrote to him to say they'd like him to visit them but they drew the line at living with him. McGahern oversaw the wording of the letter. It wasn't the first time he used his facility with words to help someone get out of a tight situation. Neither would it be the last.

His father went into a sulk about this. He didn't answer the letter. When they visited him in Grevisk sometime afterwards he stayed in his room. Agnes was left to entertain them - though "entertain" was hardly the word. She was never exactly overflowing with mirth.

Two Lives

McGahern tried to dovetail his two lives of teaching and writing over the next few years. He'd embarked on a novel round about the time he got his first job. It was in Growney National School in Athboy, Drogheda. He did his best to motivate the pupils. One of them, Paddy Duffy, remembered him giving out pencil sets on Friday mornings for the best essays. Duffy wrote one about a greyhound that was "as sleek as the wind and as clear-eyed as a fox." This was the kind of writing McGahern was always going to like – detailed, sensitive and relating to the world of nature. Duffy, needless to say, was rewarded with one of the famous pencils.

McGahern enjoyed his time in Athboy. He felt lucky to be able to work in his home country. So many people had to go abroad to teach. Little did he know this would also be his lot in the future.

He lived in the upstairs of a boarding house in Upper Bridge Street. Below him were other lodgers. They were aware of his writing. When they came in from the pub at night they used to throw their boots at the ceiling and shout out, "The poet! The poet!"[1]

Afterwards he got a job in Drogheda. When he was there he met a journalist called Joe Kennedy. McGahern and he became firm friends. Kennedy was working for a local newspaper, *The Argus*. McGahern had a lot in common with him.

He applied for jobs in Dublin when he was working in Athboy and eventually got one. It was in Scoil Eoin Baiste in Clontarf. Translated into English this was the School of John the Baptist. It later came to be known as Belgrove National School. He found himself a bedsit on the Howth Road.

He was confused in his early years teaching. Life was opening up for him but his emotions were in turmoil. Freed from the cruelties of home, different problems asserted themselves. The discipline of having to be at work at a certain time was like St. Pat's all over again. The ethos in staffrooms was almost as regressive. He found himself daydreaming a lot of the time, composing phrases and sentences in his mind, finessing scenarios in what he came to call his "private world."

He was teaching seven and eight year olds. There was no preparation and no corrections. The day ended at 2.15p.m. From then on he was his own boss. After having a meal in the bedsit he usually strolled into town. He rambled around the second hand bookshops and browsed through what they had. Some days he went to films. After he came home he wrote for a few hours but never more than that. The concentration he had to expend on it would have been too much.

He became fascinated by words, by their weight and rhythms. He played with them as he might have with jigsaw pieces. For him they were material things that had weight attached to them. He pushed them around to get the best effect out of them. If you changed one word in a sentence, he knew, everything else in it changed as well. It was like magic. Reading became like a spiritual thing for him. God wasn't behind the clouds anymore, he was in the pages of books.

He almost went into a trance when he was writing. His sisters tied his shoelaces together one day when he was in the heat of composition. He only noticed what they'd been at when he finally stood up and keeled over.

Belgrove College in Clontarf where McGahern spent
most of his teaching years in Ireland. (www.loveclontarf.ie)

They'd put a straw hat on his head as well. He hadn't noticed that either.

Many of the pupils in Belgrove were well-to-do. Others were poor. Some of them smelt badly; some looked as if they slept in their clothes. He tried to get to know them as people. That wasn't always possible. He was teaching at a time when pupils weren't encouraged to think.

In the world of teaching he had to subjugate himself to a church-run system in the same way as he had in the training college. Religion was a large part of the curriculum. Each class had to begin with a prayer. It was indeed like a "second priesthood." The manager of the school was a priest. He was involved in interviewing candidates and vetting their credentials. He also liaised with the existing teachers regarding First Communion classes and issues relating to the teaching of Catechism.

McGahern found this frustrating. He also had a problem with the amount of time devoted to the teaching of Irish. It was almost half of the day when added up. "The English beat the language out of us, he said, "and the educational system beat it back into us again." What was the point when so many had to emigrate?[2] The way it was taught prioritised grammar at the expense of speech. There was little emphasis on the spoken word except in the Gaeltacht areas. Many pupils left school hardly able to say their name in it.

Most of the other teachers happily slotted themselves into this system. McGahern saw his colleagues as being products of the theocratic regime they'd just come out of in St. Pat's. Whether they believed in it or not they acted as if they did.

In the staff-room he tried to get the other teachers away from mundane chatter. This he found difficult. He wrote about it in *The Leavetaking*: "In the green egotism of my first days in this staff room I had tried to turn the conversation to ideas and poetry, away from the continual talk of salaries or what had happened that morning in the classroom or what had been on television the night before."[3]

He intrigued them with his eccentricity. They listened to commentaries on Gaelic football matches while he sat with an earplug listening to cricket commentaries on his transistor. After a while he managed to convert the staff to the delights of the British game.[4]

He liked exposing his pupils to works outside the curriculum. One year he read them a set of German fairytales.[5] At the end of term he gave them gifts of books paid for out of his own pocket.

Declan Kiberd, a pupil of his who went on to become a friend in later life, was entranced by his work methods. He taught long multiplication by using the hands of a clock. He put one hand to twelve and the other to four and called out "Forty-eight!" One day he took the hands off the clock completely. He said, "What's the answer now?" It was of course nought. Kiberd didn't elaborate on the condition of the clock afterwards.[6]

McGahern was particularly friendly with two teachers in Belgrove who wrote. One was Tom Jordan, an ex-Christian Brother. He was very religious. Kiberd remembered him setting himself on fire one day. He'd blessed himself with such fervour he somehow managed to ignite a box of matches he had in the lapel pocket of his jacket.

Another good friend, Donncha Ó Céileachair, wrote mainly in Irish. McGahern had endless discussions with these two men about literature. He talked to them in the staff-room and on yard duty when they supervised the pupils at play. Being able to talk about matters outside the curriculum excited him. He thought maybe one day he could be like them, a successful writer who managed to hold down a day job as well.

He found teaching difficult in a similar way to writing. Both activities involved surrendering one's ego – in one case to a person, in another to a page.[7] The job wasn't stimulating for him. At times he found his patience being tested by the children. He tried not to lose his temper with them. If he did it drained him of the emotional energy he needed to write in the evenings.[8]

He burned the midnight oil many nights, either blackening pages with his writing or sampling the work of equally intense souls. The writers he liked were diverse – Kierkegaard, Rilke, Melville, Thomas Mann. The daylight hours were brain-numbing; the nights illuminating. Maybe a time would come when his whole day could be filled with reading. Was that too much to hope for?

He read Irish writers too, mainly Joyce and Beckett. He loved Yeats but wanted to get away from his ethereal flights of fancy to what Yeats himself called "the foul rag and bone shop of the heart." He wanted to use symbolism in his work but with an overlay of realism.

He also liked a Belfast writer called Forrest Reid. In 1934 Reid wrote a book called *Brian Westby*. McGahern made many efforts in the coming years to have it revived.

He also liked Patrick Kavanagh. Kavanagh was preferable to him than more conservative authors like Frank O'Connor and Seán O'Faoláin. These two were the acknowledged "masters" of the time. He didn't know why they had that status. Sometimes a writer was regarded as the best at what he did by people who didn't analyse why they held such a view. It was like The Emperor's New Clothes.

McGahern preferred the abrasiveness of Kavanagh to what he saw as a smugness in the writing of O'Connor and O'Faoláin. O'Faoláin didn't solicit any contributions from him to his magazine *The Bell* and he didn't approach him for inclusion in it. His interests lay elsewhere. He admired Joyce for *Dubliners* and *Ulysses* if not *Finnegans Wake*. The latter book he saw as an exercise in style for its own sake. Flann O'Brien he disparaged for what he regarded as laboured attempts at humour.

McGahern also admired a writer called Michael McLaverty. Like Kavanagh he'd grown up on a small farm in Monaghan. The two men, however, couldn't have been more different in personality. Kavanagh was irascible and self-pitying, McLaverty gentle and positive thinking. McGahern preferred writers with quiet personalities rather than "roaring boys" like Brendan Behan who frequented bars like McDaids. Behan, he felt, talked his books instead of writing them. He wondered what he might have achieved if he went off the sauce.

McDaid's pub, where many drinkers who liked their tipple congregated
(Patrick Donald)

McGahern liked his drink but he didn't like to mix it with his work. Alcohol was so embedded into the writing of the sixties as to be almost inextricable from it. This was the case with journalists as well as writers of literature. It was said in the offices of the *Irish Press* that any copy submitted without the whiff of Guinness on it was deemed suspect. McGahern inveighed against this culture. It didn't make him especially good company for Kavanagh or Behan. Not that these two men were friends of one another. Relationships forged in alcohol, McGahern came to realise, were fickle. Loyalties were as soon lost as won.

The bars he favoured were quiet ones: Wynn's, Larry Toibin's, Kehoe's. Fights were less likely to erupt here. By the same token, the atmosphere in them wasn't quite as electric as it was in McDaid's.

Behan once called Dublin "the biggest village in Europe." McGahern could see why. "It was easy to fall into conversation with people," he said, "sometimes it was harder not to."[9] It was easier again in a pub. When two Irishmen sat down to drink together, it tended not to be long until they found something in common. "What a small country Ireland is," McGahern wrote, "where everybody who is not related knows someone who knows someone else you share an enemy or friend with."

Kehoe's pub on Anne's Street. It wasn't quite as volatile as McDaid's
(Patrick Donald)

He became particularly friendly with a family called the Swifts. They ran an advertising business in Amiens Street. There were three boys. McGahern met Tony Swift in the bar of a dance hall in 1955 and clicked immediately with him. He later got to know his brother Jimmy. He was ten years older than McGahern and had a vast knowledge of art and literature. McGahern admired him for the way he wore his learning so lightly. They discussed life and literature in a manner that was entertaining for both of them. Before long they were meeting every Friday night. They agreed on most things, though Swift wasn't a fan of McLaverty. That disappointed McGahern.

By now he'd completed the novel he was working on. He called it *The End or the Beginning of Love*. Upon the advice of Jimmy he sent it to his brother Patrick, a third member of the family. Patrick was editing a magazine called *X* in London with a South African poet, David Wright.

Jimmy was always trying to help writers. Shortly before McGahern met him he'd collected Kavanagh's poems in manuscript and had them typed up. He was an ally to him when many of his other "friends" deserted him. Kavanagh brought a lot of this on himself due to his crabby manner but Swift knew there was no badness in him at base. He saw him as being victimised by his time. Kavanagh had little money and not much of a reputation to speak of at this time. Swift felt even sorrier for him when he contracted lung cancer.

McGahern liked Kavanagh's later poems best. These were the ones that became known as the Canal Bank poems. He wrote them after he came out of hospital. There was a line that stuck in his mind: "A year ago I fell in love with the functional ward of a chest hospital." He stayed out of his way at night but found him good company in the morning. That was before he'd had "a drop of the craythur" – whiskey.

Like Behan and Flann O'Brien, Kavanagh was an alcoholic. The demon drink basically ended the lives of all three of these men in the sixties. They provided a timely warning to McGahern about the dangers of "the high stool," something many teachers fell prey to because of the short working hours.

Anthony Cronin was another member of this set. He was the one who survived, having a talent unique for writers of this time in being able to put "a plug in the jug." McGahern saw something distrustful in him. Whatever his reservations about the other three men, at least they lived life from the ground up. Cronin he regarded as someone who viewed them drinking themselves stupid from the sidelines with a cold eye.

Cronin wrote about the drinking escapades of himself and his literary friends in a classic memoir of the time, *Dead as Doornails*. McGahern enjoyed it as a porthole into a scene he didn't want to become part of. He never liked writers who "strutted around like eminences."[10] They annoyed him as much as his father with their egotistic personalities.

He stayed away from places where such writers met: "The megalomania of these bars were as familiar to me as the air around my father. A single visit to McDaid's was enough to cure me of any desire for literary company for a month. Like all closed, self-protective societies, they believed that everything of importance took place within their circle while all of them constantly looking outwards without seeing in this any contradiction.[11]

That passage is from *Memoir*. Elsewhere he said the literary world would "bore the britches off a saint." One of the consolations of heaven, he believed, was that, "If we ever found ourselves there, there would be no writers in it."[12]

He was having a drink with some friends in Mooney's pub one night when Kavanagh rambled in. He asked McGahern to get him a packet of cigarettes in McDaid's across the road. He was having a drink there with Cronin at the time. McGahern didn't want to "dance to his tune" so he refused. Kavanagh took it badly and started abusing him. McGahern put the anecdote into his story "Bank Holiday." Kavanagh is Patrick McDonagh in it. He resisted being his messenger boy. As he put it in the story, "He could go and inflate his great mouse of an ego somewhere else." [13]

He was on the receiving end of Kavanagh's tongue more than once but he didn't take him seriously enough to be bothered by him. Cronin was quieter but more lethal on that account.

McGahern started studying for a BA degree now by night. If he got it he would be able to teach in secondary schools. It would also mean an

The Patrick Kavanagh Seat on the Canal off Baggot Street. Baggotonia, as it was called, was his "beat." (Patrick Donald)

39

increment in his pay at Primary level.

He was more impressed by his Economic lectures than his English ones. The latter, he thought, were done mainly by rote. He could have got just as much information from reading the recommended texts.

Between school and study he continued to frequent the bookshops. One of his favourites was on the corner of Henry Street. It was owned by a man called Kelly. He had many rare classics in the shop. McGahern never found out how he came by them. He assumed he stole them. Kelly was a Republican who collected money for the youth wing of the IRA. He fell foul of the organisation at one stage and was tarred and feathered as a result. He was then stripped naked and tied to a tractor in a field. His main complaint when he came out of hospital was that his assailants used car oil to assault him instead of real tar.[14]

Kelly had first editions of people like Beckett that he sold at rates not a great deal more than the regular price of the books. Beckett and Kavanagh were still the two writers he enjoyed most at this time. He read them in the "smalls," those magazines that often went to the wall due to lack of funds. He found magazines more interesting than books. There was immediacy to them. He felt he was getting material hot off the presses. "I'll never forget the excitement of reading Beckett's poem *Prelude*," he recalled, "Ignore power's schismatic sect/Lovers alone, Lovers protect."[15]

The Eblana Bookshop on Grafton Street was another place he frequented. He looked for rare tomes there. One day he found a novel that Rainer Maria Rilke had written, *Notebooks of Malte Laurids Briggs*. He became as entranced by it as he was by Rilke's poetry.

He was still writing some poetry at this time himself. It showed the influence of Yeats, the Celtic Twilight. The more he read, the better he wrote. For him the two activities would always be interlinked. "All writers begin by being readers," he liked to say. The ones he read in Moroneys stimulated him to do his own work.

He was now on a broader adventure. As well as Irish and European writers he read the Americans. He liked Richard Ford, Alice Munro, Ernest Hemingway, F. Scott Fitzgerald. He saw *The Great Gatsby* as a perfect novel but found Fitzgerald less entrancing when he strayed beyond his comfort zone of the party set in the Jazz era: "Once he moves outside that area of experience his work, though it is always carefully crafted, becomes less exciting."[16]

He liked writers who were difficult, who didn't show self-satisfaction. That was what bothered him about O'Connor and O'Faoláin. He wanted to write literature that made people sit up rather than sit back. There was too much comfort in these writers. They didn't threaten the givens. Benedict Kiely was someone else he saw as being too smug.

Writing had to have a rebellious element in it, he felt, a moving away from the known. When authors slotted themselves too commodiously into their time they compromised their ability to see it for what it was.

Two other Irish writers he started to read now were Tomás O Criomhthain and Ernie O'Malley. He read O Criomhthain's *An tOileánach* over and over again and also O'Malley's republican memoir, *On Another Man's Wound*. He wasn't generally fond of republican literature but he made an exception for this.

O'Malley's nephew was one of his pupils. One day he found him doing his sums on a discarded notebook. When he looked closer at it he saw it had Ernie O'Malley's name on it. It made him sad to think he'd faded so far into insignificance that a personal jotter would be used for this purpose.

McGahern went to the theatre a lot at this time, seeing plays by Pirandello, Eugene O'Neill, Tennessee Williams, Chekhov – all the writers he'd discovered in St. Pat's, albeit under duress.

He frequented the Gate more than the Abbey. He associated the latter venue with the cruder elements of republicanism. It had fallen under state control in 1925.[17] For McGahern that limited the kinds of plays it was able to stage. The Gate had people like Lorca. He went to Lorca's *The House of Bernardo Alba* over a dozen times.

He saw a lot of films as well. There was a cinema on the quays called The Astor. He went to many films that intrigued him there, like Jean Renoir's *The Rules of the Game*. The loose sexual morals of Renoir's upper crust lives were light years away from the kind of world McGahern was exposed to in the Ivy Leaf ballroom.

Films were very popular in Dublin in the sixties. Tickets were so scarce at the weekends they were often sold on the black market. Sometimes the touts got hard done by on slow nights if it was raining or if a given film wasn't popular. McGahern remembered being outside the Metropole one night when a pretty girl holding a bunch of tickets ambled up to him and groaned, "If I don't get rid of some of these soon I'll have to drop me drawers before the night is out!"[18]

He saw Becker's *Casque d'Or* many times. "You can go back to a movie like to a book or a poem," he said. He wasn't snobbish about the quality of literature over film: "It would be a brave man who would say any novel was superior to *Monsieur Hulot's Holiday*."

He hadn't seen many films growing up. The nearest cinema was seven miles away from where he lived. There was a travelling cinema with a tent that came to Leitrim now and then but the generator often broke down.

He didn't see his first film until his father took him to the All-Ireland Football Final in 1947. After the match they went to *Boys Town* with Spencer Tracy and Mickey Rooney.

A later generation brought rebellion to the screen. James Dean "invented" the cult of the teenager in *Rebel Without a Cause* in 1955. Bill Haley shook up the musical world with his rendition of "Rock Around the Clock" in *Blackboard Jungle*. Marlon Brando changed the landscape of acting in *A Streetcar Named Desire*.

Much of this went above McGahern's head. He was more interested in Brando's Marc Antony in *Julius Caesar* than the greasy Polack of *Streetcar* or the failed boxer of *On the Waterfront*, the film that had won Brando his Oscar in 1954. In such preference he showed his literary bias. The refined diction of Shakespeare trumped the monosyllabic grunts of a Hoboken longshoreman.

McGahern saw his life at this time as being similar to that of most men of his age: "We worked. We went to dancehalls and cinemas and theatres; the big hurling and football matches at Croke Park, race meetings in the Phoenix Park, Baldoyle or Leopardstown, we met and talked and drank and argued in bars. In hot summers we swam in the seas around Dublin or went on excursions into the Dublin Mountains. The girls we picked up we courted in doorways and back alleys, and on dates took them to cinemas or out to places like Howth by the sea."[19]

It was an era where couples met under Clery's clock and went to "the pictures" together. Sexual encounters were usually limited to heavy petting in the back row. Couples usually finished where a later generation might begin. Things might go further if the man in question had a car. If they went "the whole way," as the expression went, and the woman missed her period, an agonising wait would develop before she knew her condition. The horror of pregnancy meant she would probably take the boat to England to have the baby aborted. Ireland's Taoiseach Charles Haughey called this "an Irish solution to an Irish problem." The relief of a false alarm on the other hand would mean the couple in question could continue where they left off. If the girl had got a bad enough scare, however, she might well "break it off" with her man.

If she was pregnant he'd usually be gone anyway.

First Strides in Publishing

Donncha O'Céileachair, the aforementioned teacher McGahern worked with, encouraged him to write to Michael McLaverty in 1959. The first time he did so was in January of that year. His letter was cautious in tone but he spoke his mind in it as it went on. At one point he said McLaverty's novel *The Choice* reminded him too much of Balzac's *Le Medicin de Campagne*. He hadn't liked it. This was a cheeky thing for an unknown writer to say to his idol.

He posted the letter immediately, fearing that if he hung on to it he'd lose the courage to do so. McLaverty wasn't bothered by the criticism. He wrote back warmly to him, recommending other books that he should read. As it turned out he'd already read most of them. One he hadn't read was Dostoevsky's *A Day in the Life of Ivan Illych*. He was grateful to McLaverty for pointing him in this direction. When he read it he found he admired it even more than Joyce's "The Dead," another famous "long" short story.[1]

His first meeting with McLaverty was after a lecture he gave when he was an evening student at UCD. McLaverty had recommended the writings of Daniel Corkery to his audience in the course of it. McGahern started to read Corkery as a result. He liked his work and wrote to McLaverty to tell him so. McLaverty replied almost immediately to the letter, thereby leading to a correspondence that became increasingly prolific as the months went on. He sent him the text of *The End or the Beginning of Love* in February 1960. McLaverty was entranced by it, already aware of McGahern's genius.

Their letters became personal afterwards. McLaverty told McGahern about his life as a headmaster in Belfast. McGahern related details of his own life in Belgrove.

McLaverty knew McGahern had a quiet disposition. He advised him to stay away from the raucous pubs like McDaid's, referring him to the more sedate confines of Mary Lavin's flat at Lad Lane instead.

Memorabilia associated with McGahern from the museum
devoted to him in Leitrim (Keith Nolan)

McGahern started to frequent that. He liked Lavin and the feeling was mutual. Her *soirées* were free of the stuffiness he found at most literary gatherings. He also liked her daughter Caroline.

Caroline was only a toddler when McGahern first met her. She resented the fact that she was usually put to bed when people called to the flat. McGahern felt sorry for her and often read her stories. She remembered him reading *Rupert Bear* with his "checked yellow trousers, red jumper and trademark scarf." He acted as if he was as fascinated by the character as she was.[2]

McGahern continued to straddle teaching with writing. Often he found his mind wandering when he was at work. He spent a lot of his time gazing out the window. He couldn't see himself staying at the job forever. The "eternal scraping" of the tubular steel chairs was driving him crazy.[3]

Things were becoming tense at Grevisk now. Frankie was giving trouble in school. He was above average intelligence but was bored with it, maybe for that reason. He skipped class a lot, showing more interest in smoking and drinking than anything that went on in the classroom. His father was furious with him. At one point he asked McGahern if he'd join him in beating him up.

One morning when he was going in to work he saw Frankie in the playground of Belgrove. He seemed distressed. There was a troubled look in his eyes.

He asked him what was wrong. Frankie told him he'd fought with his father and ran away from home. He wanted to go to England. McGahern was against the idea and so was his father. They wanted him to finish his education. He managed to persuade him to return home.

A few months later he arrived back in Dublin again. He'd had another fight with his father. This time McGahern knew there was no point talking to him. He'd made up his mind. He was going to England and that was that. McGahern said he'd help him to do so. He contacted his sisters. They agreed that it was for the best that he go. Things were only going to get worse in Grevisk.

Margaret and Monica brought him to the boat. McGahern phoned Rosaleen in London to tell her what was happening. Frankie went to Holyhead. From there got the train to London. Rosaleen met him upon arrival at Heuston.

Within a week he'd found himself a job. He wrote a jolly letter to McGahern telling him how glad he was to be away from his father. He said he was happy at his job. McGahern wondered how long that would last.

By now Patrick Swift had read *The End or the Beginning of Love*. He told McGahern he'd like to publish extracts from it in *X*. McGahern went to meet him in London at the beginning of 1960 to discuss this. He stayed with Frankie during the visit. Frankie had little interest in literature so they didn't have much to talk about. He enjoyed the company of Rosaleen and Breege more.

He went to London again that summer. The "swinging sixties" were beginning and the city's vitality reflected that. He became good friends with Swift during these months. They had robust discussions, exchanging views with one another as they travelled around the city visiting museums and art galleries.

He found Swift enormously entertaining. He had a colourful way of expressing himself and a refreshing freedom from preconceptions about issues of the day. He also liked his sense of irreverence. He had an entertaining turn of phrase that appealed to the writer in McGahern. The only subject they seemed to differ on was Paddy Kavanagh. Swift thought he was "a man of genius." He advised McGahern to see him more often in Dublin. McGahern said he'd been abused by him too often to want to seek him out. He told Swift he preferred to read him than to meet him.[4]

McGahern was delighted to see his novel extract in *X* when it was published. It was a prestigious magazine that featured writers of the calibre of

McGahern at the beginning of his writing career (Bobbie Hanvey Photographic Archives, John J. Burns Library, Boston College)

Beckett and Ezra Pound. He felt proud to be in their company.

The extract came to the attention of many British publishers. One of these was Faber & Faber. T.S Eliot was working there at the time. He was coming to the end of his writing career now but was still a legendary figure.

McGahern, ironically, had started to lose interest in *The End or the Beginning of Love* by now. He felt it was too diffuse. It merged elements of what would become his first two novels, *The Barracks* and *The Dark*. He saw it as falling between two stools from that point of view. Despite Faber's enthusiasm he was already getting ready to split it up into two separate books.

He'd also sent it to Tony Whelan by this time. Whelan was the man he met in the hostel in London in 1954. He was now working in the Publicity Department of Pitman's Publishing. McGahern thought he might have some influence in "the trade" as a result of this. Whelan had literary ambitions of his own by now and was discommoded by McGahern's request. Nonetheless he agreed to help him.

He showed the book to an editor he knew but the response wasn't good. The editor saw it as flawed. McGahern was relieved. He now wrote to Whelan asking him to send it back to him. "I'm not interested in it anymore," he said, "I've disowned it for something more ambitious." Whelan didn't know what to think. What he was seeing was Sean MacEachran turning into John McGahern.

McGahern went to Faber to discuss his writing with them. He wanted to know where things might go from here between them. Charles Monteith, the commissioning editor, was away at the time. Instead he met the company's director, a man called Peter de Sautoy. He told him he wasn't interested in having *The End or the Beginning of Love* published but that he was working on another novel now. When it was finished he would offer it to them if they gave him a contract for it. He was referring to *The Barracks*. At this time it was called *A Barrack Evening*.

"Why do you want a contract?" Sautoy said. It was a silly question.

"By the time I finish it," McGahern replied, "if I have no contract from you and you lose interest in me, I'll be as badly off as I am now."

He was showing business acumen early. Sautoy agreed to give him a contract. The terms were £75 upon delivery of the manuscript. Sautoy asked him what the book was about. He said, "Boredom in a police barracks." Sautoy said, "Most novels about boredom have the habit of being boring themselves." McGahern said it depended who wrote them.[5]

Donncha Ó Céileachair died of polio when McGahern was in London. The news hit him hard. He was only 42. When he got home he struggled to complete *The Barracks*. Tony Whelan invited him up to his home in Kilkeel that September but he didn't go. A distance was growing between the two of them now. He'd been there once before and enjoyed the visit. Whelan's mother had liked him. He'd even gone to Mass up there. Back in Clontarf he'd kept in touch with Whelan, visiting him and having him over to his bedsit.

That wouldn't be the case again. Too much had happened. His career was taking off while Whelan's wasn't. He was always polite to him but their relationship made him feel increasingly nervous. McGahern was growing in confidence from the interest in his novel overseas. Whelan's own confidence was sinking. He was bored at work as well. McGahern tried to get him a job in the London publishing firm of Cassell's but it didn't work out.

McGahern was bored too. His concentration was drifting farther and farther away from his pupils. He said to Whelan, "I often fear that I shall grow old among children who care as little about learning as I do about teaching."[6] All he could think about was writing. As he wrote in the story, "Crossing the Line," "Teaching is a lousy, tiring old job and it gets worse as you get older. A new bunch comes at you year after year. They stay the same but you start to go down."[7]

He wrote a typed letter to McLaverty at the beginning of 1961. McLaverty thought it signalled a new-found professionalism in him.[8] McGahern was never a fan of typewriters either for letters or his creative work. He thought they stultified spontaneity. Carving words like hieroglyphics was more to his taste. There was a physicality with ink that disappeared with the mechanical nature of typescript.

In March of that year he wrote his first letter to Charles Monteith, a man who was to become important in his life. A Protestant with Unionist affiliations from Lisburn, County Antrim, Monteith came to publishing through a circuitous route. He'd had a military career in India cut short through injury. He was also the possessor of a Law degree.

He had an eye for good literature that passed others by. Some years before he'd rescued William Golding's *Lord of The Flies* from the slush pile at Faber. There was even a rumour he re-wrote parts of it.[9] It was the same insight that saw the potential in McGahern. Monteith would soon become a booster and good friend to both McGahern and another Irish writer who was virtually unknown before he took him under his wing - Seamus Heaney.

There was another publisher interested in McGahern at this time. Barrie and Rockliff had been behind the publication of *The End or the Beginning of Love* in *X*. They wanted *The Barracks* too. McGahern was more interested in Faber. It was a bigger company and a more prestigious one. If he was accepted by them he would be a fellow writer with people like Eliot and other major talents. He pressed Monteith for an answer one way or another. "I'm between two publishers unless something is done," he pleaded. Monteith said he'd do his best to persuade the people at Faber to take *The Barracks* immediately.

Things were starting to happen. Jimmy Swift was also making moves for him to become established in the U.S. He was consulting with an agent for the firm Abelard-Schuman but he wasn't impressed with them. He referred to them as "Abelard Shitman" in a letter to McGahern.[10] He assured him better deals lay down the line.

The writing of the book was still a struggle for McGahern. Having a publisher should have made it easier but often the opposite was the case with him. It took his concentration away from the writing and transferred it to deadlines. That made it more arduous for him. Writing was hard enough without having to think of it as a business. "If I didn't need to do it I would stop," he wrote to McLaverty, "but there seems little else."[11]

Monteith suggested he enter *The End or the Beginning of Love* for the AE Award. McGahern wasn't in favour of doing so. He didn't think he'd have a chance of winning it. Such awards were sewn up by the "in" people, he believed. There was another problem too. Up until now all the winners had been poets.

A third problem was money. If he entered he would have to submit five copies of the novel to the committee judging the entries. In the days before photocopying, this was going to be very expensive. Monteith told him he'd foot this bill if he didn't win. If he did he could repay him from the prize money.

That was what happened. He won against all the odds. The prize was £100. McGahern couldn't believe it. After paying Monteith there wasn't much left. He had just enough to promise his landlord, a man called Lightfoot, some celebratory drinks. The two of them did a jig at the bottom of the stairs in his flat. Afterwards they went down to Harry's Bar on the Howth Road to celebrate in more style.

Winning the award took away his "secret life" among his colleagues at work. Some of them looked askance at him for a while afterwards. It was the way with most writers. Spontaneity often disappeared from those they consorted with. People started to wonder if they'd be used as raw material for his books. Thankfully this didn't last long. He was soon able to relate to them in the same way as he had before he won it.

He played down the award to Monteith, saying the only thing that mattered was the work. "All success and failure are private," he said, "What matters outside that are either lucky or unlucky accidents."[12]

Lucky or not, Monteith now began to regard him as an author of promise. He knew they could both benefit one another in untold ways if his career took off in earnest.

On the Up and Up

McGahern had a love child in 1962. This is something that was airbrushed from his life before his letters were published in 2021. The mother was a woman called Joan Kelly. She was a journalist with the *Irish Press*. She subsequently became an Information Officer in the British Navy. Their relationship was brief. He had little to do with her after she gave birth.

He had little to do with the child. It was a boy called Joseph. McGahern never became close to him. For someone who dealt with children for so many years in his work life - and who had such a poor relationship with his own father - this is surprising. Could he not have used Joseph to right the wrongs of his past? Or was a child something that he saw as getting in the way of his burgeoning career? It seems the latter was the case. Having a child outside marriage at such a time would also have caused him problems in his job.

McGahern had a torrid relationship with another woman that year. She's never been named and he was never asked about her in interviews. All that's known is that she had dark hair and was the sister of a guard. It was she who ended the relationship. The parting left him in a terrible state emotionally. He mentioned her in letters to Monteith and McLaverty without going into detail. She cut in on his writing but in time she became an inspiration for it. In the immediate term her only legacy seemed to be the panic attacks he got after she left him.

He met the journalist Nuala O'Faolain when he was trying to recover from the relationship. O'Faolain was trying to recover from a failed love affair at the time too. They went out together on a semi-romantic basis over a period of two years, falling into one another's arms like twin victims of loss.

He spoke English, she said, as if he was learning the language. "Yet inside [himself] he hadn't the least doubt that he belonged in the glorious company of writers. It only remained to write the books."[1]

A shelter in Clontarf near Dollymount Beach where McGahern sometimes went walking with Nuala O'Faolain. (Patrick Donald)

They walked to the beach at Dollymount together. Sometimes they went to films in the late afternoon after McGahern's school day had ended. He knew Kevin Lehane, the manager of the Capital cinema. One day he stood them a meal. They sat at a table with a lamp on it. O'Faolain wrote about it in a memoir. She remembered looking at a rasher on her plate: "It was the luxury, the lavishness of it that made it so memorable. Because we were poor."[2]

"He looked like a typical nobody from that hard time," O'Faolain wrote, "trudging everywhere at a countryman's pace. For a while I trudged beside him, up and down and across Dublin and out along the seafront to Clontarf, learning from him about the reading that had delivered him from the terrible forge of his childhood experience."[3]

McGahern was physically attracted to O'Faolain but she seemed to only want him as a friend. One night she brought him to the flat of a man she'd been dating. McGahern suspected contrivance in this. He thought she was trying to make him jealous. They were both thinking of other people, she of the man and he of the dark-haired girl.

Another time she remembered him looking at an advertisement for women's stockings that reminded him of her. A green witch writhed over the stockings as she passed them through her hands in the ad. It seemed to bring her back to him. O'Faolain took her place for a while but in the end she wasn't enough for him. At a certain point of their relationship he wrote her a letter saying he thought they shouldn't meet anymore. There was "too much brokenness." The letter, she remembered, was blotched: "It was either rained on or I cried when I read it."[4]

Sometimes they went out to the harbour village of Howth together. They either walked the pier or climbed Howth Head, a place that evoked Joyce for him.

One of the warmest memories she had of their time together was a day they went to the seaside town of Skerries on a bus. They walked to a headland. "I remember that day," she wrote in her memoir, "because we were light-headed and friendly and not at our usual edgy distance from each other. I've seen that exact landscape in one of his marvellous stories. That's one of the pleasures of having known a writer."[5]

McGahern had begun to develop his own style of writing now, one that captured the painful time he was going through. It made socialising difficult, either with O'Faolain or anyone else.

He decided to break away from Mary Lavin now. The gatherings at her mews apartment had been boring him for some time. He hadn't liked her latest book (*The Great Wave*) either. It was difficult to meet someone and not speak of such things. Other writers could get over such situations with offhand comments but not him. He was too intense, too real. His displeasure would come out in something he said.

Howth pier, where McGahern also went with Nuala O'Faolain
(Patrick Donald)

By July he felt at the end of his tether. He wrote to Jimmy Swift, "These days are so crazed with suffering I have no calm to see anything. I have no real hope... it drags on and on. I know I'm coming to the end of my strength, I cannot endure much more."[6] This was probably a reference to the dark-haired girl.

He was more explicit in a letter he wrote to Michael McLaverty two months later. "I fell in love with someone," he wrote, "There is little end of pain in sight. I am too troubled most of the time to get any calm to work."[7]

Letter-writing filled the gap left by writer's block. Charles Monteith was a touchstone in this regard. He was able to talk to him about his work in the absence of doing any.

He addressed him by his Christian name for the first time in a letter he sent him in the September of that year. Writing "Dear Charles" was a significant moment in their relationship. It was testament to the fact that it was moving from business to friendship.

Joanna Mackle, his editorial director at Faber, was amused that he said Monteith's name as two words: "Char-less." It was the way the name was pronounced in the outlying parts of Leitrim. He pronounced other words in strange ways as well. "Gratitude", for instance, was "grahatude." "Violence" was "voilence," "Education" was "edahation." "I taught English" became "I thought English." (His spelling could also be unusual. He spelt Breege "Breedge" and Dympna "Dymphna" all his life. Edinburgh was "Edinbourg.")

Faber wasn't the only thing that was happening for him now. He started submitting stories to the *New Yorker* that autumn. One of these, "Strandhill, the Sea" was accepted, but in such a bowdlerised state that McGahern was disgusted. They "buggered it about," he told Brian Friel.[8] It was years before he approached this publication with anything again.

He received $300 for the story. It was a huge amount at the time. He met his Drogheda friend Joe Kennedy in a bar in Dublin to celebrate. During the course of the meeting he read from it. Kennedy remembered him getting so animated he reminded him of an actor delivering his lines.[9] This is probably the first example we have of McGahern the exhibitionist. It came out more in the readings he did in later years.

The Barracks was published in February 1963. He dedicated it to Jimmy Swift. The book changed both his life and the course of Irish literature. McGahern had arrived on the world's stage.

"Mrs. Reegan darned an old woollen sock," it began, "as the February night came on."[10] It's a sentence that might have come from Frank O'Connor or Michael McLaverty. Fintan O'Toole thought it depicted a world "that was even then beginning to vanish."[11] But the book doesn't always continue in this key. Elizabeth Reegan becomes a thoroughly modern heroine as it goes on.

Elizabeth is a nurse who's returned from England after a failed love affair. She marries an emotionally crippled Garda before succumbing to the cancer that's about to end her life.

The number of male Irish writers who were able to get so far inside women's heads as to become them were few. One thinks of Joyce with Molly Bloom in *Ulysses* or Brian Moore with Judith Hearne. McGahern also did so with his character here.

Reviews of the book were uniformly positive. McGahern was relieved. It made his disposal of *The End or the Beginning of Love* a wise decision. The poet Eavan Boland said, "It was the first time the powerlessness of an Irish woman seemed portrayed in a way I could believe."[12] Anthony Burgess gushed, "Nobody caught so well the peculiar hopelessness of contemporary Ireland."[13]

It was taken seriously by critics both nationally and farther afield. A writer for *The Kenyon Review* went so far as to compare Elizabeth to Albert Camus' Meursault in *The Outsider*.[14]

McGahern played down the importance of what he'd achieved. "I had extraordinary luck," he said, "Without knowing hardly anything of the business or politics of literature I was published almost immediately when I was still young, without encountering the usual barriers of rejection."[15] He was being hard on himself here. Even without the Swifts the talent he evinced would have come to the attention of the major publishing houses anyway. Cream usually rose to the top.

The book caused controversy in Leitrim. People knew he wrote but not at this level. He'd been quiet growing up. Now his name was on everyone's lips.

His Aunt Maggie was dying of cancer when it came out but he still gave her a copy of it. He sometimes showed insensitivity at times like this. Passion for his writing blotted out the human tragedy. "The story would have disturbed her," he surmised, "She probably would have thumbed through it."[16]

One passage in it amused her. It was where McGahern wrote about his father's habit of drying onions on the roof of a urinal that belonged to the guards. She went into stitches laughing about this. "John," she said, "I never thought I'd see the day when I'd see shitey arse's onions drying on the roof of a lavatory in a book!"[17] This was her nickname for him.

In another chapter a married couple make love in "affectionate tiredness" on a Christmas evening. The priest in the school in Ballinamore was so upset by this he demanded the book be removed from the local library.

Publication of *The Barracks* cemented the distance between McGahern and his father (Bobbie Hanvey Photographic Archives, John J. Burns Library, Boston College)

McGahern's aunt owned a sweet shop beside the school. She said if that was done she would stop serving the priest his cigarettes.[18] The gesture delighted McGahern. It was a small but important step in the fight against censorship.

He sent his father a pre-publication copy of it. His reaction was mainly indifference. He wrote a letter to McGahern in which he said he was sitting in "the dark" so was unable to make out the words. This is perhaps where McGahern got the title of his second novel. "I don't know if he ever read it," he revealed.[19]

One of the reviews praising it came from a journalist called John D. Sheridan. Sheridan wrote lightweight columns for an evening paper. McGahern's father told McGahern he should write like him. He didn't understand the fact that his son was on another level. Sheridan did. Now his father was conflicted. Here was "his man" praising a book he didn't want to know anything about. Sheridan's name was never mentioned in the house again.

He had a narrow-minded attitude both to literature and life. If he read the book he would have been offended by its sexual content and its comments about religion. He knew about these elements from reports of others about it.

In February 1963, he called to McGahern's bedsit on the Howth Road with a priest. The idea was to prevail upon his son to mend his ways. He still thought McGahern was the small boy from Aughawillan. It was never going to happen. McGahern gave them both their walking papers.

He wrote to Michael McLaverty the following month. Writing books, he said, was a ghastly business. He hated the bad atmosphere it created both with his father and anyone else he knew. He thought it would be a long time before he would be able to go home again.[20]

He met Charles Monteith in London that summer. Monteith found him subdued. As well as everything else he was still reeling from his infatuation with the dark-haired girl. She left a deep-seated scar inside him, one he did his best to excoriate in the relationships he depicted in his writings in the years to come.

He arranged to go and see McLaverty in Belfast after the London trip. He was looking forward to the break from his routine. "I do not get much work done," he wrote to him, "My life is in a bit of a mess." McLaverty wrote back to say he was looking forward to seeing him. "You sound a bit depressed," he wrote, "we all do – and writers more than most. In spite of yourself, force yourself to be gay. Seek cheerful company and go for a long tramp over the Dublin hills." He told him there was a man on his staff he wanted him to meet. "He has a first class hons (sic) in English," he said, "Though that may suggest he hobbles through literature on borrowed crutches, it's not so in his case."[21] It turned out to be Seamus Heaney. He would become a lifelong friend of McGahern's.

McLaverty tutored Heaney just as he did McGahern. "Look for the intimate thing," he said to him, "the worn grain of unspectacular experience."[22] It was advice he took well to heart.

The two men had much in common. Heaney was as unfulfilled in his teaching life as McGahern was. McLaverty stimulated him in the same way Donncha O'Céileachair had stimulated McGahern. He recommended the works of Joyce and Chekhov to him, and of course Kavanagh. These people were the exception rather than the rule in their places of work.

Heaney was as apprehensive meeting Kavanagh as McGahern had been. They only met twice. There was an undercurrent of tension both times. The second meeting took place at a poetry reading. Heaney drove Kavanagh home from it with his wife Katherine. At one stage of the journey she said to him, "There you are now, Paddy. It seems as if you can be a poet and have a car as well." It was almost said like an insult, as if he'd sold out.

Romantic Entanglements

Ireland was adapting to outside influences by now. Sean Lemass had become Taoiseach in 1959. Sometimes called "the father of modern Ireland," he was forward-looking and inclusive. He spearheaded free secondary education and advanced industry.

The Beatles appeared in Dublin in 1963. They sang songs about love, not necessarily free love but certainly not far from it. Philip Larkin famously wrote that sex began for him between the end of the ban on *Lady Chatterley's Lover* and the Beatles' first LP.

The showband era was about to blossom, leading to wild dancing and the expected sexual activity afterwards. Alcohol wasn't permitted in dance halls at the time but it took place before and after. Albert Reynolds, who would go on to become Taoiseach, opened many ballrooms, including one close to McGahern in Rooskey, The Cloudland. Neither were all bands male. Singers like Maxi, Dick and Twink put women into the forefront of Irish society. Women were no longer chaperoned to dances. They made their own way. McGahern's sisters had flown the coop in Leitrim, moving away from their father to Dublin and London. They took heart from him having done likewise.

The British papers were awash with stories about Christine Keeler, the call girl who'd had an affair with John Profumo, the Minister for War. It opened the lid on a Pandora's Box of sexual activity in the corridors of power. McGahern watched these developments with interest. "If they took place in Ireland," he said, "they'd probably have been hushed up."

Something else of importance happened to him that summer. The poet Richard Murphy introduced him to an American woman called Mary Keelan. His relationship with her is one of the most revelatory aspects of his recently published letters.

She was a graduate of the University of Chicago. They only spent two days together but they built up a deep friendship in that time. Much of that depth had been preserved in the letters McGahern wrote to her afterwards.

Their relationship was primarily literary. They visited bookshops together and shared their views on writers they admired. McGahern was still reading a lot of the European greats – Proust, Flaubert and the rest. He was particularly entranced by a nouvelle by Franz Kafka, *Metamorphosis*. It dealt with a man who awakes one morning to find himself transformed into a giant insect.

It's difficult to know what he found so appealing in Keelan. He hadn't met many Americans in Roscommon, certainly not many American academics. Being attracted to someone he could discuss literature with was always a buzz for him. He'd had it with Nuala O'Faolain but that relationship had gone nowhere.

He found Keelan warmer. His reaction to her shows how lonely he was at this time. The fact that he could reach out so intensely to a person he hardly knew reveals a longing in his heart. As he wrote in *The Dark* about his dreams of university, "You could walk under trees and talk with men and women who were initiates, men your own age, and walk with a girl of your own who was studying the same as you."

Lemass welcomed John F. Kennedy to Ireland in June. He was assassinated only a few months later. The country went into national mourning just as much as America did. McGahern was almost too overwhelmed by his death to take it in.

He continued writing to Keelan. At the end of the year he wrote, "I've never spoken as closely to anyone as you, and certainly never written to anyone so, not even when I was most in love." This seems to be a reference to the girl he couldn't get out of his system. In the same letter he wrote, "Love was a way into all kinds of destruction, mostly the will to destroy my art." He may have been mistaken here. Love, especially unrequited love, can also be the wellspring for art. One has only to witness the great legacy of literature Maud Gonne MacBride bequeathed to the world by rejecting the advances of W. B. Yeats.

McGahern's work is also inundated with pained treatises on "the end or the beginning of love" to quote the title of his unpublished novel. He ended by saying he would "have" to think of Keelan. The word is unusual. He seems to be speaking of her from duty more than desire.[1] She could have been excused for being confused by the sentiments he expressed in the letter. It's as if he's trying to work out his thoughts in the process of expressing them. Maybe he was.

Writing was like agony to him at this point. "I am struggling with a novel," he told Michael McLaverty that November. This was a reference to *The Dark*, his next book. He said he was "half crazy" with it. It had "no shape" yet. There was "ages of work" before him. He said he had a "sickness" too.² He was suffering from panic attacks.

He met the novelist Kate O'Brien the following month. She was a writer he admired. The meeting was arranged through another novelist, John Broderick. Broderick was a distant cousin of his. They met at a posh hotel, The Hibernian. Broderick had been drinking heavily that day. He phoned O'Brien to ask her to join them. She arrived soon afterwards. She'd been drinking heavily too. McGahern felt uncomfortable. "I was just a national teacher. I wasn't used to expensive hotels or drunk people. I had a difficult evening."³

It was made even more difficult when O'Brien started complaining about having been interrupted in the middle of a sentence by Broderick's call.⁴ McGahern hadn't read any of her books at this point. She was regarded primarily as a "woman's magazine" writer and as a result was excluded from the elite literary sets. It was only when he started reading her that he realised how good she was. Her reclusiveness put her higher up in his estimation.

"I find literary people bore me almost to the point of violence," he said at the end of 1963. A week later he wrote to Keelan saying how much he hated Christmas. Celebrations should be private, be believed, not the drunken insanity the Irish practiced. As he put it in *That They May Face the Rising Sun*, "Christmas brings out the eejit in everybody."⁵

He won the Macaulay Fellowship Award for prose fiction the following month. This was a prestigious award that was presented to him by the Arts Council. It came with £1000 prize money. This was an enormous amount at the time, almost enough to buy a house.

The Dark consumed him during the early months of 1964. He revised it endlessly, editing and re-editing it until the words came out as he wanted. At times it was almost as if he was writing poetry. Some of the letters he sent to Keelan at this time read like poetry as well.

The way he wrote to her in May suggests that their relationship was physical. "We must have some detachment," he said in one of them, "or there's merely the nothingness of the flesh."⁶ The Calvinistic denunciation of the body is like something he would rail against in *The Dark* if it came from a priest's pulpit. It's unusual to see him saying it himself. This was the part of McGahern that must have contemplated the priesthood as a way of life when his mother was alive.

In another letter he wrote to her at this time he suggested they meet in Paris. This was so they could be "utterly alone." A few lines further down he said that if they were together it would "never solve anything," that maybe they should go their separate ways. He goes on to talk about the transience of all things. Such a dramatic U-turn was typical of his confused state of mind.⁷ What's the "anything" he's referring to? He didn't speak of her as a lover any more than he did of the dark-haired girl, or Joan Kelly. We can only speculate about the details of these relationships from clues in his fiction.

There are an amazing number of innuendoes in these letters which may never be explained. Maybe it's more intriguing if they aren't. Keelan didn't "kiss and tell." McGahern was never going to either. They hint at many things that might or might not have taken place between them.

He shares raw pain with her, pain that's so at odds with the quote unquote "normal" life he was leading at Belgrove. At times he appears almost Kafkaesque in his alienation from his surroundings. No wonder Kafka's *Metamorphosis* meant so much to him. If he died young we might be commemorating him as one of those tragic writers like Keats or Byron or Hart Crane, someone who perished at the crest of an impressionistic wave. But McGahern was a survivor. He transmuted his lovesickness into stories that redeemed him through the process of creation.

Keelan met him in London that summer. They travelled to Paris in August. Keelan then went back to America, becoming editor of the *Chicago Review* in time.

McGahern left Belgrove in September, taking a year's unpaid leave of absence. This was made possible because of the Macaulay Award.

He kept up the contact with Keelan, writing to her that month, "I have resigned from where I teach."⁸ "Resigned" was a strange word to use in the circumstances. His leave of absence did eventually become final but how could he have had foreknowledge of that? He may have had an inkling *The Dark* would cause problems with the educational authorities but hardly that it would result in his removal from the school.

McGahern's aunt Margaret died later that year. When she was dying his father went up to Dublin to see her. They'd never got on. He spoke sarcastically to her from the foot of her bed. His motive seemed to be to gloat over her in her distressed condition. McGahern was livid with him. "He who would not go to see his own wife when she was dying," he wrote, "or attend his children's weddings or visit my sister in the long months she spent in Blanchardstown, could now dress up and travel all the way to Dublin to deliver himself of this poison."⁹ Margaret had contracted tuberculosis some time before. He hadn't gone near her.

Dympna borrowed money from him to go to university that year. She did an evening course in Commerce in University College, Dublin. McGahern was glad for her. He'd always been aware of her great academic ability. Now she'd be able to get away from the man who'd terrorised them all. It was a victory of sorts.

"Pay him back as soon as you can," he advised. He was aware of how much his father thrived on control over people, how money was so often the kernel of that control.

McGahern's life was about to change now. Peter Lennon, the Paris correspondent for the *Manchester Guardian*, introduced him to a Finnish woman at the end of the year. Her name was Anniki Laaksi. The meeting took place in Falstaff's American bar in Montparnasse. It was a popular haunt for people involved in the arts. Laaksi was a theatre director. Lennon knew her. He was well connected. He'd interviewed Salvador Dali and also knew Eugene Ionesco and Beckett. He was married to a Finnish woman himself, Eeva Karikoski. She knew Laaksi well enough to be able to tell her about McGahern.

As soon as he met her he was smitten. The frustrations of the past few years disappeared. He became intoxicated by her beauty.

Not long into their meeting he started talking about an ecclesiastical figure from Ireland, John Charles McQuaid. McQuaid was the Archbishop of Dublin. McGahern wasn't to know then how much this man would figure in his life.

"Have you heard the latest?" he said to her, "He's after banning the use of Tampax. He thinks women are using them to stop getting pregnant!" Laaksi burst out laughing at this. It confirmed her in a view she already had of Ireland being backward.[10]

She had an interesting background. Her father was head of the local Fascist movement when World War II broke out. He was killed fighting Russians at the front. Her mother, like McGahern's, was a teacher.

Communication with her was difficult for him at first. He had to simplify what he said so she could understand it. His teaching experience helped him in this regard. When he got to know her better he told her about his childhood. She already knew about the cruelty of his father from Karikoski.

Their relationship became physical soon afterwards. As was the case between McGahern and Nuala O'Faolain, they felt bonded by their mutually damaged pasts. Before long they started to talk of marriage. Thrust away from their moorings, they found new anchors in one another. Laaksi said McGahern was a good lover. She imagined him having had lots of women. This was hardly the case.

They married in a registry office in Helsinki in November 1964. It was a quiet ceremony. Their witnesses were two porters. There was no mention of the event in the papers.

McGahern said the reason he got married outside the church was because Laaksi had been married before.[11] She denied this. Whatever his reasons, the low key nature of the day suited him. He told Mary Keelan there was "something gruesome" about wedding receptions.[12]

It was only afterwards that they considered the ramifications of what they'd done. They hardly knew one another. McGahern had become excited by the heady atmosphere of Paris, the release from Belgrove. It was also the first time he had money in his pocket. The combination of these things with a woman as pretty as Laaksi makes it easy to see why he would have wanted to marry her.

Before long he began to wonder how the marriage would be perceived in Ireland. She was Protestant. That was a black mark against her from the off. Being foreign was another one. Marrying her in a registry office was obviously going to cause problems for him down the road. It's surprising he didn't foresee this when he was, by his own admission, employed in a priest-run profession.

A Finnish lake. McGahern never settled in Finland despite its beauty
(Pixabay)

They honeymooned in Leningrad. She introduced him to a number of Russian writers when they were there. He enjoyed their company but not much else about the trip. The weather was unbearably cold, the temperatures sub-Arctic.

Afterwards they went to Finland. Laaksi asked McGahern if he'd consider living there indefinitely. He said he was dubious about that prospect.

Laaksi wasn't keen on living in Ireland. McGahern thought London might suit both of them in the short term if she could get out of her contract with her employers. Another possibility was to have it adapted to permit her working there.

Finland didn't appeal to McGahern in any shape or form. He bridled at the fact that drink was only available at high prices in hotels, at the fact that in off-licences you had to produce a certificate attesting to the fact that you weren't an alcoholic.

The country's history of excessive drinking, Laaksi told him, caused this. He found the ploy overly dramatic. On the streets sometimes he saw drinkers in dreadful conditions, suffering hangovers from the previous night's indulgences behind closed doors. Sometimes they held their arms out in cruciform poses. He'd have preferred if the drinking was done in public and the hangovers were had in private.

The drunks he saw in Finland reminded him of similar ones he'd witnessed at home. It seemed to be the same love of the forbidden fruit, the same attempt to assert oneself against a repressive government. In both countries it was as if excessive sobriety was counterbalanced by excessive indulgence.

He sympathised with the way Finland had suffered under Russia. The situation wasn't too different from Ireland's colonisation under Britain. But Finnish people lacked passion. In that they were like the climate.

In Ireland, it's said, a person can experience the four seasons in a day. In Finland, on the contrary, it seemed like one season all the time. Such unchanging rhythms were hardly conducive to inspiration for him.

The scenery was boring to him too. There were too many thin trees without any distinguishing features. It was so unlike the trees in Ireland. Most of all, the light in Finland got to him. There was something eerie about it, especially in the hours before dawn. And how would he ever master the language?

Another thing that annoyed him about the country was the practice of his coat being taken from him in restaurants when he didn't want it to be, and then a charge imposed for such a service. Neither did he take to the national obsession with saunas. He found these to be more amusing than therapeutic. Why would anyone wish to over-heat themselves and then go through equal degrees of freezing? His upbringing had been too practical for such an indulgence.

Laaksi and himself went to St. Petersburg in December. Afterwards they travelled to Copenhagen and Stockholm. In February 1965 they went to London. McGahern got part-time work as a teacher there. There were no long term offers. Sometimes he was just paid by the day.

They stayed with Breege and Rosaleen when they were there. Both of them were working in the same hospital at Whipp's Cross. Breege was a nurse and Rosaleen a theatre supervisor. McGahern got work as a supply teacher. Rosaleen was on night duty. Often when she came in from her shift in the mornings he'd be getting ready to go to work. They'd have breakfast together. Her anecdotes about the prevalence of tragedies she witnessed in her patients made him aware of the relative triviality of his own problems. One morning she said to him, "They were falling like flies last night."

Laaski did some translating work. At the weekends they socialized with writers McGahern knew. He befriended the broadcaster Melvyn Bragg at this time. They enjoyed going to soccer matches together. It was a special treat if George Best was playing. They usually went drinking afterwards. The better they got to know one another, the more common ground they found in each other's lives.

Like McGahern, Bragg had been an altar boy in youth. He'd also been very close to his mother. Both of them had married foreign women. Bragg's wife was a French painter. McGahern and Laaksi spent many evenings with Bragg and his wife in a flat they were renting on the Portobello Road.

He also met up with him in Dublin. Bragg enjoyed watching him navigating his way around the city "like a pilot boat slipping in between a crowded fleet in a harbour." He found him to be charming company, "a singular man with a lovely smile, a bard of what can seem ordinary, a writer who alchemised much of his life into fiction."[13]

McGahern occasionally met Tony Whelan for a drink. Whelan had written a novel by now. He wanted McGahern's view of it. One night when they were in a bar he gave it to him. McGahern told him he was looking forward to reading it. When he did so, however, he was disappointed by its quality. He phoned him the next night to give him the bad news. He didn't think it had merit. Whelan was devastated. McGahern told him he'd meet him to discuss it in more detail but the meeting never took place. Instead McGahern posted the manuscript back to him.

Whelan was hurt but he trusted McGahern's judgment. He put the book away and never sent it to a publisher. He didn't see McGahern for many years after that.[14]

McGahern was in touch with Charles Monteith through all of this time regarding the publication of *The Dark*. Monteith had expressed concern about the sexual content of the book and the possible effect of this on sales. McGahern was more concerned with getting the writing right. If you did that, he felt, everything else would follow. Monteith respected his position. He saw McGahern more as a friend than a colleague. Their friendship increased over these months and also included Laaksi. On St. Valentine's Day Monteith took the pair of them on a tour of Oxford College. He'd once been a student there.

They sailed to Ireland in March. Laaksi's negative feelings about the country were fortified almost upon disembarking from the ship. One of the first things she saw was a notice forbidding the importation of "hay, straw and contraceptives."[15]

She met McGahern's father on a visit to Grevisk. He disgusted her, making her aware that the scenarios McGahern depicted in *The Dark* weren't exaggerated. The moment she entered the house she sensed "the horror and the violence." It was as if it was in the air: "I could hardly breathe, it was stifling." He reminded her of Dr. Goebbels, Hitler's right hand man. He gave her the familiar "devil's eye" treatment. Then he spoke of her as if she wasn't there. "Well, John," he said, "Is this your wife?" The question was rhetorical. He was trying to make her feel small.[16]

He then asked him what age she was. When McGahern said "Thirty," he shot back, "She looks forty."[17] This conversation mirrors one between a father and son in the story "Gold Watch" when the son presents his wife to his father.[18] McGahern seems to have created parts of this story verbatim from actual events, something he didn't usually like doing.

He visited them after they got back to London. Laaksi was amazed at how friendly Breege and Rosaleen were with him in view of the beatings he'd given them in childhood. It was as if they'd never happened. He was dangerous when he was aggressive but even moreso when he turned on his charm. That was when he could make people forget past cruelties, when he could suck them back into his orbit. When he did that, the whole treadmill began again. They became his captives – almost willing ones.

His tough side returned when he got back home. When Benedict Kiely called to the house one day he attacked him with a spade. Coupled with his aggression was a dark wit that McGahern had a grudging admiration for. He wrote to him in London, "A Mr. Kiely blew in last week. I think he was on the razzle. I'll attend his funeral if I hear of it."[19]

Patrick Gregory, one of McGahern's American editors, visited McGahern's father another day with Richard Murphy. Agnes offered them tea but he himself was like ice. No more than with Laaksi, they could almost taste the atmosphere of terror in the house.

McGahern and Laaksi spent the summer of 1965 in Spain. They were in a town called Garrucha. It was in Almeria. *The Dark* was banned while they were there. McGahern wasn't surprised. Monteith told him it probably would be. He wasn't upset from a literary point of view but he knew it could make his future complicated.

They were staying in a house that was, according to Laaksi, "like an artist's collective." It was very liberated: "There was a lot of partner-swapping going on," she recalled. Neither of them were interested in that, being "country types and rather puritanical at the time."[20]

McGahern felt strange with her in the new environment. They'd been so many places. Were things moving too fast for them? Finland hadn't really been like a honeymoon. Spain was more like one. And yet it didn't seem like it. There was a sense of unreality about everything. Would they still like one another when things became ordinary between them? That was the real test of a relationship. Maybe things would never be ordinary. McGahern didn't know if he wanted them to be or not.

He was confused. How was the banning of *The Dark* ban going to affect his future? Would it change the way he was perceived in Ireland? Various conundrums swirled around in his head as he basked in the sun with Laaksi. It was a surreal time, the beauty of the surroundings clashing with the tension of his circumstances.

Garrucha (Pixabay)

He didn't write much in Spain apart from a few stories. Some of them, he thought, might "turn into work." Not in the immediate term, perhaps, but in time. He usually had material in his head for a long time before committing it to paper. Writing he saw as a way of getting rid of material, of freeing his mind for other things.

He savoured the lazy days with Laaksi, or "Anu," as he nicknamed her. It was easier for him to say than Anniki. He'd never heard the name before. How would Leitrim people feel about her if they decided to live in Ireland? The people he knew had probably never met anyone from Finland before.

He wondered if his father would thaw out with her in time. It probably didn't matter. He doubted he'd be seeing much of him.

One day they had an accident on a scooter they'd rented. It went out of control on a sandy road. Both of them came off as it careered into a ditch. McGahern wasn't injured but the mirror of the scooter broke. It sent shards of glass into the nerves beneath Laaksi's eyes. She had to have plastic surgery on it. The feeling was slow to come back to her face.

They spent a lot of time translating a book together. It was a 1957 novel called *The Manila Rope* written by a Finnish novelist, Veijo Meri. Meri wrote comic novels to the backdrops of war. *The Manila Rope* was set during the Russian-Finnish one. It dealt with a soldier who deserts the army and then risks his life for the eponymous rope. The joke is that it isn't of any value to him. A later Meri novel, *The Colonel's Driver* (1966) featured a man traversing war zones to fetch a briefcase that's as useless as the rope of the 1957 book.

Laaksi's fluency in the language gave her an advantage over McGahern in the translating. He saw his job as putting "Irish English" on what she'd done. By that he meant adding colloquialisms and turns of phrase.[21] She tried to get the book grammatically correct while he spent his time improving it. This wasn't wise. As she said, "That's not how you do translations." McGahern was a far better writer than Meri but it wasn't his business to display this. When she tried to tell him that he became annoyed.[22] He couldn't resist the temptation to try and improve it. It was the teacher in him.

They went back to London that September. Both of them were feeling down in the dumps. They argued about where they would go from here. McGahern wanted to live in Ireland but she wouldn't hear of this. She wanted him to go to Finland with her. He said he wouldn't be able to make enough money there. She said they could live on her salary. He wasn't agreeable to that. She accused him of suffering from pride but that wasn't really the issue. His dislike of the country was a more influential factor in his thinking

She understood his problem. They'd been together long enough for her to understand how important personal relationships were to him. She knew her compatriots didn't mix as easily as Irish people: "Finnish people just do not know how to do that." She also knew the country depressed him: "So did its remoteness and darkness in winter." Neither could he write as well he wanted to there. The main reason was the intense light: "He missed the shadows and rain of Ireland." She knew he'd never settle there in the long term. "He yearned to return to Ireland to write about what he knew."[23]

London was a likelier possibility. Laaksi thought she might be able to stay there indefinitely. Her employers in Finland were interested in making her their English translator. A long time in London there wouldn't have suited McGahern but he thought he might have no choice considering what had happened with *The Dark*. His attitude to England could be summed up by Joe Ruttledge's words in *That They May Face the Rising Sun*: "It's not my country and I never feel it's quite real or that my life there is real. [You never feel] fully involved in anything that happens."

They finished their work on *The Manila Rope* in April 1966. By now he was thoroughly fed up of it. It had taken up almost a year of his life. What limited humour it contained had worn thin. He couldn't understand how Laaksi had been so patient with it. It amazed him to think she could devote her whole life to this kind of thing.

Notoriety

The Dark is a coming-of-age book full of angst and anger. The adolescent boy at its centre is the son of a widowed farmer, Mahoney, in rural Ireland. He struggles with sexual and physical abuse from both his father and the clergy, who represent another form of patriarchy. He isn't named, perhaps because McGahern wanted his plight to be seen as representative of a universal one in Ireland at the time.[1]

All the classic McGahern themes are here – parental cruelty, childhood trauma, religion, love, sex, death. It's written at a frenetic pace, shifting from first to second person willy nilly as the streams of consciousness spill over onto one another.

Young Mahoney has a sister, Joan, who's sexually abused by a drapery wholesaler. This incident was based on Rosaleen's experience after she left school. When young Mahoney reports it to a priest he does nothing about it. McGahern is prescient here, exposing the cover-up of sexual abuse that was rife at the time in Ireland, though not known generally until decades later. In *The Dark* he expunged the dark heart of a hidden Ireland, one it wasn't yet ready to confront.

Another scene has the boy masturbating into a sock. This was an act with which the book would forever come to be associated, leading McGahern to dub the book itself "The Auld Sock."

Masturbation was "the sin that dared not speak its name" at this time in Ireland. It was probably the one most confessed by adolescent boys in confession. Priests condemned it but it was still probably less frowned on than "getting a girl into trouble." In *The Dark* it becomes the sin of sins, the epitome of a lost Eden. Confessing it cleanses the boy's soul in a catharsis. Afterwards he sees himself becoming as white as snow, the world a beautiful place calling him to begin again. Paradise is Regained.

Monteith was concerned about a passage where the boy's father masturbates in bed beside him. The episode has aspects of incest and paedophilia about it. It was too graphically written not to have been drawn from life. Monteith thought it would definitely cause the book to be banned. He also feared McGahern's father would sue Faber on account of it. He'd already used his father as a model for Reegan in *The Barracks*.

Michael McLaverty flagged this. "*The Dark* could be read as a continuation of *The Barracks*," he told McGahern, "with Regan (sic) and Mahoney the same person."[2] He'd loved *The Barracks* unreservedly but some of the sexual elements of *The Dark* repulsed him.

Monteith didn't want McGahern to remove the passage, merely to tone it down. He said he'd check it out with his sisters. When he did, they reassured him that their father was too vain to sue. It would put him in the frame as an abuser and that wouldn't sit well with his reputation in Grevisk, something he guarded fiercely. As far as he was concerned, the less attention that was drawn to this aspect of the book, the better. Other abuses perpetrated by him in it are physical without being overtly sexual. The lines are blurred. One can assume there was a sexual element in much corporal punishment in days of yore. In *The Dark*, Mahoney appears to get sexual pleasure from beating the boy after he orders him to take off his clothes and bend over a chair.

The bedroom abuse was based on fact. McGahern's father slept with him. The oedipal situation is twisted here. He sleeps with the hated father instead of the loved mother. Sex compounds that hatred.

"He never interfered with me in an obvious sexual way," he wrote, "but he frequently massaged my belly and thighs... He asserted he was doing this for my good: it relaxed taut muscles, eased wind and helped bring on sleep. In these years I had only the vaguest knowledge of sex or sexual functions and took him at his word but as soon as it was safe to do so I turned away [from him]...looking back and remembering his tone of voice and the rhythmic movement of his hand. I suspect he was masturbating."[3]

In *The Dark* the sexual abuse relates to events outside the bedroom. The boy is a high academic achiever. His father isn't. The boy also has ambitions to become a priest. We can see where this all came from in McGahern's life.

The man brings both himself and the boy to a sexual climax. For him it's the only way he can humiliate someone who's outstripped him educationally. He hadn't been educated past primary school. The boy now feels unworthy to become a priest.

In another chapter a priest comes into Mahoney's room while he's staying at his house and curls up in bed beside him. It doesn't quite become sexual abuse but it isn't far from it either.

The writer Eugene McCabe saw this as prophetic of the abuse of young boys that came to light in a future era. "Mahoney unmarried would have made an exemplary Christian Brother," he suggested.[4]

McGahern knew he was tilting at windmills with the book, its sexual content being unprecedented for the time. Though Faber won a landmark case two years before with *Lady Chatterley's Lover*, D.H. Lawrence's book was still banned in Ireland. Edna O'Brien's first two books had also been banned. There was a different law for Ireland to the one in "pagan" England.

There were also many expletives in *The Dark*. "Fuck" was even used on the first page. In the pre-Roddy Doyle days of the mid-1960s, great offence was taken at this.[5]

McGahern was expecting them to shock people but he had to put them in. They weren't inserted gratuitously but at that time there was no distinction in the public eye between "good bad language" and "bad bad language." Everything went into the pot of unallowability.

Monteith told him that if he kept the expletives he was leaving the book open to the possibility of it being banned. Even if it wasn't, their presence would affect sales in Ireland.[6] McGahern was philosophical about both eventualities. Monteith suggested using asterisks ("F**K") or dashes ("F--K") to tone them down. McGahern despised this form of censorship.[7] He would have preferred not to use the words at all than to have them bowdlerised like that. Eventually Faber gave in. The book was printed almost totally as he wrote it.[8]

He advised Monteith not to circulate too many copies of it for review prior to publication. The *Irish Times* was probably all right, having an intellectual readership, but not the more conservative *Irish Independent* or the populist *Irish Press*.

On May 5, 1965, 260 copies of *The Dark* arrived in Dublin intended for distribution throughout the city. They were seized at Customs and submitted to the Censorship of Publications Board for examination. Five days later The *Irish Times* published a report that it had been censored.[9] The seized copies were pulped.

Censorship was rampant in Ireland at this time, not only in books but in theatre and the cinema too. It was ratified by a populace that desired, as the expression went, the "angelisation" of Ireland rather than its "Los Angeles-ation." The film censor James Montgomery inveighed against what he called "the morals of the poultry yard." These, he thought, threatened to pollute holy Catholic Ireland.[10]

In such circumstances it isn't surprising that *The Dark* was banned. McGahern was relieved to be geographically distant from the media storm it gave rise to. He took some responsibility for the whole business. "If I wrote the novel better," he said, "They mightn't have noticed it."[11]

He didn't take the Censorship Board seriously. Most censored books were easily enough procured "under the counter." Whether they were worth reading was another matter. Most of them weren't.

If he grew up in England he could never have written the book. There

The censoring of *The Dark* made McGahern more ashamed of his country than of himself.

would have been no need. The fact that it wasn't banned there spoke for itself. But it couldn't have been written there – by McGahern or anyone else.

He was more ashamed of Ireland than he was of anything he'd written or done. It was making a fool of itself in the eyes of the world, indulging in a form of philistinism one might have imagined it had outgrown.

The experience, he said, was "not unlike listening to a bad joke that one had learned to dismiss, and then discovering that one had become part of the joke oneself."[12]

Censorship served no purpose in his view. Banning something made it more attractive by definition. "Forbidden fruit has its own sweetness." If we wanted to have purer writers, he believed, first of all we had to get a cleaner society.

"Cleaning up literature is actually putting the cart before the horse."[13] He could have gone further and said literature actually acts as a lamp to society rather than a mirror.

His attention now turned to his job. The new term was beginning in Belgrove.

He wasn't able to attend the school on the first day of term because of an accident he'd had in Spain. He wrote to the Department of Education

Censorship of the book proved to be the least of McGahern's problems when he went back to his teaching job. He discovered he'd been suspended. (Leitrim Library)

and the school manager to advise them of this but didn't receive a reply to either communication. The letters were his way of testing the waters as to what kind of reception he'd get if he returned.

Three weeks later he wrote another letter to say he'd been passed by the doctor and would return in a week. He received a telegram from the principal of the school in reply saying, "Telephone before travelling."[14]

He wasn't sure what this meant so he asked a friend of his from UCD, the English lecturer Roger McHugh, to contact him. When he did this, the principal refused to give him any information.

McGahern presented himself for work on the morning of Monday, October 11. When he got to the school it was just like any other day. His arrival in Ireland hadn't reached the media so there were no journalists there. The staff welcomed him back warmly. When the bell rang for class he left the staffroom and walked down the corridor to his classroom. The headmaster, Mr. Kelleher, stood outside his door. He read a legal letter from the Manager, Fr. Carton, saying he was barred from entering it. McGahern then went back to the staffroom. Mr. Kelleher joined him later and offered him a newspaper to read. Fr. Carton was on holiday. He wouldn't be back until November. McGahern suspected the timing of the holiday was deliberate.

He had nothing to do all day so he just kept drinking cups of tea. He thought he'd never drank so much tea in his life. After a while he almost started to enjoy himself. The other teachers were more stressed than he was. He was reminded of an execution he'd once read of where nobody was more relaxed than the condemned man.[15] He stayed there until 2.15 p.m, the end of the school day. Then he walked out the gate with them as if he'd just spent a day teaching.

He met members of his union, the Irish National Teacher's Organisation (INTO) sometime later. It evaded the responsibility of supporting him on a technicality. He'd been away from Ireland so his membership had lapsed. He argued that it would have been senseless for him to pay his dues when he was in another country and not teaching.

The General Secretary, another Kelleher, said to him, "If it was just the auld book, maybe we might have been able to do something for you but by going and marrying this woman in a registry office you've turned yourself into an impossible case entirely."[16]

He added, "What entered your head to go and marry a foreign woman when there's hundreds of thousands of Irish women going around with their tongues out for a husband!" McGahern said he was busily chasing girls at the time but he never saw anything as "delicious" as that going around.[17]

He went back to Fr. Carton but got nowhere. He said to McGahern, "You caused a terrible schmozzle with the book. I couldn't take you back after that. There'd be an uproar." The marriage had added fuel to the flame, as Kelleher pointed out. He asked him what would happen if he regularised it. Would he be able to get a job in another school when the publicity died down? Carton replied, "Not in the Archdiocese of Dublin but maybe down the country."[18]

This statement alerted McGahern to the fact that the ripples had extended farther than he thought, all the way to John Charles McQuaid, the aforementioned Archbishop of Dublin.

McQuaid was notoriously right wing. In the previous decade he'd guillotined a proposal from Noel Browne, the then Minister for Health, to provide free medical care for mothers about to give birth. His reasons were unclear. He'd managed to find something immoral in it. What was really immoral was the huge level of infant mortality at the time. The fact that he could ride roughshod over a government minister was an indication of the huge power of the Church. The president of Ireland at the time was the equally conservative Eamon de Valera.

McQuaid's power extended across all frontiers of society from health to literature. In his biography of him, John Cooney wrote, "Browne concluded that McQuaid was obsessed with protecting Catholic Ireland from the evil nature of human sexuality. Under the country's rigid censorship laws he ensured that the majority of the world's great writers were banned on grounds of sexual indecency. McQuaid too he held responsible for the flight of Irish writers."[19]

He oversaw something else too, i.e. "the confinement by the courts of thousands of young boys and girls to virtual penal servitude in orphanages where many of them were physically and sexually abused by 'celibate' priests, Brothers and Sisters. Young men and women who did not observe the Catholic Church's strict prohibition on sex outside of wedlock were dealt with harshly and summarily. Unmarried mothers were sent away or placed in 'Magdalene Penitentiaries' where they were forced by nuns to engage in slave-labour as laundry workers and cleaning women. It didn't seem to matter if they were the victims of rape or even incest. They'd been involved in extra-marital sex and therefore they were "fallen women."

Maybe it isn't fair to just blame the church. The state colluded in this state of affairs. So did the families who threw these girls out of their homes. In many ways it was the time that was to blame. The chastisement of the body was seen as a means to the salvation of the soul, the Virgin Mary the epitome of Irish womanhood. Irish girls flocked to convents, boys to seminaries. "To direct this particular piety, McQuaid issued a series of publications which laid down a strict, all-encompassing moral code for his flock."[20]

McGahern clearly fell way outside such a code. He told Cooney he believed McQuaid was directly behind his sacking because of his obsession with what he called "impure" books. He heard privately that McQuaid told the union that if they stood behind McGahern he wouldn't give them any support in pay negotiations that were coming up for the department of education but that he'd back them to the hilt if they had nothing to do with him.[21]

Why was McQuaid so invested in McGahern's case? It was unusual for such a high-ranking ecclesiastical figure to become involved in what was hardly a matter of national importance.

If one were of a suspicious mentality, it could be suggested that McGahern was fired from his job because he was getting too close to highlighting clerical abuses. Pat Dolan wrote, "At the time *The Dark* was published and the Church banished him from teaching in Ireland, it was shielding many perpetrators of abuse similar to those outlined by McGahern in that novel."[22]

Was McQuaid himself one of these? In one part of his biography of him, Cooney suggests he sexually abused a young boy in the back room of a bar once.[23] This has never been substantiated and McGahern never heard of it.

A recently published book attests to McQuaid's kindness to the Garda Siochana. Everyone has many sides to them. Demonising McQuaid for the intellectual paralysis of 1960s Ireland – and McGahern's sacking – isn't really the issue. If McQuaid wasn't in power at the time, someone of a similar stripe would probably have been.

The church had also done a lot of good in Ireland over the years. McGahern himself acknowledged that. He also valued religion as a stabilising factor in society even after he lost his faith. His disdain for McQuaid was understandable because he'd been targeted personally by him. Such a targeting was hardly surprising. His book and art struck at the very foundations of the mores of the society to which he belonged. By refusing to give up his job he was setting himself up against a society exponentially stronger than him. It was a David versus Goliath struggle for him.

Nobody had any problem with his teaching. In fact his school had won an award the previous year for its prowess, the prestigious Carlisle and Blake Premium award. Inspectors commended all its teachers, McGahern included, for their "excellent" work.[24] The parents of the children he taught also wanted him kept on. Unfortunately they didn't carry enough weight.

The Board of Management said they'd be happy to give him references to teach in England. This amused him greatly. "It was all right corrupting the English kids," he chuckled, "but not the ones in Clontarf."[25]

It was like the Irish attitude to women who became pregnant outside marriage. Let them have their abortions "across the pond" and preserve the illusion of the home country as pro-life.

He didn't want to go quietly. It was one of the things that annoyed him about Ireland, the way problems were brushed under the carpet. Sex was one of them. His sacking was another. When he thought of it, both things tapped into the same problem – camouflage. He refused to humour the authorities by rushing off to England like so many other teachers in years gone by. Most of them had disappeared into black holes.

He hadn't committed a crime. Writing the book wasn't an offence in itself. Neither was he molesting children. His case was brought up in the Dáil, the Irish Parliament. Brendan Corish, the leader of the Labour Party, pointed out that it was an incredible system that while the state paid teachers, it was the Church that hired and fired them.

Jack Lynch, the Taoiseach of the time, refused to give a reason for his dismissal, saying the "special relationship" between church and state gave him this entitlement.[26]

The Appeals Board appointed an arbiter, Professor O'Briain, to look at the case. He went to Paris and met a man he knew called Con Leventhal, a university lecturer. Leventhal was aware of the quality of the writing. He said to O'Briain, "What in the name of God is wrong with you banning McGahern's book?" O'Briain replied, "We can't have people running around the country with their flies open!" McGahern never forgot this expression. He even used it in one of his novels.[27]

The situation had become farcical for him. He felt he was a victim of his time. His friends realised that. They wanted to make an issue out of it but by now he'd gone beyond caring.

Among all the people campaigning on his behalf, only Samuel Beckett thought to ask the question: "Does John want us to do that?"

McGahern wrote to him to thank him. He'd put his finger on the nub of the issue. It had gone beyond the book. People were using him as a puppet to further their own agendas.

Though McGahern held Beckett's work in high esteem, he showed little interest in meeting him. Beckett invited him to dinner once but he declined. He didn't see the point of going to see somebody just because he admired the way he wrote. Laaksi had been more interested in socialising with him. She'd met him through her theatre work.

Beckett had won the Nobel Prize in 1965. He hadn't wanted to take it. He only did so because refusing it would have drawn even more attention to him.[28] McGahern was delighted. So often it was given to the wrong people.

There were requests for interviews but he ignored them. He didn't want to play the martyr. Peter Lennon, the man who'd introduced him to Laaksi, wanted to politicise him. McGahern told him he had no interest in that. It was a distasteful episode in his life but not something he wanted to define him. He'd made his statement and he wanted to leave it at that. The Council of Civil Liberties asked him if he wanted to take the case to the High Court but he refused that too.[29]

He even refused a request from Edna O'Brien – a more voluble banned author – to attend an anti-censorship rally. "I felt I was being used," he said.[30] O'Brien had portrayed women in her books as sexual beings rather than primarily maternal ones. These were the images sought by McQuaid and De Valera. McGahern had done likewise for a hormonally-challenged adolescent. They were coming at the same theme from different angles. Both had got their fingers burned by an intolerant establishment. People from O'Brien's home village of Tuamgraney wanted her kicked naked through the streets. "I never understood the naked bit," she laughed. Both McGahern and O'Brien had also married people with left wing tendencies. This was tantamount to marrying communists in people's eyes.

They weren't the only two writers in the firing line. People like Lee Dunne and John Broderick had undergone trouble with the censors too. But neither they nor O'Brien had lost their jobs as a result. "The McGahern Case" got the most headlines for this reason.

McGahern's father told him hardly a day went by without his name being in the papers. The scandal the book caused was something he could never have foreseen. He'd never seen himself as a rebel growing up. He didn't want to break down the doors," as one writer put it, "just to pick the locks."[31]

McGahern described censorship as being "fascistic in the real sense of the word"[32] but he didn't make an issue of this either. If his sacking left a wound it came out in more subtle ways, like his featuring of characters called McQuaid in many of his works afterwards. They're usually unsavoury people. In *Amongst Women* a character called McQuaid is referred to as a "drunken blackguard."[33]

As for now, there was no point brooding about the problems *The Dark* caused. What was done was done. At least the reviews were positive. Alfred A. Knopf even wanted to do an American reprint. McGahern read from it in Boston University in February 1966. It was unusual for such a young writer to be getting this kind of attention. It showed how much his name had got around. It wasn't just from the notoriety. *The Barracks* had confirmed him as an exciting new voice in Irish fiction. *The Dark* copperfastened that.

McGahern pictured in Boston University at the time *The Dark* was banned (Bobbie Hanvey Photographic Archives, John J. Burns Library, Boston College)

His father gave off the feeling of being offended by the book but he enjoyed the attention if brought him. It reminded him of the hoo-ha that surrounded another writer, Brinsley MacNamara, when he wrote a similarly incendiary book some years before. That was *The Valley of the Squinting Windows*. It caused consternation in the village of Delvin, County Westmeath. That was where it was set. Many people claimed to see themselves in its pages. Some launched legal actions on that account. MacNamara became a pariah. The book was burned publicly. Children were withdrawn from the school where his father taught.

Things weren't as bad for McGahern. At least he didn't have to live in Leitrim. Brian Friel offered him a cottage he owned in Donegal where he could stay until things blew over. He was touched by the offer but didn't take him up on it.

The book became a *succes de scandale*. It was passed around furtively in boarding school corridors to be read under covers by torchlight, its title appropriate to the occasion. McGahern knew that banned books in Ireland could always be found somewhere. Leitrim's county librarian, a woman called Vera McCarthy, kept a copy of *The Dark* for "discreet distribution" for those who wanted to thwart the authorities. The Irish always had that rebellious streak in them. Maybe it was a post-colonial thing.[34]

He went back to London afterwards. When he got there he wrote to Michael McLaverty to tell him about his suspension. "The union is a paper tiger," he wrote, "the church has all the power. They'd have given me a little money to go quietly but I refused."[35] He said he was apprehensive about his future. At the end of the letter he wrote, "American universities want my manuscripts. I may be able to get a life annuity from one in return for [them], which'll save me going back to teach or some other rubbish."[36] This was an aspirational hope from one so young. It shows how confident he was in his talent, something that doesn't seem obvious in the plethora of modest outpourings that are more frequent from him.

The relationship between McGahern and McLaverty wasn't without tensions. I mentioned McLaverty's problems with sexual elements in *The Dark*. Neither did McGahern give McLaverty's work unalloyed approval. But maybe a relationship is healthier for such frankness. Neither of them

Michael McLaverty (pictured) was shocked by some parts of *The Dark*. Such a reaction caused a distance between himself and McGahern. (Literary Executors, Michael McLaverty Archives, Linen Hall Library, Belfast)

had to censor themselves with the other. They didn't take offence at any criticisms.

McLaverty was surprised *The Dark* was such a success. He believed its sexual passages – the ones that got McGahern into trouble – would have hurt its sales. When they didn't he took it as a sign that his own style of writing was becoming anachronistic. He stopped writing soon afterwards.[37] It wasn't until 1968 that he returned to it. Seamus Heaney suggested he send a story to David Marcus in his "New Irish Writing" page in the *Irish Press*. It was printed and led to others. Marcus reprinted all of McLaverty's books when he set up Poolbeg Press some years later with Philip McDermott.

Joe Ackerley, an English writer McGahern was friendly with, said to him when he heard of the ban, "That's great news. You'll get a lot of publicity and it'll increase sales."[38] He didn't think of it that way, being more concerned with the disgrace it would bring on him.

His sisters were accosted at a wedding one day by a man who asked them if they were related to "the fella who wrote the dirty book." They were very upset by his comments.[39]

Joe Kennedy, the journalist he'd known since his time teaching in Drogheda, went to London to interview him. The interview criticised both the church and the teacher's union. As such it was deemed unfit for publication. The institutions that had been instrumental in his dismissal couldn't be advertised in this capacity in his newspaper, the *Evening Herald*. McGahern was too much of a hot potato. It didn't appear until after he died.

Many people expected McGahern to be more bitter about the church than he was at this time. One of them was Gay Byrne, the host of *The Late Late Show*, a programme on which he appeared one night.

Byrne expected him to come out against religion but he refused to do that, emphasising how much the church had meant to him all his life. Byrne then asked him if he ever put in "spicy bits" in his books to gain attention. It was one of the worst insults he'd ever received and a total misunderstanding of his work. He replied, "If you ever wrote sentences and paragraphs, you would have enough to do to keep the rhythm and images and grammar in order without thinking of whether it would make you famous or not."[40]

The show was coming from Belfast that night. A Unionist in the audience was disgusted with him. "There's a man," he said, "whose book had been banned by the Southern government, who has been sacked from his school by the Archbishop of Dublin and he comes to Belfast and gets up on his hind legs and praises the Catholic Church. Could Moscow do a better job of brainwashing than that?"[41]

Another episode of the show aired at this time had Byrne engaging in a fun quiz with a husband and wife. Each was asked questions the other had to answer to find out how well they knew one another. One of the questions concerned the colour of the nightdress the wife wore on her wedding night.

The woman in question, Eileen Fox, said she couldn't remember. She speculated that she may not have worn any night dress at all. A ripple of laughter cascaded through the audience at this. The next morning at Mass, a bishop called Thomas Ryan denounced the show from his pulpit in Loughrea, County Galway for its "objectionable" material. The Loughrea Town Commissioners backed the bishop, describing the programme as "dirty." They said it should be taken off the air. Other groups rowed in behind them. The "Bishop and the Nightie Affair," as it came to be called, turned into a "national incident."⁴²

Bishop Ryan became a figure of fun as time went on. People laughed at him. This was the "new" Ireland, a country where a woman – shock, horror – was entitled not to have anything on her on such a night. The affair became national news. The story of "The Bishop and the Nightie" was talked about for years as a watershed. McGahern wrote about a similar situation in *The Leavetaking* years later, telling a story about a woman who wanted to wear nothing on her wedding night but her "birthday suit."⁴³

The attitude to the bishop signified a change in the country's mood. The practice of saying the rosary also died off. It had once been an almost mandatory practice in Catholic households, including McGahern's one. Now it was only recited here and there. Instead of saying it, most Irish families now sat down to watch television.⁴⁴

Brian Lenihan, the then Minister for Justice, replaced members of the Appeals Board with more liberal people. The times they were a-changing, as Bob Dylan said. This affected films as much as books. Banned films became viewable underage restrictions. In the past this system had been rejected out of hand. Reactionary people argued that a certificate like "Over 18s" would only make a film more attractive to viewers. It was a form of thinking that treated the populace like children.

Legislation for the unbanning of books was introduced now too. It resulted in the release of a staggering 5,000 titles over the next few years.

Memorabilia from the McGahern Museum in Leitrim (Keith Nolan)

James Joyce's *Ulysses*, strangely enough, wasn't one of them. It had never been banned in Ireland, though it as only available under special order in bookshops.[45]

McGahern was in Paris when *The Dark* was unbanned. There was a media circus surrounding the event. He was invited to join it but demurred. It would have been wrong to make money out of such nonsense, he said, just as it would have been to gratify the original banning with a sense of importance. He felt staying put and keeping quiet was a more dignified response.[46]

The fact that *The Dark* was banned for its sexual content led people to think McGahern had an obsession with this subject. Nothing could have been farther from the truth. He didn't approve of sexual hedonism anymore than he did of sexual repression.[47]

"We got an appalling sexual upbringing in Ireland," he said once, "Sex was exaggerated out of all proportion instead of being given its normal place in life, like food, water or air."[48]

His rural roots gave him an earthiness that saw sexual behaviour as being as much a part of life as anything else. "Either all of life is sacred," he said, "or none of it is."[49] Sexuality was part of that.

According to Jesus, the Ten Commandments could be reduced to two. In the Ireland of McGahern's youth, those two would have been the sixth and the ninth. He regarded the church as being responsible for this misplacement of values which resulted in so much Catholic guilt.

His life had been dictated to by the church, first as an altar boy who was expected to become a priest and later as a teacher when he was expected to guide the new generation in the same way as he had been, with all its mores. Being fired from his job by an Archbishop put the final seal on that influence.

Or did it? Some of it continued even after *The Dark* was published. This was made clear to him from a story he heard from a friend concerning its appearance. Apparently, a Galway man made a special request to his local bookshop. He asked the shopkeeper to send him a copy of the book with the dust jacket torn off. He also wanted the spine removed and the book to be torn in two, after which it was to be sent to him in separate envelopes. McGahern wondered if it was the bishop of Galway.[50] The incident shocked him when he heard it. After the shock subsided, he thought it epitomised many of the issues he wrote about in the book.

Exile

McGahern had more reason than Joyce or Beckett to be bitter about Ireland. Their comments on the country have been well documented. Joyce once called Ireland "the old sow that eats her farrow." When Beckett was informed that he was teaching the "cream" of Ireland's youth in a post he had in Foxrock once, he replied, "Yes, rich and thick." No such pronouncements emanated from McGahern. Bitterness he once described as "a failure of understanding."

Losing his job meant he had to forage for work outside the Republic. He asked Michael McLaverty if he could scout around for teaching posts in the north of Ireland. He was offered academic posts in American universities but they didn't interest him at this time. They would later. When McLaverty didn't come up with anything he wondered how he was going to support himself. Even though *The Barracks* was selling well it wasn't enough to live on.[1]

He found it difficult to write after his sacking. He often worked at a manuscript for hours and eventually threw it into the wastepaper basket. He asked Faber for an advance on future royalties so he could buy a house but his request was turned down. It was feared this would create a precedent for other writers. The only option available for him to earn a living was to continue teaching in England.

Most of this was done in London's East End. It was pressurising in a different way to Belgrove. The Church was less of a dominating force in England than Ireland but the children were more difficult there. He found himself giving them articles on football to try and arouse their interest.[2] Often even this proved futile. Neither did their parents seem to care much how they performed.

He felt like a gypsy going from school to school. As was the case with his mother, no job seemed to last long. It meant he didn't get a chance to establish himself with the pupils. He found himself unable to build up a bond with them. His spirits dropped as a result. He became a worker for hire. "One place is as good as another," he wrote to McLaverty, "to keep stupid flesh on the stupid bone."³

McGahern had a complex relationship to educational institutions right through his life. Primary School was enjoyable for the first few years but then he moved to a school where he was beaten and he became traumatised by that. His later years in Primary were taken over by his mother's cancer. That introduced a new horror to it. There was also the constant moving between schools which prevented him being able to settle anywhere.

He enjoyed secondary school because it allowed his mind to develop but St. Pat's was a backward step from that point of view. Added to the intellectual repressiveness in Pat's was a strict regime that intensified the tension of the place. The transition from pupil to teacher removed that to an extent but he still felt pressure, especially when Belgrove grew in size and he moved from the Junior School to the Senior one. The older boys gave him discipline problems and sometimes he let his temper get the better of him with them.

One of the most neglected aspects of training college, as I found myself, is the excessive amount of time devoted to pedagogical theory and the relative dearth given to behavioural problems teachers face. In Primary school, as the saying goes, one teaches pupils whereas in secondary one teaches subjects. St. Pat's didn't pay enough homage to this fact, skewing the curriculum far too much towards the academic side of things.

The pupils in London gave him different kinds of problems. In September 1966 he claimed to be teaching "15 special morons."⁴ The sarcasm was out of character, the term not one he would normally have used. Those who knew him expected him to show an extra concern for weak pupils. It's a sign of his frustration at the way his life was going that he used language like this.

The schools he taught in at this time were either elitist, which meant the pupils were often pampered, or poverty-stricken, which meant they were likely to dress (and even smell) badly. It brought him back to the class divide of Belgrove. Here it was more extreme.

He spent more time trying to discipline the pupils than he did teaching them. He was reminded of Darwin. He wrote to McLaverty, "It's a real killer. The poorer five-sixths [of the class] are almost illiterate. [It's] more a willpower struggle – who'll dominate – than teaching."⁵

The pupils in one school were so unattuned to the world outside them, half of them couldn't even remember the colour of their front doors.⁶ In another one the parents of three of his pupils were in prison. He performed a minor miracle on one of them. He was a boy who'd been given up on by the other teachers. McGahern gave him individual attention over a period of time using experimental methods to teach him to read. One day he threw a bottle at him that fell on the ground and broke. He said to the boy, "B for Bottle, B for Break, B for Bits."[7]

He noticed the boy was more interested in looking at his face than at pages in books so he made a mask for himself to try and inspire him. He told him to write letters on pieces of paper and to stick them onto the mask. The boy put three letters on it and read out the word "BAT." They continued in this vein. After six months the boy was able to read the headlines of the newspaper. One day his father came up to the school to thank McGahern. He had tears in his eyes.[8]

Things weren't going well with Laaksi at this time. She thought he was spending too much time with his sisters. He saw a tough side to her, something he hadn't witnessed in Paris or Finland. The honeymoon was over now. Reality bit.

Going out to dead-end jobs every morning might have been bearable if he had something to look forward to in the evenings but that wasn't the case. They argued a lot and that drained his spirits for the next day's work. The same applied to Laaksi. She became hot-tempered. No matter how nice his sisters were they were still his sisters. A sister *in-law* was different. Being put up by them wasn't a good situation for her. If she was paying rent at least she'd have had her pride. If something wasn't to her satisfaction she could have complained about it. McGahern's closeness to them increased her discomfiture. She felt he wasn't being a "real" husband to her. Maybe he never got a chance to. They were never in any one place long enough for him to adopt that role, or for her to adopt the role of wife. There were too many displacements – domestic, national, international. Something had to give.

In July 1967 they moved from his sisters' house to a flat in Gore Road. The question of where they were going to live permanently was like a running sore by now. McGahern was determined it wouldn't be Finland. Laaksi was equally intransigent about Ireland. She still saw it as a provincial backwater. Even though it had made some liberal strides in the recent past it still had a large core of conservatism attached to it.

Earlier that year, the actress Jayne Mansfield, regarded primarily as a sex symbol, had arrived in County Kerry. She was due to make an appearance at the Mount Brandon Hotel in Tralee but it was opposed by the local priest, Monsignor Lane. He argued rather dramatically that her appearance would "besmirch the name of our town for the sake of filthy gain." She never got to appear, despite arguing that she was "a good Catholic" and the sole supporter of her five children.

Even if Laaski liked Ireland it would have been difficult for her to make a living there. She might have got translating work but little else. London was always going to be only a temporary bolthole for them. Either their work or their natural inclinations would have drawn them back to their native shores in time.

Both of them knew they couldn't go on as they were. Their love for one another, if it had been there at all, was long gone. They were at each other's throats all the time, tied together by circumstances but having little to say to one another. Laaksi travelled from London and Finland on various assignments. It didn't seem to matter to either of them if they were together or not.

McGahern met the woman who would become his second wife on a trip to New York. She was American. Her name was Madeline Green. She was a statuesque beauty who was well-to-do. She had kind eyes and strong features, reminding him of those New England intellectuals he saw sometimes in films. Her grandfather had been the Danish ambassador to the U.S. She was referred to in newspaper articles as a photographer but she didn't like that description of herself, preferring to say she didn't have any profession.

She was everything Laaksi wasn't – good-humoured, witty, encouraging about his work and friendly to his sisters. He was attracted to her but the timing wasn't good. He was still living with Laaksi even though it was a dead relationship. Madeline moved to Paris later that year, taking up a job with her father. He owned a recording studio there. He was a difficult man and she argued with him a lot. McGahern went to see her there in 1967. Her father didn't like him, thinking he was after her money. She moved to London in August of that year. McGahern re-kindled his friendship with her there. Not long afterwards they became lovers.

The relationship with Laaksi, meanwhile, grew steadily worse. Both of them knew they were headed for the divorce courts. It was only a matter of time. Their *folie a deux* was ending.

Distrust of one another became an issue. Suspicious that she was opening his mail in his absence, McGahern asked people who were writing to him to address correspondence to the school where he was teaching rather than to Gore Road. He feared she would use anything she could against him in any future legal proceedings. Laaksi denied this, countering with an allegation that McGahern was writing to her friends to find out things about her.

She admitted she became difficult towards the end of their relationship. McGahern said she reminded him of his father. She put it down to frustration over where they were going to live. This was obviously only the

The break-up of McGahern's marriage to Anniki Laaksi traumatised him. (Bobbie Hanvey Photographic Archives. John J. Burns Library, Boston College)

tip of the iceberg. People don't become as angry as she did over a geographical circumstance. She seemed to resent his literary success, his personality, even his popularity with his sisters.

They broke up in the summer of 1969. As they emptied the apartment of their belongings, McGahern was reminded of the emptying of the Aughawillan house when his mother was dying. Divorce was a different kind of death.

She spent the summer of 1969 consulting with her lawyers. McGahern was relieved when it all ended in the September. "It's good," he wrote to Patrick Gregory from Paris, "To wake up in the morning without the certitude of some violence before night."[9] It was time to put the seal on their relationship for good.

That was easier said than done. Divorce wasn't legal in Ireland at the time. It was something that bothered him about the country. Nobody divorced without good reason in his view. The breakdown of a marriage was like "death without a body. You've let yourself down and someone else down."[10]

Though the marriage officially lasted five years, they'd spent very little of that time together because of her frequent sojourns to Finland. She went back there again. She left in a bitter frame of mind, destroying all their love letters and photographs before she got on the plane.

McGahern said she re-married after they split up. She denied this. She also continued to deny his claim that she'd been married before, a rumour she said he put about for reasons best known to himself. And she denied his claim that she was going to a prestigious post in the theatrical world in Finland. She insisted she was just a translator and director of radio plays. Any embellishment on this, she alleged, was McGahern engaging in his favourite hobby of writing fiction.[11] Embellishment or not, however, she went on to translate over forty Russian plays into Finnish after moving out of London.

McGahern was upset by the divorce even though it was necessary. Everything was changing around him, both in his personal circumstances and those of his siblings.

Dympna became bored with Ireland and moved to London in the sixties. McGahern often stayed with her there. He loved all his sisters but he had a special affection for Dympna. Because she was the youngest girl in the family he felt she suffered more under their father. He felt protective towards her for that reason. They always had a lot to talk about any time they met. Another thing he had in common with her was that she wrote poetry. He always believed she had untapped potential. He encouraged her to develop her academic side as well as her creative one. He felt she was wasted in the Civil Service when she got a job there. In time she came to agree with him. After she moved to London she did a degree in English at Reading University, getting a job teaching in the city afterwards.

Margaret didn't marry. She remained in the Eastern Health Board. Monica worked in the Civil Service in Drogheda and later in Donegal.

Frankie went to night school. After getting his GCE he studied accountancy. In later years he became manager of a number of factories and small businesses. He eventually became a Financial Controller in BBC Radio. Breege and Rosaleen lived together with their husbands and families in the same house in London.

Breege's husband Con worked on the buildings for a time but then tired of it, and of London. They were saving for a house at the time but he wanted to come home. They had a daughter at the time and Breege was pregnant. He spent all the money on a fish and chip van. He made some money at this but then developed a drink problem. One night he crashed the van after falling asleep at the wheel. Later they returned to London to start again. They had two daughters now and no money.

McGahern felt like a rabbit in the headlights. His family was in flux. He didn't know where he was going to live. First he'd lost his job; now his marriage had ended. But there was a new woman on the horizon. And possibly a new career. He felt positive. He was coming out of a tunnel. Soon he might be able to write well again. It was pointless to look back.

Maybe he'd secretly wanted to get out of teaching. It had probably been draining him more than he realised. His sacking could have been a blessing in disguise, a ticket to a new life.

He came around to this way of thinking more and more as the years went on. One day he even felt confident enough to say, "Whenever I pass a school and see the teachers' Volkswagens parked outside, I say a silent prayer of thanks to John Charles."[12]

Emerging from Writer's Block

Two of McGahern stories were published in the *Atlantic Monthly* in 1969, "Bomb Box" and "The Recruiting Officer." The latter story, he told Patrick Gregory, had originally been "600 pages" long.[1] It's possible he meant to write "60 pages." McGahern was a painstaking reviser of his work but it's difficult to believe he would reduce a manuscript of that size – it would have been huge even as a novel – to the length of a short story.

Hugh Leonard adapted *The Barracks* for the stage as part of the Theatre Festival that year. McGahern hadn't much respect for Leonard, regarding him as something of a hack writer. He'd done television scripts and an adaptation of Joyce, *Stephen D.* McGahern hated it. In February he got a letter from Colgate University asking him if he could fill in for a lecturer who'd let it down. Thus began a visiting professorship that lasted many

Colgate University, where McGahern spent many productive years

years. He referred to it jokingly as the "toothpaste university."²

Teaching literature hadn't been on his radar up to this. "I don't believe in schools of writing," he said once, "The God cannot come out of the machine."³ As he got older he compromised that view. In Colgate he could exchange ideas about subjects close to his heart. He was able to engage in open-ended discussions with his students about things that concerned him deeply and also do some writing on the side. He was also getting paid for it. What was there not to love?

One might have thought the groves of academe to be anathema to such an earthy soul as McGahern. This wasn't the case. The bookish side of him that the Moroneys gave birth to found a different way to blossom in an atmosphere where he was called on to make classic texts relevant to a new generation.

Colgate ticked all the boxes for McGahern. There were trees, a lake, a convivial atmosphere. Being a lecturer was more like fun than work. Between classes he played handball, a game he'd loved growing up.

He found America a more liberating country than England. It was "the land of the free." There had always been something servile about taking the boat to England.⁴ It was the reluctant destination of so many of his forebears when no other option was available. Trips to America, in contrast, seemed to be taken as much for pleasure as necessity. And, needless to say, a prestigious lectureship was somewhat more fulfilling than trying to cram facts into the heads of listless pupils in East London.

America was changing in a way that was exponentially different from Ireland. A man had been put on the moon. Films like *Easy Rider* had brought the counterculture into the forefront of society. There was an appetite for new ways of seeing things. It was a young country and, like most young countries, hungry to sample the traditions of older ones - like Ireland.

McGahern decided not to give his pupils what previous lecturers had. He recommended some traditional texts to them but also some unique ones, mixing the mainstream with the eclectic. His fondness for traditional writers like Proust and Flaubert was offset by texts like Nathanael West's *Miss Lonelyhearts*. He conducted robust debates with his students. They were pleased to have their voices heard by him. In his dissertations on writing he placed a lot of emphasis on original thought, encouraging them to say things that were unconventional.

Some of his students had a commercial approach to literature that he believed to be born of America's lack of tradition. Without condescending to them he guided them towards an appreciation of it that was nuanced and layered, free of bombast and rhetoric.

He didn't write much at this time. It was almost as if he was too calm. He liked to say, "Happiness writes white." If one was feeling too well, a blank page was the result.

His contented frame of mind was bothered by the almost aggressive friendliness of some people he met who had "Have a nice day" bromides ever at their lips. If he felt like being melancholy he liked to think such a mood wasn't socially forbidden. "Have a nice day" wasn't the only phrase that annoyed him. He also hated when they said people "passed" rather than died. If sex was a taboo in the old days, dying seemed to be the latest one that had to be euphemised. Neither was he a fan of people who wished him a "merry" Christmas rather than a "happy" one.

He liked the explosion of energy he found in America but sometimes it was excessive. Democracy had come at a price. The free speech that was denied him in his youth was often too strident in Colgate. Confidence sometimes failed to camouflage empty minds.

The attitude to religion in America was markedly different to what he'd grown up with. It was strange for him to see Jesuits dressed like they'd come from Carnaby Street instead of seminaries. The round collars of his youth were gone and so was the solemnity. A part of him missed these things. "The changes in the liturgy, he said, "are just one more example of emptiness, like restaurant owners who re-decorate after losing business."[5]

Trendy priests with colourful sweaters instead of the dour soutanes of Ireland were refreshing, at least in the short term, but he found something bland about the American clergy. Had they put the baby out with the bathwater? In many ways the magic of religion was absent from America. Mediocrity had replaced fear for these ministers. It was as if they were toadying to a generation raised on Benjamin Spock and James Dean.

He joined Madeline in Paris after his tenure in Colgate came to an end. By now her father had divorced his wife. He then got married again, this time to a much younger woman. Despite this he was as difficult as ever to get on with. He verbally abused McGahern on a number of occasions. Afterwards he was capable of putting his arms around him. There were always these mood fluctuations to be contended with.

Madeline lived in a separate apartment to him in the same building. She and McGahern later bought an apartment of their own in the area. It was on Rue Christine, an address they would occupy on and off for many years. When they weren't there they rented it out. The money helped when royalties were low. It was here he embarked on a collection of stories, one he would call *Nightlines*. It made him feel good to be writing again. Maybe the new decade would be everything the previous one was supposed to be but wasn't.

Panther reprinted *The Dark* in 1970. The cover featured a priest leering over a scantily dressed woman. It fed into all of the sensationalist attitudes that had caused the book to be banned. McGahern was disgusted. He felt the cover should have been banned, whatever about the book.

Nightlines was published by the Atlantic Monthly Press that September. It was a collection of stories he'd been compiling for some time. Patrick Gregory had left the company by now. A man called Peter Davison took over from him. McGahern thought he didn't understand the book. The cover he put on it reflected that. It had a peasant woman wearing a shawl and carrying a stick down a path from a thatched cottage. He was reminded of something from *The Tailor and Ansty*. It fed into all of the clichés he was trying to eradicate from his writing. "Lovely mist that do be rising from the bog," he wrote to Davison in a derisory letter, "Top of the morning."[6] Davison took his point on board, replacing the cover with a plain black one instead.

Nightlines was the least controversial of his books so far. *The Barracks* brought him fame; *The Dark* infamy. The reviews of this book focused more on its content rather than its author. He was able to read them without thinking of the circumstances of its composition. Hopefully this would be how he would be from now on, a professional writer practicing his craft, anonymous behind the prose.

He dedicated the book to Monteith. It was a gesture of the respect in which he held him. Such was his reputation by now, however, Monteith should have been more honoured to have him as a writer than McGahern should have been to have him as his editor. A measure of his confidence now was that he asked for a copy of the book to be sent to Samuel Beckett. The great man replied positively.

In his stories McGahern presented us with grim tableaus of modern Ireland. Fathers tyrannise sacrificial women and long-suffering children. Young men on the cusp of adulthood make commando raids to dimly-lit ballrooms where love may or may not follow flustered conversations on dance floors. Sexual congress sometimes resembles glorified cattle marts in his stories rather than romantic interludes. In the city, civil servants push pens in dead end jobs. In the country, farmers scratch out livings on small freeholds. Abroad there are prostitutes, building site labourers, diasporic refugees.

There's a joke on John Charles McQuaid in one of the stories, "Lavin." It recalls Joyce's "An Encounter" from *Dubliners* in its tone. "John Charles" becomes a reference to a penis in the course of it. This was a Dublinism. At one point a boy touches another boy's fly with his fingers and asks, "How is little John Charles coming along? Sprouting nicely?"[7]

Here as in later books we get homespun wisdom mixed with profound deliberations. In "The Recruiting Officer" McGahern gives us a picture of what a life in education is like for a Christian Brother. "Wheels" explores a familiar dynamic – the tension between a father and son. "Peaches" documented problems between a married couple in Spain.

Some of the stories seem to end in mid-air. That was how he liked it. "I don't think a short story is ever ended," he maintained "It's like an explosion. The energy it attracts throws light back to things that happened before it began and after it ends."[8]

His world is one of transitoriness. Sex is snatched at bus stops, in alleyways, in dowdy bedrooms. Unemployed workers get the boat to England but can't shake off their home country. They feel the tug of the past more than the promise of the future. Dreams nearly always crumble into dust.

"My Love, My Umbrella" captures that transitory world *vis-à-vis* a sexual relationship that's presented tragi-comically. There's an element of mockery in the story that's apparent from the title, the mention of the umbrella undercutting the romance of "love." It's almost as if he's being satirical to stop himself from feeling the pain of the couple's break-up. The sex scenes are described almost animalistically at times. It's like a protective coating for the couple. They've "fallen into the habit of each other."[9]

The story gives us a very vivid picture of McGahern's horror at the prospect of the dull routines of married life: "Fear of a housing estate in Clontarf, escape to the Yacht [on] Sunday mornings to read the papers in peace over pints, come home dazed in the midday light of the sea front with a peace offering of sweets to the Sunday roast. Afterwards in the drowse of food and drink to be woken by, 'You promised to take us out for the day, Daddy,' until you backed the hire-purchased Volkswagen out of the gateway and drove to Howth and stared out at the sea through the gathering condensation on the semi-circles the wipers made on the windshield, and quelled quarrels and cries of the bored children in the back seat."[10]

The most talked about story in the book was "Korea." It concerned a young man's terrifying realisation that his father wants him to join the US Army so that, in the event of him being killed in action, he'll receive a large pay-out. He's initially against the idea of him joining but when a neighbour's son is killed and his family get a substantial payment from the American government he changes his tune.

The "cruel father" was a trope in many of McGahern's stories. Its origin was obviously his own one. There's no direct reference to him in "Korea" but another story in the collection references his hypochondria.

"The Key" was based on actual incidents. "My father decided he wasn't getting enough attention," McGahern recalled, "and that he was going to die. He left instructions for his funeral and set off for the Garda hospital in Dublin. There was nothing wrong with him and they kicked him out after a week." He was in a rage when he came home. McGahern's aunt Maggie made fun of him. She said things to him like, "Well, Frank, may I enquire where is the pain located today?"[11] McGahern exaggerated these events for comic effect in the story.

His father knew he was being satirised. He threatened to sue him over the story. Neither McGahern nor Charles Monteith were as worried about this as they had been about his threatened legal action over *The Dark*. In the end, as was the case with that book, he did nothing.

A writer called Bernard Share, the then editor of *Books Ireland*, thought he was praising McGahern when he put him "in the great tradition of Irish short story writers" in his review of *Nightlines*.[12] This wasn't praise as far as McGahern was concerned. His ambition had been to break out of that tradition. Neither did he see it as necessarily "great." Much of it was sullied by cliché, laziness, conformity.

Share didn't realise that he was trying to clear the decks of this kind of writing, to rid people's minds of the idea that people like Frank O'Connor and Sean O'Faoláin were his benchmarks. Yeats and Joyce were giants, to be sure, as was Beckett, but he refused to subsume himself under these lesser figures.

He wanted to be free of anything that had stage-Irishry in it, be it the stories of O'Faoláin and O'Connor or the Synge-song rhythms of *The Playboy of the Western World* – what a character referred to as "eejity stuff" in a later novel.

O'Connor and O'Faoláin were like blancmange to McGahern. As someone whose mind was a cauldron of emotions, he thought they smacked of complacency. They fed into the stereotypes of Irishness fomented by the theocracy of Eamon de Valera and his ecclesiastical cohorts. As such they were preaching to the converted.

He was once asked what he thought of O'Connor and O'Faoláin. He replied tartly, "I don't think about them at all."[13] He hadn't intended to sound rude. What he was intimating was that he saw himself as part of a new era in writing, a new mode of expression. It would be less user-friendly than the one that went before. There would be more angst in it, more alienation.

He won an Arts Council Award for *Nightlines*. It meant he had money in his pocket again, an unusual situation for him. He asked Madeline if she'd be interested in going to Ireland with him. She said she would.

After all the problems he'd had with Laaksi as regards where they were going to live, he didn't want a repeat of that with Madeline. He was assured that would never be the case. She had no nostalgia for America. Paris could always be a stopping point for them if they wanted it. She liked Ireland as a country. It was worth keeping in mind as somewhere they could live in the longer term. "What about my father?" he asked. She said she didn't see him as a problem. It wasn't as if they'd be living with him.

They left Paris towards the end of 1970. Their destination was Cleggan, a harbour village in West Galway. It was the first step towards a permanent move back to Ireland.

Cleggan was like paradise to him after the alienation of the London years, its scenery a tantalising antidote to the dull concrete of his urban schools.

The harbour village of Cleggan. McGahern and Madeline joined Richard Murphy here for the best part of a year. (Galway Tourism)

He didn't need a car to get around, cycling or taking the bus when he needed to. He fished in the ocean and frequented the musical bars at night. He didn't have a great singing voice but that didn't bother him. He melted into the environment.

His writing improved. He was able to function in other countries but not as well as in Ireland. The details of land, sea and sky – not to mention character – were better captured in the land where he was born.

He wanted his return to be quiet but an article that appeared on him in The *Irish Press* put paid to that. He knew his father would read it or hear about it. He hadn't wanted this, not having told him anything about his relationship with Madeline up to now.

He was gruff when he met her for the first time, almost triumphal in his sense of superiority over her. They called to him with a priest McGahern knew who had a car. He spent most of the visit talking to the priest. When he was alone in the room with her he stayed silent, trying to freeze her out, but she was as good as him, not speaking either. Eventually he caved in. Whenever he lost a power struggle with someone – McGahern included – he always showed increased respect for them afterwards. In this he probably resembled most bullies. In later visits he flattered her to try and gain a different kind of control over her.

McGahern was put down in a similar manner. Any tensions were smoothed over by Agnes. She rose to his defence any time he played the victim, something he was a past master at doing. What she didn't know was that he planned to disinherit her. In a previous era he might have got away with it.

Madeline was more confident than Laaksi. Laaksi had been threatened by him during her one-night stay in Grevisk. There were a few reasons for this. She'd met him at a time when McGahern's confidence was low. He'd come back to Ireland on a visit rather than to stay. With Madeline it was different. He was more secure now, both in his relationship with her and his general situation. He saw his father as a man to be pitied rather than feared. Such an attitude transferred itself to her. She was more curious about him than intimidated. She sat out the situation and he caved in as a result of frustration.

Such frustration informed most things he did now. He was capable of losing his cool at the most trivial events. One day his car broke down in the middle of the road when he was with his relative Liam Kelly. When Kelly fixed it for him he lost his temper with him, never liking someone to be able to do something he couldn't. McGahern focused on this side of him in his story "Gold Watch." One day when he was in Kelly's house his bicycle was stolen from outside the door by someone who had a grudge against him. (McGahern thought it was a Crombie coat before Kelly corrected him.) The incident was reflective of a growing resentment against him in the area. Ever since he retired there were more people who wanted to settle scores.

He was enveloped in his own world by now, his main ambition being to create as much trouble as possible and then deny any complicity in it, adopting a siege mentality that shifted the blame to others instead. He moved from aggression to persecution complex to mordant self-pity, marshalling his "troops", as he called his children, against McGahern at every opportunity. He gave out to him for not calling more but when he did he abused both him and Madeleine in any way he could think of.

They only saw him now and again, preferring the spectacular scenery of their surroundings in Cleggan. They'd moved there upon the recommendation of the poet Richard Murphy. McGahern knew him slightly. He lived there himself. In 1962 he'd entertained Sylvia Plath and Ted Hughes. Plath fell in love with the area but her relationship with Hughes was about to crumble at the time. He'd fallen for a woman called Assia Weevil and would take up with her after the Irish trip. He was distant from Plath even when he was there. She made romantic overtures to Murphy as a result but he didn't respond. His indifference irritated her and spoiled her visit. She cut it short and headed back for London, committing suicide the following year.

Both McGahern and Madeline loved Cleggan as much as Plath did. The island of Inishbofin was only six miles away. They took trips there in Murphy's hooker the Ave Maria. There were also trips to Clifden, Yeats' Tower, the more outlying areas of Connemara. Galway city was another port of call. It was always abuzz with activity. No more than with Cleggan, people broke into song at the drop of a hat. You could make friends for life there in a night.

Murphy lived in a blacksmith's cottage. He'd "gone native" in a self-conscious way. McGahern liked him but he didn't take him seriously either as a person or writer. The Aran jumpers and seaman's boots put him off. He once remarked that he liked him better when he wasn't seeing him than when he was. He told Patrick Gregory once that he felt embarrassed being left "along" with him.[14] He probably meant "alone." The more time he spent in his presence the more he feared becoming infected with the sense of preciousness that attached itself to him. He referred to him either as The Bard of Cleggan or Kissy Dicky.

The two monikers testified to his exaggerated self-image both as a writer and a lover.

McGahern thought Murphy's writing was too soft. He said of one of his poems, "You've given it a rose at the end – I'd give the knife another twist."[15] Good writing was nearly always difficult, he believed. If a writer enjoyed it too much, the likelihood was that the reader wouldn't.[16]

"Only a fool would write out of happiness," he said once.[17] He told Murphy that his main impetus was pain. He didn't begin his books until he found that.[18] The only nice thing about writing was that it made everything else seem so easy by comparison.[19] He liked to quote Thomas Mann's dictum, "A writer is a person for whom writing is more difficult than it is for other people."[20]

Murphy never knew what to make of his pronouncements. They seemed to make writing into a negative pursuit. McGahern said to him,

"Art is as mortal as life whether it lasts one year or a million years. Like us it must die. It's a game, the most interesting game there is. It's not religion, but false religion."[21] Elsewhere – in perhaps a dig at Murphy's messianic sense – he said, "The writer sets himself up as God, king and counsellor. A man who takes a pen in his hand has already convicted himself of egotism. We write to please ourselves. It's amazing that someone should want to publish it."[22]

Back to Leitrim

McGahern spent a year in Cleggan. After he left it he bought a house in Leitrim. It was only seventeen miles from where he grew up, located at the end of a side road behind a mountain on the banks of Lake Laura. The original plan was to settle in Clifden but Madeline found that town "too fashionable."[1] The house they chose had previously been occupied by a childless widow.

It was a low bungalow that afforded him a lot of privacy. That was what he wanted. Every lane could jog his memory with an anecdote, every view of the lake call up a potent anecdote. Madeline liked it just as much as he did. It was near the Ivy Leaf Ballroom. This was where he'd courted women as a young man.

Joe Kennedy visited him when he was moving furniture in. He couldn't understand why they weren't going to some exotic place like France or Spain. Why choose an undistinguished cottage in dire need of repair? Kennedy was shocked to see a jackdaw's skeleton in the fireplace.[2] McGahern's father referred to the house as a "snipe run."[3]

They didn't plan to occupy it straight away. The buying of it was enough. McGahern asked Monteith for an advance on his next book to help him with the cost. His cousin Emmet McGarry, a builder by trade, was recruited to renovate it before he moved in.

Before he did that he took up another lectureship. It was at Reading University. He taught there for an hour a week in the autumn of 1971.

Before he started work he asked the professor of English, a man called Donald Gordon, what he should teach the pupils. He replied blithely, "Anything you like. I've been teaching them for the last 28 years and they haven't understood a word I've said. Assume they won't understand a word you say either."[4]

He was back in Colgate the following January. By now he'd become so familiar with the place he could almost have given the classes in his sleep. He brought an air of simple wisdom to weighty topics, gaining popularity with his students because of his unassuming personality and personal interest in each one.

Writing occupied him as much as teaching. He did a dramatisation of Tolstoy's *The Power of Darkness* when he was at Colgate, trying to adapt the material to an Irish context. He'd started it when he was in Cleggan. Other adaptations consumed him over the next two decades.

By June he was back in Rue Christine with Madeline. The tenants had just vacated it, leaving it in a terrible condition. They would become more familiar with such delinquent behaviour as the years went on.

In September the Abbey rejected *The Power of Darkness*. Lelia Doolan, the artistic director of the theatre, was so virulent in her comments that McGahern was shocked.[5] The following month he had an extension put on to the Rue Christine apartment. It was with the "toothpaste" money.

A painting of McGahern from Leitrim artist Colleen Quinn. (Colleen Quinn)

Undaunted by the Abbey's rejection of *The Power of Darkness* he now wrote a dramatisation of *The Barracks* for BBC Radio. "I disliked the Hugh Leonard version of it," he wrote to Susanna Capon in June 1971.[6] Much of the novel was comprised of Elizabeth Reegan's soliloquies. McGahern resisted the temptation to reprise these in the play.[7]

An adaptation of Joyce's story "The Sisters" followed. He was happy with *The Barracks* but not "The Sisters." He blamed himself. He was one of many writers who were adapting stories from Joyce's *Dubliners* at the time. He took some comfort from the fact that nearly all of the other adaptations were as bad as his one. "The only qualification anybody needed," he chirped, "was to know nothing about television."⁸ He'd done it for the BBC.

His father had a heart attack at the beginning of 1973. It resulted in him losing his speech for a while. His daughters danced attendance on him as he recovered. McGahern imagined the old rascal making the most of this, exaggerating his symptoms for the effect.

One day soon afterwards Madeline told him she'd like to get married. He said, "I hope it's to me."⁹ She assured him it was. They tied the knot in Paris on February 3rd. Soon afterwards they went back to Ireland.

He was working on another novel by now, one about his sacking. Enough years had elapsed for him to be able to deal with it impartially. Distance lent objectivity to the eye.

In *The Leavetaking* Patrick Moran, a teacher, returns from a year's leave in London in the course of which he marries a woman called Isobel, a wealthy American divorcee. He then faces dismissal from his school. The plot is taken almost directly from McGahern's life, at least so far.

From the very first sentence we're aware that this is going to be a work of prose poetry: "'I watch a gull's shadow float among feet on the concrete as I walk in a day of my life with a bell, its brass tongue in my hand, and think after all that the first constant was water."¹⁰

We learn he's about to be sacked on the second page of the book. This acts as a spoiler to the plot, throwing all the responsibility on McGahern to compensate readers with the power of his writing. This he more than does. He works a variety of thoughts into his sentences, threading them into eccentric unities. There's often a thesis, antithesis and synthesis in their structure. They're given a tenuous unity by dint of his phrasing. He ranges from the famous plain style to the equally famous heightened one.

The book also gives us the inside story on the details of his sacking, including the conversation with the priest who oversaw it. Apart from the book and the registry office marriage, he had problems with McGahern teaching Catechism to children while, as he put it, "living in sin."

The Leavetaking has much autobiographical content in it apart from his life in teaching. He writes about his father trying to get him to live with him in the barracks when he's a young boy. There's also a lot of material concerning his relationship to his mother, his promise to her that he'll be a priest and the emotional devastation he undergoes when she dies.

The subsidiary characters in the book are sketchily drawn. This is unusual for McGahern. Normally with a stroke of the pen – his short story genius coming to his aid – he's able to create a character in a few lines. In *The Leavetaking*, for some reason, we don't really get to know Patrick's father, or indeed Isobel's.¹¹

His writing of it was delayed by an unfortunate event – the theft of his typewriter at Customs when he was leaving Paris. He finished it in the summer of 1973 in Achill, an island off the coast of Mayo that he went back to many times in the years ahead. Madeline and himself stayed at a holiday home lent to them by Niall Walsh, a Ballinamore pathologist he'd been friendly with since the sixties. He re-connected with him after he went to Cleggan.

Charles Monteith paid a visit to them in Achill. When he was leaving, McGahern gave him the text of the book. He read it when he got back to London and was enthralled.

McGahern and Madeline stayed in Achill until October. They then went to London, spending six months there with his brother Frankie and his wife. While he was there he was diagnosed with gout. It would be a problem for him throughout his life from now on.

They went to Leitrim afterwards. The postal address was Foxfield. In September a BBC producer called Barry Hanson dropped in on him to discuss a radio adaptation of his story "Swallows." *The Leavetaking* was entered for the Booker Prize around the same time. He hadn't been in favour of this and wasn't surprised when it failed to be shortlisted.

The fact that it wasn't meant Faber didn't have to publish it that year. Instead of doing so they delayed it until 1975. The decision disappointed McGahern. January was as bad a time for book sales as it was for anything else. Few people had money after the spending that always went on at that time of the year. "After the Christmas stocking," he wrote to Monteith, "comes the graveyard."¹² He found it difficult to see the book in the shops. People he knew also had trouble ordering it. As a kind of consolation he won the Society of Authors award that year. It netted him £500.

Terence de Vere White rubbished *The Leavetaking* in all ill-thought out review in the *Irish Times*, of which he was then literary editor.¹³ Brian Friel thought it was the best book he'd ever written. In a sideswipe at De Vere White he told McGahern he felt sorry for "any poor bastard" who failed to appreciate its riches.¹⁴

"Swallows" was aired two months later. McGahern was disappointed with it. Hanson put its failure down to a poor cast. "If you think you'll get poetry out of these guys," he said to him, "You'd better start thinking about the transmigration of souls."¹⁵

McGahern became a Northern Arts Fellow at Newcastle University for the academic years of 1974-76. He loved Newcastle. It had a warm atmosphere and many entrancing villages surrounding it. The Norman influence of the city also impressed him, as did the constant hive of activity he found there. He saw it as a dinosaur of the Industrial Revolution, "a gorge ripped with terraced houses and spanned by mighty steel bridges with the mighty Tees below."[16]. Madeline worked on the campus with him this time, having secured a job as secretary to the head of the Economics department.

Eamon de Valera died in August 1975. He'd been synonymous with Ireland since its independence. A symbol of rebellion in 1916, he went on to become the quintessence of conservatism over the next six decades. He presided over a country in which church and state sat teeth in jowl with one another, a country that had repressed people's natural instincts – and liberal books. McGahern wasn't sad to see the end of his tunnel vision of what constituted Irishness. De Valera, as one writer put it, was "quite willing to bend down and kiss a bishop's ring, and to be photographed doing so."[17] McGahern imagined him drinking cold tea in heaven. For better or worse, the "devil era" was over.

The following year began on a poor note for McGahern. On January 3, Terence De Vere White reiterated his poor opinion of *The Leavetaking* in a general piece on books that had been published the previous year. "If this was the first novel by an Irish country boy about his experience in a wicked city it would be understandable," he wrote, "but Mr. McGahern is within a few years of the age at which Balzac died."[18] His attitude beggared belief. If this was the review of a cub reporter it might have been understandable but White was a seasoned author...within a year of the age at which Balzac died.

Friel sympathised with him again. So did Seamus Heaney. They both knew how good the book was. The person who really needed sympathy, as Friel pointed out, was De Vere White for his lapse of judgment.

McGahern was seeing quite a lot of Heaney at this time. As well as both of them having been nurtured by Monteith they shared lectureships in the U.S., capitalising on the huge appetite for Irish studies there.[19]

They both became judges of the Hennessy Awards in 1976. These were literary awards presented to young writers who'd had work published in the "New Irish Writing" page of the *Irish Press* during the year.

Heaney bought a house in Dublin now. He'd just moved there from Belfast after getting a lecturing post in Carysfort College in Blackrock. McGahern helped him move in, ceremoniously crossing the threshold with another writer, Alan Sillitoe. McGahern sensed that he'd be there a long time. He said to him, "Well, you've bought the coffin."[20] Heaney was a little taken aback by the comment but when he thought about it he had to admit that he was right. Maybe McGahern knew him better than he knew himself.

His story "Wheels" was made into a television film that year by Cathal

Black. He invited himself to stay with McGahern and Madeline for a week to celebrate after it was aired. They didn't appreciate this. He had to be "kicked out," as he put it, for overstaying his welcome.[21]

McGahern's former Belgrove pupil Neil Jordan reviewed the film kindly. He maintained McGahern's work was ideal for cinema because of the graphic manner in which he captured daily life.[22]

Neil Jordan was a pupil of McGahern's when he taught at Belgrove.
He now became a reviewer of one of his books. (Photocall)

Jordan was now a writer himself. He'd published a story collection, *Night in Tunisia*, earlier that year. The stories were brilliant, especially the title one which was more like a novella. Sean O'Faoláin praised the book, citing him as being in the tradition of Yeats and Joyce in his style. His comments represented the confluence of two eras.

Jordan had been instrumental in setting up The Writers Co-Op two years before, seeing it as an antidote to conventional literature. Emerging authors like Des Hogan, Fred Johnston, Peter Sheridan and Ronan Sheehan joined him in the enterprise. McGahern welcomed the changing of the guard in Irish Letters. New voices were being heard, new ways of seeing life that detached themselves from the O'Faolain influence even as they were being commended by him.

I'd had a short story published in the "New Irish Writing" page that year but it wasn't shortlisted for the award. Neither had I got anywhere with anything I sent to Neil Jordan at the Co-Op. I'd just graduated from university with an M.A. in English. My thesis had been on the literary style of Ernest Hemingway. For a time I considered doing a Ph.D. My tutor, Seamus Deane, encouraged me to. I asked Denis Donoghue, the head of the department, if I could. He said he wasn't sure if my M.A. grades were good enough. When I asked him what they were he said, "I can't give you chapter and verse." Deane didn't know why he was being so vague. He advised me to push him for a final decision.

I always enjoyed going to Deane's tutorials. He had great insights and a mellifluous voice to deliver them with. After one tutorial I showed him some poetry I was writing. He was a published poet himself. Seamus Heaney, a former classmate of his from St. Columb's College in Derry, had shown McGahern his work. McGahern admired it, as he did Deane's prose memoir *Reading in the Dark*.

In the end I decided against doing the Ph.D. Instead I applied to St. Pat's Training College to be a teacher. In my spare time I wrote. It didn't matter to me if I wasn't up to the standard demanded by Jordan or McGahern. I was reading McGahern's books avidly now but I never thought of approaching him for an appraisal of my work.

Jordan lived near me. I met him at a party one night and told him I was going to be a teacher. "Not another one," he said. He'd met too many of the breed through his father. "My main ambition is to write," I said. I wasn't doing as much of that as I should have been at the time. Most of my spare time was spent going to films. I was also reviewing them for a university magazine now. Little did I know then that in the future Jordan would become more famous as a film director than a writer.

To cap a busy year for McGahern, extracts from *The Dark* were aired on the BBC as part of a schools programme for twelve to sixteen year olds. He was amused. "God help us," he exclaimed. The book that caused his removal from teaching was now being used as part of its infrastructure.[23]

He moved into his Foxfield home permanently now. He'd been there off and on since he'd bought it but never for long periods. There were too many disruptions. These had eased off in recent times.

He needed to be grounded somewhere. In the previous eleven years, he said, he'd lived in eleven places. That was mainly for financial reasons. He was more secure that way now. Both he and Madeline wanted to put down roots in the house they'd bought some years before. They were "tired of climbing other people's stairs."[24]

"My wife and I were beginning our life together," he wrote, "We thought we could make a living on these small fields. It was a time when we could have settled almost anywhere. If she hadn't liked the place and the people, we would have moved elsewhere." Where he lived wasn't as important as how he felt. He felt the comfort of the familiar in looking at the sky and the fields but he could have felt equally comfortable with other skies, other fields: "If you happen to live on the moon you'll learn to love it. You don't change your life by changing the externals of it."[25]

Electricity was installed in his house now. He also drilled a hole for water. The operation cost him £600, a costly sum at the time. As he learned later, he would have been better employed drawing it from the lake nearby. Renovations on the house cost him a lot of money at this time. His builder was frequently absent. When he turned up, McGahern had to stand over him to make sure the work was done right.

McGahern happily twinned the two pursuits of
writing and farming after returning to Ireland. (Pixabay)

He bought some cows and sheep and also kept cats. They were treated royally. Madeline kept bees – like the Moroneys.

The house became a farmer's house – wellington boots inside the door, a range in the kitchen, concrete floors. The image was softened by art on the walls and a wealth of books in his library. He carried the contrast in his appearance too, his soft writers' hands offsetting the weather-beaten complexion.[26]

He didn't install a phone. He was generally uncomfortable talking to people on the phone. It went back to the days when he had to answer calls on it for his father in the barracks as a child.[27] He liked the house for its primitiveness. It reminded him of his past. He'd missed that in England and America. Now he could experience it again.

The pace of living was slow. He liked that too. "I have no ambition," he said, "I used to be ashamed of that but then I came across the word in an old dictionary and looked up its etymology. It comes from the Latin word *ambitio* which means, 'Walking around looking for votes.'"[28]

He was able to joke about his neighbours. Leitrim people, he said, spent so much time walking behind their bullocks that in time they'd come to resemble them. He had a relaxed attitude to them, enjoying their unfussy attitudes. Many of them would find their way into his writings in years to come. Though outwardly conservative, they carried independence within themselves that they didn't feel constrained to advertise.

You could set your watch by their daily routines. Little happened. Local news was gobbled up and rehashed in the pubs and houses over pints or cups of tea. Trivial happenings were analysed to the nth degree. Everyone knew everyone else's business but they didn't shout about it. There was a veneer of diplomacy to protect the privacy of those who got into trouble with money or sex or anything else that made tongues wag.

News was conveyed with a nod or a wink. It was like the secret codes of cattle deals. On the surface nothing changed but the weather but many things bubbled under the surface, the thoughts and dreams McGahern portrayed in his writings to capture the richness of the simple lives around him. He became like Chekhov, like Carson McCullers, like William Faulkner – anyone who amplified the ordinary into art.

He never played the role of the writer in Leitrim. It wouldn't have worked. The flowery locutions of a Wordsworth or a Coleridge wouldn't have "done" down there, he once told an interviewer, but if writing cut to the nub of an issue they'd admire it.

The people he socialised with may not have been to university, as he put it, "but they met the scholars coming out." Their folk wisdom spoke more to him than any number of university theses.

He wasn't a celebrity to them. He was a neighbour who'd do them a turn if they needed it. If a writer in the area had "notions," they'd soon be knocked out of him.

"Notions," he said, "are easier grown than daffodils."[29] Writing was seen as an activity like farming to the Leitrim people. Blackening pages was just another job. Any award or commendation that came his way was treated nonchalantly. The county was free of any kind of class, be it of social caste, money or employment. People were evaluated for what they were, not what they had. The most important things were genuineness, authenticity, being there for your fellow man. For most people, their word was their bond. If that was broken it cast a long shadow.

McGahern was looking forward to writing productive books in Foxfield. He told his friend Paul Muldoon he once bought an hour of silence from a juke box in San Francisco. That was what he was looking for here too.[30] He hoped it would be a base for the images he had in his head to blossom, providing the platform on which he could make them take wing.

He wrote facing a wall. One might have thought the landscape surrounding him would have inspired him. It did, but not while he wrote. For this he needed the concentration of a samurai. Nothing could be allowed to invade it, not even beauty.

The only furniture in the room was a divan bed and a formica table. "All a writer needs is a cell," he said. It wasn't like someone selling turnips who had to live near the market where they were sold.[31]

Seamus Heaney was aware of the way McGahern became totally immersed in his work, how it was probably an effort for him to drag himself away from it whenever he called to his house with his wife to see him. "When the gate was unbarred," Heaney said of these visits, "the penman became the countryman, the novelist became the neighbour. Although he managed the change with ultimate grace, I was always convinced that work had been suspended once we came into view, absorption had been abandoned."[32]

Madeline tried to keep visitors to a minimum. She typed up his manuscripts, taking great care to have them to his liking. Their love for one another, Declan Kilberd wrote, "was simple and majestic, rooted in the belief that life is best shared quietly day by day."[33]

People called every now and then to update them on local news. Once a week they went to Enniskillen to do their shopping, afterwards dropping into Blake's pub for a drink. In time it would become a treasured watering hole for him.

McGahern became involved in local events. If there was a book or a film to be plugged he would be behind it. His photograph often graced the pages of the *Leitrim Observer* in this capacity. He didn't have a problem being in the company of the parish priest at such events. Despite not being a believer he recognised the importance of religion in people's lives – for sociable reasons if nothing else.[34]

Tony Whelan bought a house in Leitrim now, thereby becoming a neighbour of his old friend. They visited one another in their homes every so often and also ran into one another in the adjoining towns of Enniskillen, Sligo, Carrick. They had lively discussions about literature whenever they met. McGahern wasn't slow to tell Whelan if he disagreed with him about anything but he never acted as a know-all.

Madeline stayed in the background. She was a gracious hostess who enjoyed listening to her husband entertaining visitors. She chipped in at select intervals. McGahern welcomed her contributions.

They continued to rent out the Paris apartment. There were many bad tenants over the years. The distance from Leitrim to Paris made it difficult to supervise people if they weren't behaving properly or defaulting on the rent. They often made the property available to friends for visits. Occasionally they dropped in on it themselves when McGahern's work called for him to be there. They liked to get away as much as they could but it wasn't always easy. Trips away involved arranging for the cattle to be taken care of, and the cats.

McGahern's move back to Ireland didn't get many headlines. Having left the country with such drama some years before, he slotted himself back into it like a key in a lock, a hand in a glove. He wasn't the sacked teacher now. He was the smallhold farmer.

The prodigal son had returned to his homeland not to kill the fatted calf but to raise it.

Change of Direction

McGahern's father died in May of 1977. The man who'd been so huge a part of his life had almost dwindled into insignificance in recent years. They were superficially polite to one another when they met but nothing more. Tension always hovered beneath the surface. It was a different kind of tension from the old days. There was more jealousy on his father's part and less fear on his. Ice had replaced fire.

He showed little emotion when he heard the news. There had been too much suffering at his hands. His sisters were calm too, calmer than they expected.

Maybe he'd dramatised his impending demise so often over the years that his death came as something of an anti-climax to them.

The house was left to Frankie. Because of The Family Protection Act he wasn't allowed to occupy it while Agnes was alive. He disputed this. Against McGahern's advice – he was the executor of the will – he contested it in court. The case rumbled on for years.

McGahern started to be published in the *New Yorker* from 1977 onwards. He struck up a warm relationship with its editor, Frances Kiernan. She published his story "Sierra Leone" that year and many others afterwards. The *Atlantic Monthly* rejected his story "Getting Through" that year. The disappointing news ended his relationship with that publication.

He made this the title story of his next collection the following year. There may have been some indignation in the gesture. *Getting Through* was a book that showed him at the height of his powers. There are classic stories in it – "The Beginning of an Idea," "All Sorts of Impossible Things," "Faith, Hope and Charity,", "The Wine Breath." "Sierra Leone" was the one that stood out most. The backdrop to it was the Cuban crisis of 1962, something that impacted hugely on people who witnessed it, as he did.

He dedicated the book to Robert Woof, a colleague from his time at Newcastle. He'd written much of it there. Neil Jordan reviewed it in the

Irish Times. He said it represented a change in the coalface of Irish writing. "The Sligo boarding house could be on America's east coast," he wrote, "the Leitrim farms could be set in provincial France. The weight of association that has too often crippled these familiar landscapes has fallen off for good." [1]

The review pleased the pluralist in McGahern. It had always been his ambition to slough off the constrictions of the past. To have a member of the new order of Irish writing praise him was particularly welcome. Jordan's own writing also outgrown these "familiar landscapes," as Sean O'Faoláin had noticed.

He did a reading from the book at Nun's Island in Galway. It was attended by Colm Toibin, someone who would become a big fan of his in time. He was amazed at McGahern's confidence during the reading. It was so at variance with the persona that came through the stories. It was as if a different person took over. Maybe it was the teacher in him, he concluded. Teachers liked audiences too. [2]

He gave a talk afterwards. In it he reflected on the way Ireland had changed so much in recent years. He'd been born in a country that was still going through the nineteenth century. Now we were nearing the end of the twentieth. Where were all the missing decades? [3]

Ireland, it seemed, had turned from black and white into colour. It had changed more in the past twenty years than in the 200 preceding that. [4] As he said, "The sixties came to Ireland in the seventies."

One of the main ways it had changed was in regard to sexuality. He didn't have to worry about bans when he wrote about such matters now. The shutters had come down. There were no bishops and nighties anymore, nor any John Charles McQuaid either.

An aspect of his life that still remained closed, however, was the child he'd had outside marriage. He hadn't disclosed this to anyone except close friends.

In November 1979 he went to see Joan Kelly and their son Joseph in Portsmouth. McGahern still hadn't acknowledged him. He said Joan was "beautiful but impossible." Joseph he described as "nervous." [5] His attitude to him was distant. In his letters he referred to him as "Joseph Kelly" or "the boy." It's as if he saw him as a remote acquaintance rather than his own flesh and blood. Was this true or did he secretly guilt-trip himself about his treatment of him?

His friend Jimmy Swift interceded for him in his assignations with Joan and Joseph. "Does he feel he should have a father like others," he asked Swift in a letter to him, "rights to assert?" The question is astounding for a man of such empathy. One would have imagined he took such rights as to be automatic. One would have imagined he'd have insisted on them for Joseph.

His attitude is so different to the one he showed to the boy he taught to read in East London by giving him so much extra attention. He walked the extra mile there for someone who had no blood connection to him nor wasn't even Irish. Joan Kelly never spoke to the press about any of this. It's possible he was kind to Joseph behind the scenes. We have no right to judge a pattern of behaviour that seems so out of character.

The theme of an unwanted child was at the core of his next book. *The Pornographer* gives us a new McGahern. Set mainly in Dublin and London, it's bereft of most of the lyrical descriptions that inform his previous works. The tone is harder too. He seems to be reaching for a new voice, that of the urban realist. There are no country lanes here, no herons flying majestically across lakes to the backdrop of a setting sun.

The main character has an aunt who's terminally ill. A girlfriend, Josephine, gets pregnant without him wanting her to. He writes pornography for a man called Maloney. Maloney is a poet *manqué* who's transferred his interests to business. He's world wise and world weary. His speeches to the narrator are full of droll cynicism.

At one point of the book the narrator wants to use a condom when he makes love to Josephine but she makes him take it off, finding it mechanical. He tells her he won't marry her if she gets pregnant. Sex, he tells her, is just a need for him, "like food or drink." [6]

After she becomes pregnant he thinks he'll have to marry her to give her respectability. He could leave her afterwards. The prospect of marriage is as negative here as in any of McGahern's books. When he decides he won't enter into it he becomes filled with happiness. It's like a liberation. "We were not caged," he writes, "in any nightmare of the future." [7]

His character breaks out in a cold sweat as he contemplates such a scenario: "The grey suit, the church, her friend the boozy priest, her doting father above me as I place the gold ring on mother's finger, and afterwards the prawns, the long-stemmed wine glasses, the toasts, each cliché echoing its own applause."[8] He evades her overtures to permanence. "You can't," he says, "do the loving for both of us." [9]

She's older than he is, and emerging from a sheltered past to embrace liberalism. "I was wasting my life," she says. Now she's doing what's natural: "I don't feel dirty or sinful or anything. I just feel that I have a great deal of lost living to make up for." [10] Despite his writing about pornography – or maybe because of it – he's more puritanical, more analytic. Sex is the thing that causes pregnancy. Children are the price you pay. It's a different kind of guilt than we've been proffered in *The Dark* - but no less Catholic.

The Pornographer gave us a new McGahern – more visceral, less lyrical. (Pixabay)

He advocates abortion. She's against it. When he tells Maloney he's going to be at the birth, he says, "Well old boy, you're crusading off to London then. You'll be in illegitimate attendance while another white hope of the human race comes squawking into the world."[11]

He refuses to see the child after Josephine gives birth to him. Marrying her is the last thing he wants but he doesn't "ditch" her either.[12] "Don't you want to see your child at least once?" she asks him. "No," he replies. On the following page McGahern writes, "I found myself completely indifferent to her." As for the child, he tells her coldly that it should either be "adopted or kept." He doesn't really care which option she chooses.[13] She thinks he might have picked up his cold-bloodedness "writing that pornography stuff."[14] McGahern doesn't go the obvious route of making that link.

He has an affair with a nurse afterwards. He does the chasing this time. She's dark-haired. Is she modelled on the woman who broke his heart back in the sixties? It's possible. We can even see Joan Kelly in Josephine, who's a journalist.

McGahern changed his *modus operandi* to write *The Pornographer*. This was important to him. He even went so far as to say he would have stopped writing if he hadn't done so.[15] He believed *The Leavetaking* paved the way for such a change. "I couldn't have written *The Pornographer* without having written *The Leavetaking* first," he claimed. It's a looser style but behind it we can see familiar themes coming through. One of these is death. McGahern was once described as Ireland's greatest "connoisseur" of death along with Beckett.[16]

In one chapter he walks through a hospital ward seeing newborn babies close to where his aunt lies dying. It's a familiar dynamic with McGahern, birth and death intermixing as the twin planks of existence. They'd been connected for him ever since his mother contracted cancer from having had one too many children.

"It seemed felicitous," he writes, "that our going out of life should be as similarly staged as our coming in." [17]

He brings brandy to his aunt as an anaesthetic for her pain. It's "one of the great greasers of the slope we'd all slide down anyhow."[18] He gives her reassurances that she's going to recover but he knows it's hopeless for her, as hopeless as the marriage dream of the other woman in his life.

He's in charge of both relationships. Both women are desperate in their way, one to hang on to life, the other to hang on to him.

The dialogue in the book is more crisp than usual. There's an urgency in it, an urgency brought about by the impending birth and the imminent death. It's been said that McGahern prefers rumination to narrative.[19] That's true but here the plot keeps driving the book forward. It's because he's away from the usual rural backdrop that causes him to indulge his descriptive powers in such detail.

The Pornographer has often been called McGahern's "European" novel. It's free of the limitations some readers find in his other works, the familiar characters and locales, even the mode of writing. It's a more commercial mode. This alienated as many readers – his loyal fan base – as it entranced. The pornography is probably a reaction to what happened to *The Dark*. As one viewer expressed it, it's as if he's saying to the Censorship Board: "If you thought that was something, look at this!"[20]

He spent a long time agonising over the title of the book, eventually settling for the one that appeared. This was more from a lack of alternatives than anything else. He never liked it. The overtones were as unsavoury to him as he thought they would be to his readers but he couldn't think of anything else. His history of putting the definite article in his titles may have been a factor. It was like his signature tune by now.

He found the titles of stories easier to come up with than novels. "A story generally chooses its own title," he said. "That's because it's dramatic and usually only makes one point." Novels were different: "A novel reflects more varieties of experience. It's more closely connected with the whole of society. The story is a fragment."[21]

The title tempted those who had a narrow view of him to go back to the days of *The Dark* when he was seen as a "dirty" writer. One reviewer dismissed the book as being "blue comedy" instead of black.[22] This was to trivialise it. The phrase might account for his whimsical attitude to the sex in it but this is mere scaffolding to the main plot thread.

The ambition of most pornographic writing is to excite. McGahern uses it more for farcical purposes here, especially when his two characters, Mavis and the Colonel, take a cruise on the Shannon. This is the stuff of high comedy.

The book had its origins in the story "My Love, My Umbrella." Here McGahern wrote about sex with the same sense of abandon he used there. It's like a literary version of *Last Tango in Paris*. Freed from a world where the spectre of guilt hung over sex, he can now write about it without trappings. There's still poetry in the writing but it's released from its ethical overtones. As with *Last Tango*, the characters in his pornography don't even have names, at least until Maloney comes up with them. His characters aren't people, he tells us, they're athletes.[23]

His research for these scenes was comprised of magazines bought from a stand near the university where he was teaching in Newcastle and others ordered through the post using Madeline's name.

After sampling as much pornography as he could stomach for his research he concluded that most of it was very poorly written. If he'd read it in any detail before writing the book he would have known that already. If *The Pornographer* has a weakness it's that his writing on the subject is *too* good!

McGahern could never resist writing well. We saw that when he wanted to "improve" on Veijo Meri's work in *The Manila Rope*. It's difficult to see this kind of writing appealing to people who would buy snuff magazines. Maloney shouldn't be happy with it. He's streetwise enough to know what was likely to work for his readers. He needed to tell the book's narrator to adopt a style more in keeping with what they might have wanted.

The Mavis and Colonel episodes read like a novel within a novel. They jar with the rest of it like the subsidiary characters in *The Leavetaking*, making it into a book of two halves. They're more like characters from a French farce than real people. If McGahern was looking for a MacGuffin (to use Alfred Hitchcock's phrase) he would have been better employed having his narrator write a different kind of fiction.

The Pornographer was so explicit in its sexuality it made *The Dark* look tame by comparison. And yet there was no shock among the public when it was published. By now Ireland had become desensitised to books about sex. Nobody in the church or government cared much about it. Charlie Haughey was in power and, according to reports, having more dalliances with women than any number of Mavises. That posed a different kind of problem. People wouldn't be outraged by it but would they be bored?

The book performed better in Germany when the title was changed to

Love in Winter. In America it sold more copies than all McGahern's other books put together.

The French edition of it had a rainbow arched over a thatched cottage. McGahern was amused. Journalist Eddie Holt remarked, "It looked like a cover more suitable for *Peig*."[24] *Peig* was a traditional Irish novel that Irish schoolchildren were force-fed for decades. The presence of anything approaching sex in it would have been anathema.

A writer in the *New York Review of Books* castigated *The Pornographer* for its crew of "tortured celibates." This was to misread it. The treatment of sex in the book is more playful than tortured. McGahern tries to demythologise it, not set it up as a holy grail. In private correspondence he referred to the book as "The Porno Man." It was the same self-mocking tone he used when he called *The Dark* "The Ould Sock."

He thought *The Pornographer* was the best book he'd ever written but was open to the fact that his view may not have been shared by the reading public. "Authors," he declared, "are as untrustworthy as lovers."[25]

The novel was regarded as "existential" in France. He said he wasn't sure what that word meant.[26] It was even compared to *The Outsider*. We can see Camus' Meursault in McGahern's narrator. He enjoys sleeping with Josephine but he says he doesn't love her just as Meursault does with Marie in *The Outsider*.

The book almost cost McGahern a friend in Joe Kennedy. Kennedy saw himself as the character of Maloney in it. McGahern denied this, adding that Maloney was one of his favourite characters. He may have been but Kennedy could hardly be expected to like being identified with someone who made statements like, "Ireland wanking is Ireland free."[27] He stopped communicating with McGahern for years as a result but the wound healed eventually, Kennedy accepting that he'd been wrong in his assumption and wrong to be "thick" with McGahern on account of it.[28]

John Updike found the narrator unlikeable.[29] It isn't difficult to see why. McGahern worked hard to create an unappealing character as his central figure. Josephine makes him look bad because of his irresponsibility regarding the child. This doesn't sit well with his other traits. His failure to take care of her is inconsistent with his sensitivity elsewhere. The McGahern emphasis, if you like, clashes with the Camus one. Maloney describes him as "a corrupter with a priest's face."[30]

Updike also had problems with McGahern's way of writing. He didn't like his habit of using a comma after sentences instead of the conventional full stop: "It was great to see you," he shook hands.' " He found this to be an "over-indulged mannerism."[31]. McGahern also used it in most of his other books. But it's extremely effective when it works. Another mannerism is his fondness for the word "and." He liked to use this at the beginning of sentences. It's often the most potent word in them.

Sometimes it's a thematic non-sequitur. He often uses it to link two dissonant sentences, thereby creating a musical effect, as in the story "Doorways" from *Getting Through*: "Another time you can take me if you wish," and when we were outside I said, "It's only a few streets. I'll walk you home."[32] A few pages later he writes, "All I'd ask is that between certain hours I could come to him if I was tired," and she looked at me so steadily that I began to feel uneasy."[33]

McGahern's eccentric phraseology made his work difficult for translators. His French translator told him once that it took her three times longer to translate him than any other novelist she worked with.[34] Considering that, maybe the French title of *The Dark* – *L'Obscur* – was appropriate. Any translator would have had problems with the expressions he used from rural Leitrim. They're in most of his novels and stories, expressions like "the whole shoot" (meaning "all") or "he was full of himself," or "anyhow," which he preferred to "anyway." In *The Pornographer* he uses expressions like "I ran them," meaning "I got rid of them" and "He got a land" meaning "He got a fright."[35]

He's even more difficult in some of his other books. One wonders, for instance, what a translator would make of terms like "dawnder" or "frigger" from *That They May Face the Rising Sun*.[36] What would they make of expressions like "He was full of himself" or terms like "gom" or "amadhaun" (both meaning "fool"). They'd probably scratch their heads over terms like "being fed royal" (being well fed) or "They lapped it up good-o," meaning "They believed it."

Phrases like "He had little shout," meaning he had little influence, or "She was a middling cook," meaning she was a mediocre one, were straight out of the Leitrim heartland. An expression he used often in his work, when someone was castigating someone else, is "That'll do you now." It's a lovely way of saying "That's enough out of you" but it would probably mean nothing to anyone not familiar with it.

McGahern got a new translator in 1980. His name was Alan Delahaye. He'd worked with writers of the calibre of Updike and Roald Dahl in the past. Having such a track record gave McGahern confidence in him. It was more than rewarded in the years ahead. He became a close friend to him in time, as most people who worked with him became friends if they were in any way personable. He always tried to break down barriers. If he liked a person he usually extended an offer to them to visit him at his home.

New Decade

He worked at Colgate again in 1980. In June of that year he fell through a trapdoor on a visit to Frances Kiernan's house in New York. She was his editor at the *New Yorker*. It had been left open for cats to go through. He was hobbling around the place for weeks afterwards on crutches but he wasn't seriously injured.

It could have been a lot worse. People had died in such falls. Perhaps the most tragic incident of this nature occurred in 1946 at a party in the house of the film actor Tyrone Power. It was during a game of Hide and Seek. Primula Niven – David's wife – was the seeker. All the lights in the house were out. She saw what she thought was the door of a cupboard and opened it. It turned out to be a staircase leading to a cellar. She fell down and landed on a concrete floor, fracturing her skull. She died the following day.

The accident, McGahern claimed, gave him prestige. He was now able to play the role of the absent-minded professor to those who thought intellectuals shouldn't be practical. "Several distinguished ladies in their late seventies," he wrote to Neill Joy, a colleague at the university, "seemed disappointed when they heard I was married. If you ever have a favourite candidate at Colgate, make sure you throw him down the stairs before the interview."[1]

The Dark was published in France later that year. McGahern hated the cover. It had a graveyard on it. It wasn't quite as bad as the titillating Irish one that had annoyed him so much a couple of decades before but it wasn't far off it. "I'd certainly not want such a person in my house!" he exclaimed.

The title of the book lent itself to such morbid overtones. People who read his works without getting to know him expected him to be a more dour individual when they met him. They were heartily relieved when he regaled them with humorous anecdotes, flashing that infectious grin at them as he spoke.

He met Joan and Joseph Kelly a few times towards the end of the year. The meetings, like their earlier ones, were more functional than anything else. In his letters he still referred to Joseph as "the boy" or "Joseph Kelly" rather than anything more familiar. There seemed to be no hope of closeness between the two of them nor indeed any desire for it, at least on his part.

McGahern's friend Kevin Lehane published a memoir of Dublin, *Tom Corkery's Dublin*, that year too. It was full of vignettes from "the rare oul' times" but thankfully free of the kind of touristy clichés this kind of coffee-table book generally invited.

Tom Corkery was Lehane's pseudonym. He went racing with McGahern a lot in the sixties. They also went drinking together and visited one another's homes. McGahern listed Lehane, Jimmy Swift and Tom Jordan as his three best Dublin friends at this time. Lehane managed various cinemas in between capturing city lore in his journalism. The book was a collection of his *Irish Times* pieces from the forties and fifties.

He was one of the first cinema managers I met when I started reviewing films in the 1970s. I found him to be very personable – and eccentric. He wore a crumpled suit and was refreshingly bereft of the slickness that characterised most of his breed. I remember having a cup of tea with him one day from a cracked cup in a rundown room in Pearse Street as he told me the film I was about to see wasn't very good. Such honesty was also very unusual.

McGahern liked the bohemian flavour of Stoneybatter, where he bought a house in the early 1980s. (www.daft.ie)

McGahern reviewed the book favourably in the *Sunday Independent* in 1981. His only caveat was the epilogue. Not being a lover of the kind of writers who frequented pubs, especially in groups, maybe he didn't like Lehane saying things like, "The poet could and did share the same pub with the peasant, and no man had need of looking up, down or askance at his fellow man."[2]

McGahern bought a house in Stoneybatter that year. By a strange coincidence, so did I. His sister Margaret shared the cost of it with him. I wasn't aware of his purchase. It would have been a strange experience for me to see him around the area. I could have passed him on the street any day of the week on my way to work. I often kept his books in the glove compartment of my car. That year I had *The Leavetaking* in it. I re-read it many times at various intervals, opening it at this or that page to savour the sentences, their rhapsodic flow. The fact that it concerned teaching meant I talked about it sometimes to some of the teachers. Not many of them were 'into' literature but nobody could be blind to the beautiful way McGahern used language, how he wrote effortlessly. At least it seemed that way to me then. It was only later I learned how strenuously he worked to achieve his effects.

Stoneybatter is a trendy area today. People like solicitors and university lecturers live there. In 1981 it was often inhabited by those of limited means. The houses were mainly artisan dwellings, small red-bricked terraced houses.

Was McGahern's choice of the area a result of Lehane's fondness for it? He'd delegated him to find a house for him in Dublin in the sixties so it's not beyond the bounds of possibility, especially when we look at passages like this from *Tom Corkery's Dublin*: "Smithfield still carries a faint dying odour of horses and hay. Stoneybatter and Oxmantown still considers itself cattle country, and its people are still called cowboys."[3] McGahern wrote in his review of the book about an episode where a man goes to Smithfield to buy a piano. When he finds it he sees straw sticking out of it. He then goes into a bar. Here a customer offers to sell him "a clatter of ducks."[4] It's clear he enjoyed the sense of the past that the area still possessed. McGahern would have too.

The Stoneybatter house was useful to him as a base from when he was in the city for events. It was near the markets and within walking distance of town.

Living in what he called the "unfashionable" part of Dublin suited him. He enjoyed browsing the second-hand shops, walking the cobbled streets past houses that called up the TV series *Coronation Street*. He even liked "the dirty Liffey." The psychiatric institution of Grangegorman was also nearby.

"No nation needed it so much," he surmised, *a la* Jonathan Swift.[5]

He was reminded of the bedsit he once lived in on the Howth Road when he was teaching in Belgrove. That was within walking distance of the city as well. His life had changed so much since then. How many of the Belgrove staff would still be there? What would happen if one of them wrote a book like *The Dark* now, or married in a registry office?

He got the answer to these questions the following year when a secondary schoolteacher called Eileen Flynn was fired from her job for co-habiting with a married man by whom she had a child in New Ross, County Wexford. The incident became almost as controversial as McGahern's 1965 one. She brought an Unfair Dismissal case to the Employment Appeals Tribunal but was unsuccessful. She said she didn't expect to win because of the power of the church.[6]

Neil Jordan turned from writer to film director in 1982 with the Republican thriller *Angel*. It won him the *London Evening Standard* "Promising Newcomer of the Year" award. *Angel* was the first in a series of ground-breaking films made by the debutante director. He ran his literary projects in tandem with his cinematic ones in future years.

McGahern re-wrote *The Leavetaking* in 1983. He said in a characteristically humble Preface that he felt lucky. His second chance at writing it, he felt, was undeserved. "It should have been written right the first time," he wrote, "What is still uncertain is whether it is right even now. That will rest with whatever readers it may find."[7] Carlo Gebler did a televised adaptation of it that year. It was broadcast on RTE.

The second half of the book was seen as being dissonant with the first by some critics when it came out. One writer even went so far as to say it was the weakest of all McGahern's books on this account.[8] McGahern claimed the main reason he re-wrote it was to improve the second half. "It was too abstract," he said. He compared it to the second half of Camus' *The Outsider*. That to his mind also had a weak conclusion. Asked how pleased he was with the amendments he said, "Moderately." Delahaye thought the re-write made it into a completely new book. McGahern didn't go that far. He thought he was being over-generous.

Real life drama came to Leitrim the following year when a businessman called Don Tidey was kidnapped by the IRA. There was a shoot-out not too far from McGahern's house between the kidnappers, the Gardaí and the Irish Army. In a letter to Monteith, McGahern said some of the soldiers were said to have dropped their weapons at the sound of gunfire. A soldier and a guard were shot dead by IRA men when it broke out. They took refuge in a house in Claremorris, County Mayo. Gardai surrounded it but they still managed to burst out. They fled into nearby woods. The escape was a cause of great embarrassment to the Gardai. They were never caught.

Madeline brought McGahern to California in April 1984 to visit her mother but it wasn't a pleasant trip. He found her even more difficult to deal with than her husband. "It may be luck," he reflected, "that we have no children."[9] This was a curious comment to make in the circumstances. One might have expected him to say instead how distressful it was to have such a parent. He would love to have had children with Madeline. So would she with him. Alas, it wasn't to be, but neither of them brooded over the fact. The absence of a family can drive some couples apart and bring others closer together. In their case it was the latter. In many ways books became their children.

In the same year a court ruled that Frankie wasn't allowed take possession of his father's house while Agnes was alive even though it had been willed to him. McGahern warned him that this would be the outcome when he began his action in 1977. He'd put himself to a lot of needless expense over all those years for a case that was futile – and cruel.

McGahern's story "Crossing the Line" was published in the *Irish Times* the following month. It concerns a teacher who's ostracised by his colleagues when he refuses to support a salary strike. Its publication was arranged by Caroline Walsh, the daughter of Mary Lavin. She was literary editor of that newspaper now. McGahern remembered her from the days he used to visit Lavin at her home in Lad Lane, reading stories to her as a toddler. She became close to him in adulthood as well, even visiting him in Leitrim after their relationship was re-established.

In January 1985 Ann Lovett, a fifteen year old girl from Granard, County Longford, died giving birth beside a grotto. Her baby also died, thereby giving rise to a furore about women giving birth outside marriage. The incident came just four months after an abortion debate in which those advocating for the right to life of the unborn prevailed by a two-third majority. McGahern witnessed these events with interest. They made him aware that even if Ireland appeared to be liberal on the surface, there was a quiet majority hanging onto the value system that made sex into something dirty, especially sex outside marriage.

He submitted his story "Like All Other Men" to the *New Yorker* the following month. It featured a woman who had a sexual encounter with a man on the night before she entered a convent. The editor thought this was highly implausible. McGahern didn't agree. She was ending one kind of life and starting another. If the situation seemed unlikely, the writing compensated. He often said that the difference between life and literature was that life wasn't believable and literature was. The editor's attitude disappointed him. It made him realise it wasn't only Ireland that had narrow-minded attitudes to sex.

A story broke later that year that made him aware how primitive parts of Ireland were. A brutally murdered baby was found on a beach in Kerry. At the same time a woman called Joanne Hayes gave birth to a stillborn child. She was falsely accused of having had twins and murdering the other baby. Her family was dragged through the mud in a case that showed the police force up in all its worst colours as false confessions were wrested from them. McGahern was interested in it for the light it shone on a hidden Ireland. It was "A national scandal in a society that tries to pretend sex doesn't exist outside marriage." The manner in which the Gardai demonised Hayes and her family was seen as the last stand of Irish patriarchal attitudes by Tom Inglis in his book *Truth, Power and Lies*.[10]

McGahern's friend Michael O'Regan wrote a book about the subject. McGahern made an overture to Faber on his behalf for its publication with them but they didn't bite. It went to an Irish publisher instead. The story remained a talking point for decades before the police accepted the fact that they'd all but destroyed the Hayes family. Joanne was financially compensated for her years of distress but money could never blot out the pain of situations like this. After Eileen Flynn and Ann Lovett, McGahern felt he was back in the sixties again.

Another issue that bothered him at this time was the threatened pollution of his beloved Lake Laura from a proposed pet food refrigeration plant. The Fianna Fáil politician John Ellis wanted to build one in the area. McGahern objected to it. He didn't normally become so voluble about such matters but he did in this instance, soliciting the support of his neighbours to mount a campaign against it. Ellis was livid, saying of him in a phrase he thoroughly enjoyed, "That writer bastard has them all riz."[11] In the end the plan to build the plant was abandoned.

McGahern's third collection of short stories, *High Ground*, came out that October. It included some of his best work, including the aforementioned story, "Crossing the Line," which Caroline Walsh had published in the *Irish Times*. It also had the disputed "Like All Other Men" which failed to find favour with the *New Yorker*, and a second story that had been rejected by it, "Bank Holiday." That decision flummoxed him. He'd laboured long and hard over it, re-writing it no less than fifty times before he was satisfied with it.

"Bank Holiday," as mentioned earlier, featured a character based on Patrick Kavanagh. He's called Patrick McDonough here. The first draft was completely different to how it finally turned out. In the original version a man who abused women got married. On the wedding night he was warned by some instinct that his wife intended to harm him. After getting into bed with her he pulled back the sheets and saw she had an open razor in her hand. This material was scrapped for the version of the story that was printed.

The last story in the book was "Gold Watch." Once again it dealt with the theme of friction between a father and son. It had also been published in the *New Yorker*. It was one of McGahern's favourites and one of his most loved generally. He cared so much about it he wrote a special letter to Frances Kiernan asking her to change just one word in it, a preposition. The sentence that ends the story contained the phrase "time which does not have to run to any conclusion." He thought "which" sounded awkward so he asked her to change it to "that."[12] This kind of perfectionism is so typical of McGahern. One is reminded of Harold Pinter faxing a semicolon from Berlin to London one time.

The term "epiphany" was suggested for the book's blurb. McGahern disapproved. It called up too many echoes of Joyce – echoes he'd already been over-saddled with in reactions to *The Dark* if not his total *oeuvre* up to this. "It might sink our frail vessel," he warned Monteith, leading to the term being replaced.[13] McGahern was only seven when Joyce died. His writing cast a shadow over his work, perhaps leading to a defensiveness about him. (Was this why he told Michael McLaverty he preferred Dostoevsky's "The Death of Ivan Illych" to Joyce's masterly short story "The Dead"?)

He was sad to hear of the death of Philip Larkin at the end of 1985. He'd always been one of his favourite poets. Like McGahern, Larkin had enshrined the ordinary at the centre of his canon. Unfortunately, after his death many substandard works of his were published to capitalise on his passing. It upset McGahern to see this "posthumous crap." There were collections of unpublished verse and some trivial juvenilia. Afterwards came biographies, letters, memoirs of the various women in his life. There was even a collection of his writings on jazz music. Publishers rarely resisted the opportunity to flood the market with subsidiary works of dead icons. McGahern was disturbed by their opportunism.

Such opportunism had a bearing on his own work when Faber discovered to their horror that Philip McDermott, their Irish representative, had secretly printed copies of *The Pornographer* and *Getting Through* with his own imprint of Poolbeg. He was selling them at remaindered rates and pocketing the proceeds. Not surprisingly, they immediately launched legal proceedings against him.

Farmer John

McGahern bought the farm next to him at the beginning of 1986. He'd been having problems with the owner of it over the years due to the amount of activity at his house. Now that would be over. The purchase was a sign that he was here to stay for the rest of his life.

The land was poor. To live in Leitrim, he said, was like putting animals on roofs. The beauty of the county, he claimed, was only on the surface. The soil was like plasticine – too muddy in the rain and too hard in the sun. It wasn't suitable for raising stock.

He kept about two dozen sheep and a dozen cows. He sold the wool every year, and/or the lambs that provided him with it. The neighbours complained that the cattle were too well fed.[1]

His daily routine was simple. He fed the sheep and cattle first thing in the mornings and then went into his study to write. He revised as much as ever. The waste paper basket, as he put it, often became his publisher.[2]

He wasn't a famous writer to the people among whom he lived, he was "yer man who lived out the road beyond the Ivy Leaf Ballroom."

People saw him as a simple man with a simple lifestyle. His nephew Patrick Gilligan remembered dropping in on him every so often on his motorbike. "He'd pop on the back with his cap on and come for a spin," he recalled.[3]

In his poem "Epic," Patrick Kavanagh wrote that Homer wrote the *The Iliad* from a "local row." Elsewhere he referred to World War II as "that bit of Munich bother." The rural sense of pulling down the mighty, of making global events subservient to local ones, was something that was ever-present in McGahern. "All good writing is local," he said, "and by local I don't differentiate between Ballyfermot and North Roscommon."[4] When he talked to his friends, their eyes glazed over if the conversation drifted away from gossip about people they knew to anything that was happening in the wider world.

Another fine evocation of McGahern's sculpted features from Leitrim artist Colleen Quinn. (Colleen Quinn)

McGahern was part of that world because of his writing but he kept talk of it to a minimum. People were aware that he disappeared for weeks or months but they didn't ask him for details of these disappearances. If he was on a lectureship or some kind of speaking engagement it was seen as a diversion from the important business of life - farming.

The wider world came to his doorstep when visitors called. They might have been from the BBC or some publishing house in Dublin or London. It didn't matter to the locals. They were just people to them.

Visitors negotiated the potholed roads leading to his lakeside retreat and were rewarded with warm welcomes and vivid anecdotes. His sheepdog was probably the first thing they saw, trotting up the lane with his inquisitive eyes. The dog was more a friend to McGahern than anything else, a companion on walks as much as a functionary.

He talked about his life in Leitrim in an interview he gave to *Magill* magazine in 1987, sounding off about anything and everything in a more revelatory way than usual.

He didn't talk to the other farmers much about writing: "If you did you'd be run out of town, and quite rightly so too." Writing consumed him so much that life outside it, by contrast, was "like living abroad." There were times, he said, when he wrote for six months without having a word to show for it.[5]

His characters, he said, had a life of their own beyond him. It wasn't a writer's remit to judge them. "They make their own lives and their own mistakes within the framework he creates."[6]

He was asked how he felt about living in Ireland. He said the world in which he grew up had an insular-looking mindset. It was a world that enshrined misery almost as a virtue. "Good manners and going around with gloom all over your face."[7] Things had changed now. The country was more multi-cultural. It accepted all classes and creeds.

The Ireland of his youth was featured in a TV play he wrote that year called *The Rockingham Shoot*. It centred on a teacher who's an extreme nationalist. He warns his pupils not to stay away from school to work as helpers on the local lord's estate during a pheasant shoot. They've been asked to drive the birds from trees for a half crown so a visiting ambassador can shoot them. Their teacher, Reilly, is totally against this.

They disobey his order and the following day he becomes enraged, beating the children to a pulp. He says this is because they've failed to answer educational questions but the real reason is because they missed school to take the British "shilling." He knows he's over-stepped the mark. Parents of the pupils threaten to beat him up. There's even a threat of legal prosecution.

McGahern based him on a teacher he had in his youth who behaved in this way, delivering "unmerciful" beatings to children who'd stayed away from school for the shoot. He fulminated against British colonialism with questions like, "Is this what Padraig Pearce (sic) died for?" But amazingly, he remarked, this teacher expected the pupils to salute him if he passed them in his car outside school, "as if he was a member of a new aristrocracy."[8]

McGahern described Reilly as a "mixture of sexual asceticism, blind Irishness and a particularly puritanical brand of Catholicism."[9] His Anglophobia foreshadows the Moran of *Amongst Women*. It was the attitude that said, "Burn everything English except their coal."

At the end of the film a troupe of travelling entertainers arrive at the school and put on a performance of tricks and stories that entrance the children. "Imagination triumphs over lies," McGahern said. He remembered such entertainers from his youth: "These itinerant magicians were a permanent fixture of the countryside in the forties. They were probably down-and-out actors coming to the schools to earn some drink money. They used to learn a bit of Irish to get by."[10] They infuriated his teacher with their illiteracy but to him they were glamorous figures.

McGahern didn't condemn anyone for their views except fanatics. The irony of the piece is that the teacher is one of the most intelligent people in the county. "Lies are the oil of the social machinery," he said, "Fascism is rooted in the way intelligent people can get drawn into inhuman ideas."[11]

He was determined not to make the same mistakes on *The Rockingham Shoot* as he had on "Swallows." He insisted on being more hands-on with this production, overseeing everything. It paid dividends. The film was praised, especially for the performance of Bosco Hogan in the main role.

McGahern was also taken with Kieran Hickey's direction. At one stage he intercut the hands of the children beating the birds out of the bushes with Reilly raining blows down on those same hands. McGahern always welcomed the grammar of cinema to enhance texts.[12] McGahern liked the film. Hardcore Nationalists weren't happy with it. He was placed on a blacklist by the Republican newspaper *An Phoblacht* after it was aired.

McGahern believed Protestants in post-Independence Ireland were "devoured" by the new Catholic state.[13] This was mostly done through the marriage laws. These required them either to convert to Catholicism and/or raise their children as Catholics if they married a Catholic.[14]

The following year brought another school memory to him. A woman called Maguy Deschamps wrote to him asking him for information on Neil Jordan. He told her he'd taught "Niall" (sic). He said he'd come to him at nine years of age from a Montessori school but found it difficult to assimilate himself into the system in Belgrove. McGahern recommended to his father Michael that, despite the boy's intelligence, he be placed in a lower class for a year to help him settle.

Michael Jordan had been one of his lecturers in St. Pat's College when he was training to be a teacher. McGahern was asked to give a model class in the college's main hall one day in front of a number of lecturers. Jordan was one of them. He found the idea embarrassing. Teaching, he knew, was about a continuum of behaviour throughout a year, not some aspirational idea of perfection squeezed into a half hour.

With this in mind he decided to give an *im*perfect class instead of a perfect one. He asked the children to simulate drunkenness. This they were delighted to do. It was an example of the rebellious spirit in McGahern that he kept under wraps in Pat's before unleashing it on a wider society in his post-graduate years. He won himself a lot of favour with the pupils that day but not many with the staff of the college.

He showed a similar interest in the pupils of a writer's workshop he directed in Galway in the spring of 1989. A young poet called Paula Meehan attended it. She was fascinated by him both as a writer and a man. One of the first things he did was rush through a series of cheques for the students to fund them for the course when the money wasn't forthcoming from the Arts Council.

One of the other writers at the workshop, by coincidence, was Neil Jordan. He read from *Night in Tunisia* and also from a novel he was about to have published, *The Past*. Meehan knew of his double connection with McGahern. She loved these "loops and connections."[15] Nuala O'Faoláin was also at the course. She provided another link to his past.

He became a kind of shaman in that environment, finding pearls in unlikely oysters. Meehan was impressed with many of the things he said, like, "Judge yourself not by your success but by the grandeur of your failures," and "The proper territory of the writer is doubt. The moment you're sure of what you're doing is the moment of greatest danger.[16]

These weren't unusual sentiments from him. He believed a writer was always a beginner. The day you stopped learning was the day you were finished. He never saw a book as something that could be defined like other finite things. It was readers who gave books their essences. Theoretically they could mean as many things as the readers they acquired.

He claimed he never wrote about anything that wasn't in his head for a long time beforehand. Writing about it was a way of getting rid of it. It was a form of burial.[17]

Joyce once called music "the coffin of the soul." In the same way, McGahern regarded books as coffins of words.[18] Once a book was completed, it no longer belonged to the writer. He ceded that ownership to whatever readers it might find. He liked quoting something Rilke said, "There are certain books that must long for the death of their authors so that they can assume their own lives."[19]

Meehan was both confused and fascinated by his obliqueness. Sylvie Mikowski, who met him when he visited the university where she taught in France, said he delighted in giving cryptic answers to questions from her students. She said he fended them off with jokes, insisting that his job wasn't to interpret his work but merely to write it.[20]

He told Meehan not to be afraid to revise her work ruthlessly, even up to thirty times. And to beware of publishing it too soon. Abandoning a work was something therapeutic. It enabled a writer to move on to something else. Books were resurrected by readers but by the time they got to them the writer of the book they were reading wasn't really interested in it.[21]

McGahern travelled a lot that year. In the autumn he was a keynote speaker at a convocation of university lecturers of English in Chantilly, France. He visited Newfoundland as well. It didn't take him long to fall in love with it. He also fell in love with the writing of one of its native scribes, Alastair McLeod. His style echoed McGahern's own lyricism. (He always hated being called lyrical, finding it to be a lazy cliché). He recommended McLeod to his friends in subsequent years just as he'd recommended Michael McLaverty to people in the sixties.

The year ended on an amusing note for him when a deputation of people came to him from Cootehall to ask him if he wanted to buy the barracks where his father worked. It had fallen into disuse and was up for sale. He told them in no uncertain words, "I've spent the best part of twenty years trying to get out of the place. I have no intention of buying my way back into it!"[22]

Moran and his World

McGahern received a proof copy of Colm Toibin's debut novel *The South* from his publicist Marsha Rowe towards the end of 1989. The idea was that he would provide an endorsement for it to be used on the dust jacket. He demurred, despite being a friend of Toibin's and an admirer of his earlier work, *Walking Along the Border*. McGahern was always leery of writers praising the books of their friends even if they liked them. He thought it compromised both the friendship and the books. The previous year, he told Rowe, he'd been sent a proof copy of a book which he found unreadable, only to see it being lavishly praised by Anthony Burgess and others afterwards. If he wasn't suspicious of puffs up to now, this experience certainly made him so.

Toibin didn't mind his hesitancy. He was more amused by it than anything else. It was almost enshrined in Irish literary life that writers scratched one another's backs in a kind of Old Boys Network. He wasn't surprised that McGahern didn't want any part of this. He continued to communicate with Toibin in an affectionate manner and to offer him private praise of his work any time he met him.

Like McGahern, Toibin was living in a house in Stoneybatter at this time. McGahern visited him for supper one night. He hadn't published a novel in ten years. They didn't discuss his writing over the meal but as he was leaving Toibin's house he indicated an envelope he'd left on the hall table on his way in. "Have a look at that," he said shyly. It was the text of *Amongst Women*. Toibin spent all of the next day reading it. By the time he was finished it he felt quite sure it was a masterpiece.

It was the story of a widower, Moran, who fought in the War of Independence. He's now in the autumn of his years and married to a second wife, Rose. He's struggling with the dying of the light and with a family he feels is drifting away from him. In an almost literal manifestation of "Home Rule," the old Republican tries to make his home into another kind of "republic."[1]

Colm Toibin was one of the first people to see a draft copy of *Amongst Women* in 1989. He became a close friend of McGahern's in subsequent years. (Photocall)

Moran is as disenchanted with the legacy of Republicanism as he is with life itself. His patriotic ideals disappeared with the foundation of the Free State. He's now concerned about a family that's growing up too soon. He may have won the war but he can't win the peace, his clear-sighted vision of a united Ireland having been replaced by what he sees as a disunited family.

He thinks the dream he fought for in his teens has been hijacked by the greed of the business class in modern Ireland. His days in the IRA's Flying Column have dissolved into a country run by, as he sees it, gangsters. Such a breed have spent their time fumbling in greasy tills, the "cure" of independence being worse than the disease of colonialism. His world has shrunk from the national fervour of rebellion to the four walls of his home; here he presides over a personal kingdom of young girls. Through them he seeks to recover feelings of glory, the freedom fighter of yore replaced by a man in search of a new form of control.

McGahern has softened Reegan from *The Barracks* and Mahoney from *The Dark* to create this character. Just as he needed the artistic distance from his sacking to write *The Leavetaking*, time also enabled him to subdue the anger he felt at his father to make him into a more multi-layered person.

McGahern had been presenting readers with Moran clones long before *Amongst Women*. By now he was so familiar with the character he was able to adapt it to his wishes. Here he becomes more paternal. He isn't the harrowing figure of *The Barracks* or *The Dark*. We understand how he can be hypnotic to his daughters, how he can hold such sway over them. Moran

McGahern's writing reached a high water mark with *Amongst Women*. (Photocall)

also experiences religious doubt. This would have been unthinkable for either of the other two characters.

His relegation to domesticity in the aftermath of his Flying Column escapades is a mark of disempowerment for him.[2] He seeks to reinforce that power by a nightly saying of the Rosary, the "father" becoming a substitute for the almighty father in heaven. The plethora of Hail Marys in the prayer makes it more like a dedication to Our Lady. His paternalism flies in the face of this lip service to motherhood.[3]

Amongst Women is as autobiographical as *The Leavetaking*, even moreso when we take into account the amount of detail in it about McGahern's family. He may have written about his father many times before, either overtly or covertly, but he hadn't featured his sisters up to now, or his stepmother. There are as many echoes of Agnes (and Susan?) in Rose as there are of Margaret, Monica, Breege, Rosaleen and Dympna in Moran's daughters. Sheila is almost directly based on Dympna. Maggie and Mona are composite characters. We can see McGahern and Frankie in Moran's two sons.

The original starting point of the book was a lorry outside an urban park with green tarpaulin over it. That image stayed in his mind for months. It eventually became replaced by Moran and his family.[4]

Amongst Women was seven years in gestation. It originally had a section dealing with ancestors of McGahern's who went to England to live, what he referred to as "the lost generation of the 1950s and 1960s." This comprised over 200 pages of his first draft. It became dispensed with by his Irish family in the finished novel.[5] The original title of the book was *Monaghan Day*. This might have been suitable for a chapter but certainly not the whole book. Julia Kilroy, Tom's wife, suggested the eventual title. McGahern immediately went for it.[6]

He spent two hours every morning seven days a week working on it. He knew he was onto something special with it from early on. He revised all his books with great precision but this one specially. He sent it to Seamus Heaney when it was in proof form. That in itself was evidence of how much he thought of it. Heaney was entranced.

The book is a little like *The Old Man and the Sea*. Ernest Hemingway was also in his fifties when he wrote this simple book, the one that's seen by many as his purest. It took him all his life to be able to write it, to be able to say more with less words. To be – as Yeats might have said – as cold and passionate as the dawn.

Hemingway's Santiago is an elemental character like McGahern's Moran. Both of them battle things they can't defeat – in Santiago's case a shark, in Moran's his own overweening egotism. And both of them lose.

Santiago is destroyed but not defeated at the end of *The Old Man and the Sea*. Moran is both destroyed and defeated at the end of *Amongst Women*. His dying words, "Shut up!" confirm that.

McGahern and Hemingway dispensed with first person narration to write these books. It gave them a more universal edge. John Updike didn't like the persona McGahern created in *The Pornographer* as we saw but that's not a problem when one writes in the third person. In this mode a writer can judge his characters without committing himself. It's a more subtle way of doing it. It can be done in the first person too of course. Camus did it with Meursault, hiding his shock at this character's lack of feeling behind a slew of prosaic pronouncements and appearing to be one with him. McGahern did it with his main characters in *The Leavetaking* and *The Pornographer*, if less obviously. His transition from the "I" to the "Other" is seamless in both cases.

Amongst Women was published by Viking in 1990. The cover showed three women sitting under a tree. For McGahern it was a clichéd image. He suggested the publishers didn't understand what he was trying to get at in the book. It annoyed him almost as much as the botched cover of *The Dark* all those years ago. He thought about leaving Viking after he saw it.

The book struck a chord with readers all over Ireland. He got many letters about it. His favourite one was from a woman who lived in Tubbercurry in Sligo. She said her father was like Moran, only worse. She was one of eight daughters. He wanted to get them off his hands. He advised them to "find a piece of land with an unattached man attached to it." He brought some of these kinds of men home with him. The woman ended her letter by saying, "If you saw what he brought in that was attached to the land, you wouldn't wonder why we're all in England!"[7]

Only a few people registered negative opinions of it. Denis Donoghue, my former UCD lecturer, inveighed against McGahern's supposed naiveté about the War of Independence. This was a strange criticism, one he'd never been confronted with before. McGahern hadn't liked Donoghue's memoir, *Warrenpoint*, published some years earlier. Donoghue didn't specify what McGahern's "naiveté" entailed. He'd been accused of living in an ivory tower himself for many years. He was normally an insightful reader of books but in this case his judgment let him down. It's possible he confused McGahern with Moran.

Another reader accused McGahern of glorifying the IRA in the book. This again was something that applied more to Moran than him. More often than not he saw Republicanism in a poor light. It led to an alliance of church and state that carried a dangerous orthodoxy with it.[8]

These kinds of criticisms were rare. Most people loved the book. Any hostility that remained towards McGahern from "the bad old days" was firmly and finally removed with its publication. He was now an elder statesman of letters rather than the *enfant terrible* of yore. It was even nominated for the Booker Prize.

It should have won. It came as close as possible, being narrowly defeated at the very last hurdle by three judge votes to two. McGahern was always a good loser and proved to be so again here. He said he was glad that he'd been in the running rather than deflated that literature's ultimate accolade had eluded him once again. His publishing director Joanna Mackle believed he was more disappointed for Faber than for himself.[9]

Antonia Byatt won it that year for her novel *Possession*. But *Possession* couldn't match *Amongst Women* for sales. It was now in its sixth printing and was also the beneficiary of many other awards for McGahern.

He was amused by the night. It had nothing to do with writing, he claimed, and everything to do with publishing. At one stage he noticed a photographer lying on the floor beside him with a camera in his hand, presumably watching him to pick up his reaction when the winner was announced.[10]

The event went out on television. After the programme was over the BBC producer Nigel Williams told McGahern he thought he was Ireland's

McGahern hadn't much time for Charlie Haughey when he was Taoiseach. (Photocall)

greatest writer since Joyce. McGahern replied, "You left out Beckett."[11]

Sales of the book continued to grow after that night. They topped 33,000 by the beginning of 1991. It stayed on the best seller lists for months. McGahern travelled overseas for signings and readings.

Charles Haughey, Ireland's Taoiseach, even presented him with an award for it. Like many people, McGahern thought of Haughey as a man more interested in feathering his nest than the good of the country. Posterity has borne out that view. His final fall from grace was in 1992 but in 1990 he was still riding high on a tide of support from his grassroots supporters.

Despite a plethora of rumours about him – and a sacking for suspected involvement on running guns for the IRA in his past – he continued to be the great escapologist of Irish politics. His saving grace was the fact that he had the common touch. Many people were charmed by this but McGahern wasn't. He'd seen too much chicanery in his time to be taken in by it. When Haughey said to him, "I was down in your county last week and I praised you," McGahern shot back, "I heard that. You also praised the football team. They haven't won anything since 1938!"[12]

Amongst Women was subsequently read on BBC's show *Books at Bedtime*, running over ten episodes. The programme brought McGahern to a much wider audience than his books. He wrote them himself, paraphrasing his material in ways that didn't always please him. They were read by Tony Doyle. Doyle also played Moran in the TV version of the book.

I was asked to interview McGahern about the book for the *Evening Press* in 1990. When I rang him he was friendly, speaking to me as if he'd known me all my life. When he heard I had roots in Roscommon and that I was a teacher as well as a journalist he became even more friendly. He asked me to write out some questions and to post them to him. He said he would send the answers back. He was too busy with interviews to meet for a few weeks. The answers he sent gave me the basis for my article on him. The fact that I'd have the back broken out of it when I met him meant we would be able to talk in a more relaxed way at the meeting. I told him I would be bringing a tape recorder. He said that would be fine even though he wasn't too fond of such contraptions.

He replied immediately to my letters even if it was to postpone the interview. He was out on his tractor sometimes when I called on the phone. If I left a message he would always return it. His main worry was the cost of my phone calls. He was unfailingly polite.

A date for the interview was finally arranged when he became free. We met in the North Star Hotel on Amiens Street on a wet Thursday. When he swished in the door I felt a sense of excitement. I was finally meeting my favourite writer.

He had an air of crumpled grandeur about him. The red farmer's face, the tweed coat – he might have been a country squire up from the country for the day, a gentleman farmer like Andy Moroney. When I put it to him that he didn't look like a writer he threw his head back and laughed. "Someone once described me," he said, "as the kind of fellow you'd see around a building site any day of the week. I took it as a compliment."[13]

He didn't seem to be interested in talking about writing at first. He spoke about his brother Frankie, what he was doing in England. He mentioned a weekly salary he was getting. What did I think of it? Was it generous? I felt I was being brought into his world immediately – and it wasn't a literary one. His manner was courteous and old world, qualities that were fast disappearing from the literary world even then. It gave his words an added resonance for me.

He asked me about my teaching. I was having trouble with it at the time. It was affecting my health. He said it did that to him too. I said it was the best job in the world when it was going well and the worst one when it wasn't. He agreed. I said it was affecting my mental health as well as my physical well-being. He said he'd gone through that in the years when he was "a clock watcher." He wondered if I'd fallen prey to the "high stool" - shorthand for the pub. I said I had. There was too much free time. It was one of the reasons both of us had chosen it as a career. "And one of the reasons I now want to leave it," I said.

He asked me if I'd enjoyed Pat's. I said I found it a welcome antidote from university in one way and a step backward in another. The atmosphere was friendly but it also seemed juvenile to me in ways. "You weren't encouraged to think in my time," he said. It put it in a nutshell. Not much had changed between the fifties and the seventies.

I told him I'd got into trouble with the authorities during the year I was there. It was when I was in the Gaeltacht in Kerry on a course with classmates. One day myself and some friends went down to a bar when we should have been at a lecture. We were playing pool. The lecturer left his rostrum and followed us down to the pub. We hid in the back but he saw one of the pool cues up in the air.

He went behind the counter and confronted us. "An bhfuil sibh ag freastal ar an gcúrsa seo?" he asked. ("Are you attending this course?") One of my friends said, "Tá and Níl." ("Yes and no,") I thought it was a good answer.

The lecturer said, "Caillfidh sibh an deontas." ("You'll lose the grant.") We'd been subsidised by the college to go down there. McGahern said to me, "Ni bheidh sibh ar ais." ("You won't be back.") He said that was the phrase used to students in his time if they misbehaved.

I asked him if he'd fallen foul of the establishment when he was there. "Only once," he said. It was when he'd been asked to give the class by Michael Jordan. "I didn't like the idea," he said. "I told him I wouldn't do it. He said if I didn't I would be reprimanded. I decided to do my own thing with it. I made a farce of it. I had the pupils running around the hall like drunk people, kicking chalk. He was furious. He said he was going to expel me. He was strutting around the place like a turkey cock. It got around that he hadn't approved of me. Some of the students refused to take notes at his lectures afterwards. The tide turned in my favour. He had to back down. He hated me even more after that."

I was curious to know if the incident affected his relationship with Neil when he got to know him. "Not at all," he said, "He had problems with him too." In retrospect did he see these events as prophetic of his problems with authority in the future? He asked if I meant in relation to his sacking. I said I did.

"You could make that argument if you wanted. I suppose I was never going to be able to fit into the system in the long run. It was so restrictive and I had so much living to do." How did he feel about it all now? "I've dined out on these stories too often to think about it much. All things return to laughter, as Kavanagh said. Whenever I can I make a joke of the whole episode. It's too long ago to have any effect on my life now. At times it feels as if it happened to another person."

Did he feel any anger about it still? "No. When you're angry about anything it gives it the power to hurt you. I try not to let that happen, either with the educational system or anything else."

I told him I'd heard about his campaign to stop the pet food plant being built beside the lake where he lived. Had he become embroiled in many other local issues over the years? "None at all. I felt strongly about that one but it's all over now. I have nothing against John Ellis. People accused me of having a grudge against him. That's the bad part of living in a small area. Things get blown out of proportion. My problem was with the factory, not John Ellis."

I was sitting beside someone whose rhythms had been dancing in my head for as long as I knew what it was to read. I thought of him creating those rhythms, putting words on pages in his little room in Leitrim and taking them out again, playing with the syllables as the great world revolved around him.

Had he always wanted to be a writer? "No," he said, "I was the first writer I knew." Would he have been one if it wasn't for the Moroneys? "I imagine I would but maybe not as soon. There would probably have been other Moroneys. What's inside you will come out one way or another. But I loved that time in their run-down mansion. It was like a banquet of riches for me. I was able to see worlds inside pages. In later years I created my own worlds on different pages."

I thought I should ask him about *Amongst Women*. It was, after all, the reason he'd met me. I felt bad that I hadn't enjoyed the book as much as I should have. I'd been reading a proof copy of it that was sent to me from Faber. That never sat well with me. I'd never regarded proof copies as "real" books. Such is the simultaneous blessing and curse of being a reviewer. You get to read books before everyone else but you don't enjoy them as much.

I asked him if he thought it was the best book he'd written. "That's not for me to say," he replied. Was it the most difficult? "It almost killed me," he said, "There were times I thought I'd never finish it." He basically saw it as a book about power. Moran has had it all his life. By the end it's transferred to the women. That happened in life too.

I asked him why he hadn't featured his mother in it. "She was there in an earlier version," he said, "As Moran became more central she was eliminated. I wanted to focus on his hatred of the past, his demand that his life be seen as a continuous present."[14]

Moran's second wife, Rose, is given some of McGahern's mother's qualities – patience, loyalty, the ability to "read" a situation so that she can save her husband from doing damage to himself or others – but her role as stepmother tempts us to see her more as Agnes McShera than Susan McGahern.

Was he ever afraid people would recognize themselves in his books? "It's happened," he said, "but I've never built a character on a single person. People as we see them don't make great fodder for art. Life is too thin to furnish a writer with a character. There's generally four or five people in any one of mine. And of course there's a large dollop of myself in everyone – including the villains."[15]

Did that mean he had villainous traits in him? "None of us is simple. We all have both poles." In what way? "It's like love and hate being part of the one coin. Or fiction and life." Where did he draw the line between them when he was writing? "The basic distinction is that fiction has to be believable and in my view a lot of life isn't. That's why I tend to look down on the current fixation with biography, the treatment of life as a set of bald historical facts. A fiction writer has to establish the kind of belief that comes to a biographer ready-made."[16]

So the book wasn't based on reality? He paused for a few moments before he replied. "The act of writing is, by its nature, artificial. It's forcing life into the form of an idea, or vision. Life will never give you this. If it

McGahern turned from being a rebellious figure to an iconic one as he aged. (Photocall)

did there would be no point in writing. A writer works out of an inner world, the same world with which we read. The writer just has the knack of dramatising it. You have to lose yourself in the material so that it can find space to breathe."[17]

He weighed each word as he spoke, testing it like he did in his written work, formulating the sentences as he would have if he were writing them, each one having a structure almost like mathematics.

He said he edited his work mercilessly: "I've often written for three or four months with what I thought were good ideas, only to find the prose dead on re-examination. When this happens you have to throw away what you've written. Sometimes you might find a few living sentences scattered pell-mell among the dross. If you're lucky you can lean on these to deepen the truth of the shallower bits."[18]

Considering the theme of *Amongst Women*, how important did he think the family unit was in Ireland? "Sometimes I feel the whole country is like one extended family," he said. "Ireland has always held something sacrosanct about families. They bring out distinctive traits in people. I've often noticed how people not given to reflection can turn out to be brilliant psychologists when talking about members of their family. And I've noticed how families often have a different code of ethics to society, how certain behaviour will often be tolerated that wouldn't be accepted outside, how strong or bad people can bend the family to their will."[20] He was probably thinking about his father here. He was on record as having described families once as "little republics."[21] He summed up by saying, "I see families as strange stopping posts between the self and society."[22]

I'd been reading his stories in various publications in the previous years but it was a long time since he'd written a novel. What did he see as the main difference between the two forms?

"Novel writing is loose and relaxed," he said, "the short story is more like a sharp point. The prose has to go to that point and then away from it. If you had that kind of intensity in a novel it would eventually become very tiresome writing."[23]

He spoke of getting a novel or a story "right," as if it was a problem in mathematics that had only one answer. I put it to him that what might be right for one writer might not be for another. He took the point. "It's not forensic," he said, "it's intuitive. I know when something has to be changed but often I can't explain why."

I wondered how he saw poetry in this matrix. "It's more like the short story than the novel," he said. "I suppose that's obvious. It captures moments more than conditions."

Did he ever regret not writing more of it? "No. I wasn't comfortable with it over the long term. Very few writers can do poetry as well as prose. Hardy was an exception in that. He made the transition so easily you hardly noticed it. Most writers don't have that ability. I don't find Yeats' prose very good, for instance. Philip Larkin wrote two poor novels."

Did he see himself in the tradition of these people? "Every writer has his own voice but we're all readers before we become writers. I've probably borrowed from them unconsciously. I don't see this as a problem. As Chesterton said, we have no right to a life unless we've broken bread with the great dead."[24]

The more he talked, the more animated he became. Sometimes he seemed to be reaching for words he wasn't able to find. It made him look agitated. I could see what he meant by his private world. He seemed to be in it.

How long did he spend writing every day on average? "Only an hour or two." If he did more, the standard fell. That was because he put so much into it. Did he enjoy it? "The more a writer enjoys what he's doing, I think, the less a reader does. Writing is the most difficult thing one can do. If you could get out of it you would." So why didn't he? "It's an addiction now."[25]

It seemed like masochism to me. He relieved me of that notion. "It's not all pain. There are times when two hours have passed and it seems like as many seconds. That's as close as I've ever been to happiness."[26]

He talked about his travels abroad, the years in Europe and the U.S. Did he ever think he'd like to live abroad permanently? "No. There used to be a cult of exile in this country when I was young. It was as if all the good writers went to express their Irishness. That was nonsense. Imagine someone telling Philip Larkin he had to go into exile to be a writer."[27] Larkin, I knew, was no lover of travel. He once said he'd like to go to China, but only if he could come back the same day.

McGahern looked on the idea of exile as being part of a post-colonial mentality. "We have our own country now. We have to take responsibility for it."[28] Did he like that country or was it just somewhere he happened to live?

He said he liked Ireland for its classlessness. Leitrim was particularly renowned for that. The people there didn't care what job you had as long as you behaved well: "It doesn't matter whether you're a farmer or an archbishop. If you're a bastard you'll be targeted early."[29]

Did he find it difficult to combine farming with writing? "One of the advantages of farming is that you can use it to escape writing. There's always something to be done on a farm. I find that relaxing. Writing is more tense. When you're writing you have to shut everything else out."[30]

I was surprised to hear him saying he preferred writing in the city than the country. "Believe it or not it's easier, even though there's more noise there. People are always dropping in on you in the country."

Sometimes they were too shy to tell him what they wanted. They'd just stand there until eventually he'd have to confront them with a straight question. Everything became straightforward afterwards but it took him a long time to learn how much interruptions were a part of life in Leitrim. If someone was looking for help you gave it to them. "The advantage of working in the city is that you can control your time. People aren't as interdependent."[31]

I asked him if doing publicity for his books cut in on that time much. "Writing and reading are both parts of a private world, as I said. It disappears after publication."

Did that bother him? "Marketing has become an empire today. It's the rock on which it could founder." He found literary gatherings off-putting for the same reason. "When people are together, whether they're dentists or writers or engineers, they become almost automatically less interesting. To use Jung's phrase, 'If 100 intelligent men are put in a room together, the level of conversation will fall into that area of the brain where waters gather.' "[32]

Writers' festivals were in the same barrow for him. "Basically I look on them as an excuse to kick up one's heels. If religion has its churches and sexual intercourse its dance-halls and discotheques, I suppose writers should be allowed their conventions. You can have a good lark at them if you're in the right company." He said he was fond of a place in France called Aix-en-Provence. "I have friends there that I would never have met if I hadn't been invited to a literary conference in that town."[33]

Public positions for writers were dangerous in his view. "A writer's opinion on anything isn't necessarily more important than a footballer's." Notwithstanding that, many of them liked "strutting around like eminences." McGahern tried his best to stay away from such people: "I've always found the shade a more hospitable place for the muse than the light. You can see the sun better by not looking at it."[34]

Some critics saw his writing style as dark. Did he suffer from depression? "I've never been depressed, at least not for long." Had he ever experienced suicidal thoughts? Some friends of his killed themselves over the years, he said, and while he understood why, he never felt that low himself. "I'm too curious. Curiosity must be one of the most powerful forces in life. To die is not to know what's going on."[35]

His favourite optimist, he said, was a man who threw himself off the Empire State Building. As he passed the 42nd floor a window washer heard him say, "So far so good!"[36]

He enjoyed his joke. The red face broke into a laugh. A different kind of laughter was coming from the people at the bar, the raucous jollity of people discussing a football match. He was dropping pearls of wisdom on me in his faint voice and I was finding it difficult to hear him, his words drowned out by their guffaws. Maybe it was time to wind it up. "I think I have enough," I said.

We'd been talking for over an hour. I turned the tape recorder off. He seemed relieved. He started chatting about more ordinary things – his farm, people he knew, the burden of interviews.

He bought me another drink. I spoke about my teaching, how difficult it was to keep the children quiet. He said he had that problem too, especially when he taught in England. He was glad to be out of the job now. Did he ever think about how it ended for him? "Not much. I suppose the main thing I feel is relief. I was freed really. It was probably going to get harder for me to combine it with the writing as the years went on. I'm sure I'd have left eventually anyway, one way or the other."

I stood up, putting the tape recorder in my pocket. The night drinkers were starting to come in, the bar filling up. For some reason I felt I was in a McGahern short story. The rain, the noise, the false sense of gaiety around us. I thought of the worlds of "Peaches," Gold Watch," "My Love, My Umbrella."

He gave me a warm handshake. "I enjoyed the chat," he said, "Good luck with your article." I told him I'd send him a copy of it. "Don't put yourself to the bother," he said, "We get the *Press* down below." With that he swished out the door.

I imagined him walking across the road to the train station, getting a ticket for Leitrim, sitting in the train with the other passengers, taking note of how they looked, how they dressed, how they talked – all of the details that might find their way into a future story or novel.

My article appeared the following week. I only sent the paper a fraction of what we'd talked about. I'd been given a moderate word limit. Anything beyond that, I was told, would be cut out.

He rang me to say he liked it, "I get misquoted a lot of the time," he said, "It's almost a relief not to be."

A few months later, some more of what he'd said appeared in another publication, the *Hot Press*. I hadn't mentioned this to him as I hadn't been commissioned to write it. It was done "on spec." I sent it down to him. It gave him a pleasant surprise. "I liked it even more than your other piece," he said. So did I.

Mary Robinson became president of Ireland that year. She was the daughter of a doctor from Mayo. He was our family doctor. In fact he delivered me. McGahern was surprised to hear that. He saw her as being the harbinger of a new Ireland, one in which women weren't going to be the second sex anymore. They held that role in all his books. This was reflective of their general status. In the church, the home and in politics they ministered to their men folk. Robinson promised to change that. From now on, she said, women would rock the system instead of rocking the cradle. It became her clarion call to a delayed emancipation.

Some emerging women writers believed McGahern's vision of women was anachronistic. Not just Rose Moran and her step-daughters but a large swathe of his female characters.

Elizabeth Reegan, Eilís Ní Dhuibhne pointed out, is a "woman as a mother, not as a wife or partner."[37] Ní Dhuibhne was a university student when she started reading his books. She found his women in general, with their "old time frocks, their high heels, their nondescript jobs, their bed-sitters and their squinting window landladies" had nothing to say to her. She was of the flower power generation. Many of her friends had been to San Francisco. They worked in hotels for the summer holidays.[38] It hardly needs to be mentioned that McGahern was writing of the women of his era rather than Ní Dhuibhne's so her criticism of him is unfair.

Ní Dhuibhne was discommoded by the way McGahern wrote about men too. His male characters, she noted, almost had a predatory attitude to women as they sized them up at dancehalls. She mentioned his reference to a woman in *The Pornographer* as "a wonderfully healthy animal." In "My Love, My Umbrella," she quoted him describing a woman as having hips that gave promise of "a rich seed-bed."

In this mode, she suggested, he was like a farmer at a mart. Or, more ominously, "a python measuring his next meal." This is something of an overstatement. His language isn't politically correct but it isn't meant to be. He was writing about hormonally-charged young men in an erotic way. Ní Dhuibhne found this "scary."[39] It's as if she's charging McGahern with the same attitude as his characters. There was nobody more gracious to women than he was, no one more respectful of their bodies, so this was off-kilter.

He didn't portray women in the way she suggested. They often take control of the relationships in which the McGahern character is involved. They're in control in *The Leavetaking* and in stories like "Doorways," "My Love, My Umbrella," Bank Holiday," "Along the Edges" and "Like All Other Men." Often they're bored, angry with their landladies and uninterested in marriage. Ní Dhuibhne shouldn't have identified them with their circumstances. A novel featuring women with flowers in their hair in San Francisco would have had much less to say to a reader than his "anachronistic" ones.

Writers like Ni Dhuibhne would probably have been enraged to see *The Pornographer* made into a film. It almost was. McGahern was commissioned to write one in the early months of 1990. He had high hopes of it coming about but despite numerous re writes over the best part of the next year he couldn't get it to the satisfaction of the people who commissioned it. They wanted him to juice up the sexual scenes. Since these were largely written in a tongue-in-cheek manner it was difficult for him to oblige.

They kept changing their requirements and that frustrated him. He found himself working at a snail's pace. He was used to this for his novels and stories. A screenplay was different. He'd done screenplays before but mainly for radio and television. The demands were more stringent here. In the end he couldn't make it to the final cut.

"I'll never put couples into bed again," he remarked wryly after his year's fruitless labours, "It's so hard to get them out."[40]

From Page to Stage

McGahern attempts to finesse Tolstoy's *The Power of Darkness* represent one of the few failures in his career. Its rejection by the Abbey in 1972 cut deep with him but he refused to let go of it. In subsequent years he re-wrote it over and over again with an almost samurai-like concentration.

His first stab at it was for BBC Radio 3. "They wanted a work which showed a peasant society where religion was a living presence," he explained. The people who commissioned him to write it thought its material would translate to an Irish context because of its religious fervour and its absence of class – two prime characteristics of old Ireland.[1]

On paper he looked like the ideal candidate to carry such an ambition to fruition but maybe he tried too hard to bring it about, resulting in a laboured text.

The Power of Darkness had all the elements of *grand guignol* – murder, adultery, infanticide. McGahern wanted to play these down and get at the underlying characteristics of the Russian peasantry. This was too big an ask. He even referenced Joanne Hayes in it. "The confusion and guilt that surrounded sex," he maintained, "turned men and women into exploiters and adversaries. Amid all this, the sad lusting after respectability, sugar-coated with sanctimoniousness and held together by a thin binding of religious doctrine and ceremony, combined to form a very dark and explosive force that went inwards and hid. For anybody that might imagine this to be a description of a remote age, I refer them to the findings of the Kerry Babies Tribunal in 1985."[2] The ingredients were there for a hit but he over-egged the omelette, his revisionist attempt to write the past into the present falling between two stools.

Things went from bad to worse when Field Day rejected his 1988 rewrite. Brian Friel was the man tasked with giving him the bad news. He thought the main problem was the size of the cast – thirteen characters in all.

The Power of Darkness was one of McGahern's few literary frustrations. No matter how many times he re-wrote it he could never get it to his satisfaction. (Photocall)

"The touring costs alone," he said, "would absorb all our grants for five years."³ Tom Kilroy helped McGahern narrow this number down to six.⁴ But the play was still problematic, having too much stage-Irishry about it. The desire to remove such elements from literature was the very reason McGahern became a writer. Why couldn't he do it in the play? It was almost like a blind spot with him.

Field Day turned it down again in 1991. McGahern told Michael Colgan, the director of the Gate Theatre, that he believed Friel was behind the decision, being the most high-profile member of the Board of Directors and a successful playwright himself. He was a founder-member of Field Day. Indeed, it had sometimes been called "Friel Day." McGahern couldn't understand why he would have rejected it, especially when he'd worked so hard to improve it from its 1988 format.

He remembered Friel's kindness to him around the time of the banning of *The Dark* when he'd offered his holiday home in Donegal to him to retreat to until the controversy blew over. He'd also helped him when he sought advice on tax once. He was surprised that he'd use his casting vote to ensure the play wasn't selected for production. He thought of him as a friend. They'd had minor issues with one another in the past but nothing worth talking about. He saw himself in a similar light to him. Both of them had given up teaching careers to become writers.

Colgan told Friel what McGahern had said to him. Friel then wrote to McGahern to say he was wrong. He'd done his best to get the play accepted but was over-ruled. He said his influence on the Board was over-rated. But he had good news for McGahern. The play was going to be staged at the Abbey as part of the Dublin Theatre Festival.

That took place in October 1991. The "curse" surrounding the play infected this too. It bombed. Once again McGahern scratched his head in confusion. Was his radar on the blink? Could he have got it wrong three times in a row? It wasn't as if he was working with amateurs. The director, Garry Hynes, had a wealth of experience, and the cast was first rate too. He blamed himself for its failure, saying he'd been too melodramatic in his approach.

Some people didn't mind this. Nicholas Grene said Tolstoy's novel was melodramatic. The problem of McGahern's play was that it failed to replicate it.[5] Desmond Rushe wrote a particularly scathing review of it in the *Irish Independent*, castigating it for the "broken, soulless world its purports to portray."[6]

One reviewer said the play would have been more suited to the Abbey of the 1930s than the 1990s.[7] These were hard words for McGahern to read. Cynics speculated that he'd tried to jump on a bandwagon, that he thought he could step sideways from his fiction and emulate the theatrical success of Friel and Kilroy. He was aware that he was going outside his genre but he didn't do so from greed. It was from a long-term obsession with a text, one he thought he could update and hibernicise. He now realised that was an impossible dream.

The production had other difficulties. At one stage an actress became pregnant and had to be replaced. McGahern travelled to Dublin to oversee the change of cast. "As a writer of fiction," he remarked sardonically, "One never imagines these excitements."[8] Behind the sarcasm he was glad to be involved with people. Writing books was a lonely life. Theatre took it into a different dimension. Books may have been dead to the writer after they were published but plays weren't. *The Power of Darkness* lived anew for him with each performance.

The British Press was kinder to it. Hynes printed an excerpt from a review in *The Observer* to try and stem the flow of abuse levelled at it but this backfired. Paddy Woodworth, writing in the *Irish Times*, justifiably pointed out that its melodrama might have jibed with British myopia about what constituted Irishness.[9] He thought McGahern suffered from a similar condition and that Hynes added insult to injury in her direction by exploiting the shock value of the play. That was the rock it perished on.

She lost her job as a result. The theatre critic Emer O'Kelly – a friend of McGahern's – blamed her for parodying his message.[10]

The negative publicity accorded to *The Power of Darkness* brought McGahern back to the bad old days of *The Dark*. His subsequent books had given rise to the occasional barb but nothing major. This was more widespread and therefore more disheartening. He didn't mind so much for himself as for the cast. They had to go on stage every night feeling there was all that negativity in the audience.

The play had better success during its London run, playing for a month there. The reviews obviously helped – if not the depiction of the Irish that Paddy Woodworth indexed. McGahern felt he was beaten before he began with the Irish critics. He believed they pigeonholed him as an ageing novelist desperately seeking to reinvent himself as a playwright. He thought some of them damned the play even without seeing it, a familiar sin of reviewers.

His *Collected Stories* came out in 1992. It was a huge compilation that was well received. Penelope Fitzgerald wrote, "McGahern is a realist who counts every clean shirt and every pint of Guinness but who writes at times, without hesitation, as a poet." This was only possible because of his "magnificently courteous attention" to language.[11]

His writing presented readers with a new kind of Ireland. Fitzgerald said it was a country where teachers were no longer paid at the back door by the priest's housekeeper, an Ireland where "the strange, living light of television" replaced the red lamp in front of the Sacred Heart.[12]

In his story "Crossing the Line," McGahern wrote, "One of the great early things the INTO got for the teacher was for the salary to be paid directly into his own hands – to get it through the post instead of from the priest or his housekeeper."[13] The INTO was the Primary teacher's union, as mentioned earlier.

In "Oldfashioned" he wrote, "In every house across the countryside there glows at night the strange living light of television sets, more widespread than the little red lamps before the picture of the Sacred Heart years before."

He did a series of readings to promote the book. Tony Whelan saw an advertisement for one of them on London's South Bank. He decided to attend it. McGahern was glad to see him. He was wearing the insignia of the *Chevalier de L'Ordre des Arts et des Lettres* at the time. He'd been awarded it the year before in the French Embassy. It was a reminder of how popular he was in that country. Maybe it wasn't surprising that such a bastion of liberalism would take him to his bosom.

Whelan bought his book. McGahern signed it for him after the reading. "For Tony," he wrote, "with constant affection." He was always polite to him but Whelan still felt an awkwardness with him that was caused by his outstanding success and his own stalled literary career. McGahern didn't discuss that. He was hoping to have a drink with him but McGahern said he was going for a meal with his family. Going home on the train that evening Whelan reflected, "I knew that we could not have the same easy relationship that we once had."[15]

Like Colm Toibin years before in Galway, he'd been amazed to see McGahern reading with such confidence. It was a far cry from the time in the London hostel when he'd shaken hands with him so shyly.

He did more readings as time went on. They attracted large crowds. He had a way of enunciating phrases that excited people, a sense of pacing that was almost theatrical. His voice was also very engaging. When he picked humorous pieces it read he was especially entertaining. It gave him a chance to show a penchant for mimicry that only a few of his close friends were aware of. Classmates from St. Patrick's College testified to it. He used it to mock people he knew – lecturers in Pat's and writers and neighbours afterwards. Such mimicry, unfortunately, was conducted mainly in private so we have no record of it.

An interviewer once said to him, "When you do a reading you get many laughs. Do you think it's important to have laughter in your work?" He answered by saying that humour couldn't be added to a work if it didn't fit.[16] It wasn't like baking a cake where different ingredients were added to taste.

Madeline didn't go to his readings, preferring to let him plough that furrow on his own. She respected his private space and he hers. There was nothing she would dislike more, she claimed, than to be known as "the writer's wife."[17]

He wasn't formal in his daily dress, looking more like a farmer than a writer, but he dressed up for the readings. When John Montague asked him why, he said, "The priest always dresses for the altar."[18] He was still seeing writing as a "second priesthood."

McGahern was also giving English classes at this time. The writer Joan Dean attended the ones he gave in University College Galway in 1992. She was impressed by his lack of fussiness. He was more like a secondary teacher than a lecturer. The classes, she recalled, were "Socratically driven." The students sat around him in a circle as he chatted with them about his favourite writers – Proust, Flaubert, Richard Ford, Ernie O'Malley. All he carried with him was an ordinary copybook in which he'd written notes. There were no exams. Students were graded on an essay they wrote at the end of term.[19]

McGahern was the recipient of many accolades by this time of his life. Here he is with a Degree of the Doctor of Laws from the Higher Education Training Awards Council. (Photocall)

He won the lucrative Guinness Peat Aviation Award that year too. John Updike presented it to him on RTE's "Late Late Show". Updike had long been an admirer of his work. Here was a chance to show that.

Michael McLaverty died that year as well. McGahern penned a tribute to him attesting to his conservative beliefs. "As well as being a source of strength," he wrote, "they may have taken some toll." Such a toll, he thought, affected both his thinking and his writing:" In the novels in particular there's a turning away from any disturbing grain in the material."[20] In the end it was what drove them apart intellectually. But he never lost his affection for him.

Colm Toibin sent McGahern a copy of his second novel, *The Heather Blazing*, towards the end of the year. Mindful of his cool reaction to the overture made by his publicist for *The South* three years before, this time it was a published copy of the book that arrived in McGahern's door. He praised it but in a qualified way. In all of McGahern's comments to writers he knew regarding their works there was always a "yes, but" tone to them.

He was still nervous about being quoted, even after publication. Such qualifications cut down on the risk of that.

Toibin admired him for his reticence. "It's almost a ritual between writers who are friends," he said, "that they will think of something good to say about each other's books around the time of publication no matter what." McGahern didn't believe in that: "He told you bluntly what he thought of your book in a letter. I was not alone among Irish writers who waited for such letters with trepidation."[21]

The main reason many people remember 1992 is because it was the year that Ireland had to face a rash of sexual scandals. The first of these concerned a 14-year-old girl who was raped by a neighbour. When she went to London to have an abortion her father informed the Gardai. As a result she was brought back to Ireland, abortion being against the law at the time. The incident caused a national uproar. It came to be known as the "X" case.

A few months later the Catholic Church was in the firing line when Galway bishop Eamonn Casey was found to have fathered a child by an American divorcee, Annie Murphy. He'd also misappropriated diocesan funds for the upkeep of the child. The scandal was the first of many to hit the church in the following years, causing many worshippers to fall away. Child abuse cases in these years made the Casey story seem almost tame by comparison, the cover-ups by the authorities being as bad as the offences themselves. For McGahern it signalled a seismic shift in society. Church authorities had to relinquish the power they once had when their word was law and "a belt of the crozier" to be much feared. The fact that a sexual scandal was the catalyst for this was something nobody could have predicted.

For McGahern the irony was rife. The crime Casey was guilty of was sex – the sin the church never stopped talking about. It was also the one that resulted in McGahern being fired from his job. Now the boot was on the other foot. The laity could bring ecclesiastical figures to court for sexual misdemeanours.

The horrific child abuse of another cleric, Brendan Smyth, added to the disdain many felt about the church. Smyth was a notorious paedophile who was protected by his order, the Norbertines. His case opened the floodgates to a tsunami of abuses.

Once again the cover-ups seemed almost as heinous as the original offences. Offenders were moved from parishes when revelations about their abuse came to light instead of being defrocked. The authorities hid behind their solicitors, behind the abstruse nuances of something called Canon Law.

Divorce was legalised in Ireland in 1995. A referendum to legalise it had been defeated a decade before. Its passing now was evidence of the growing distance between church and state.

The Church was hit by a further scandal in 1995 when it emerged that Fr. Michael Cleary, who'd died two years earlier, had fathered two children by his housekeeper, Phyllis Hamilton. The television presenter Joe Duffy had stood on a podium with Fr. Cleary and Eamonn Casey during Pope John Paul II's visit to Ireland in 1979, "Of the three of us," he said, "I was the only one who wasn't a parent." Hamilton was homeless when Cleary employed her. He was seen as a Good Samaritan when he took her in. After he died, she sold her story to the *Sunday World*. It was headlined, "My Secret Life as Priest's Wife for 27 Years."

McGahern refused to take the easy attitude of condemnation for any of these cases. He realised the church had learned hard lessons from such incidents, that it had brought in measures to ensure they didn't recur.

"The priests had terrible authority," he said, "Some of them were very frightening but there were also good ones. Nothing in human nature is simple. They had very hard lives in that they were cut off from the people they served. And then there was celibacy. There was much sexual frustration."[22]

Priests were gods in his youth. That was of course wrong but in the modern era he thought things had gone to the other extreme: "Everything religious is now held in deep suspicion."[23]

He felt the tide had turned too far. People were now embracing anti-clericalism in the way they once did its opposite. Agnosticism had become the new faith. People may have had a sheepish mentality during his formative years but it was no less so now; they were just jumping on a different bandwagon. It was many years since McGahern had lost his devotion to the church but it hadn't, as was the case with so many, been replaced with anger. Many of his friends in Leitrim were priests and he saw no problem with that. He wasn't a believer but he still felt religion served a function in society. It was a stabiliser.

He thought of it as a Beautiful Lie, saying, "I don't think the Catholic Church is true any more than Buddhism is true or any of the other [religions]. They all express in different ways the same human need and I see it as an important and essential need."[24]

He liked to mock religion in a mischievous way, telling a joke about a Marxist priest who said to his congregation one day while leading them in a recital of The Stations of the Cross, "Christ falls the third time, and if he was as badly fed as you lot, he'd be dead by now!"

McGahern may have been a lapsed Catholic but he never became an ex-Catholic. It was like the old Jesuitical maxim, "Give us the boy at seven and we'll have him for life." That also applied to non-believers. He was still showing himself to be resoundingly free from bitterness considering how the church had been responsible for stopping his career in its tracks in the sixties.

Such a quality was also in evidence when he reached sixty and applied for his teacher's pension. For some unknown reason it was withheld.

Forty years after his sacking the wounds still festered. Being the kind of man he was he didn't push it though he could have done with the money. Joe O'Toole a former general secretary of the INTO said, "John was such a polite man. The creaky hinge gets the oil. He didn't complain and he was left without."

O'Toole didn't think it was a politician who was responsible, just some "zealot" in the Civil Service.[25]

Charles Monteith died of a heart attack in 1995. He got the attack in his London flat. A woman who was clearing it heard him falling. She ran to get help but forgot to bring a key. By the time the police managed to break down the door it was too late to resuscitate him. Rosemary Goad, his colleague at Faber, said he wouldn't have wished to be resuscitated, preferring to live life to the full or not at all.[26]

McGahern was sad to hear of his passing but he didn't attend the funeral. That was surprising considering all they'd been through together. He'd been more a part of McGahern's career than anyone. He was there at the beginning, and through all the wars he'd fought with censors, reviewers and the public. But Monteith had been retired for many years now. They hadn't been in communication much since then.

Monteith didn't live to see Seamus Heaney, another of his prize acquisitions, win the Noble Prize the following year. This came as a surprise to many. There was some begrudgery in Ireland. He was on holiday in Greece when the announcement came.

McGahern was more amused than anything else. "Nobody," he said, "will enjoy it more."[27] There was little doubt about this. His merry eyes twinkled at Dublin Airport after he returned from Greece with his wife Marie. "Champagne had to be drunk," he said, "You had the feeling the world was pressing its nose to your window."

McGahern's comment highlighted the difference between them. It was as if Heaney's gregariousness in some way mitigated against his seriousness as a writer. Would Famous Seamus now spend more time partying than "digging" with his pen? Nobody knew. McGahern certainly wouldn't have in such circumstances.

Colm Toibin wrote about him attending a Heaney reading once. He went home alone afterwards instead of attending a dinner to which he'd been invited. At that time Toibin described him as being "a connoisseur of quietness.[28] There were overtones of high seriousness about him in contrast to the winsome folksiness of his Faber colleague. Did he feel he was more worthy of it himself? His respect for Heaney's work had started to wane in recent years.

Seamus Heaney with his wife Marie at Dublin Airport after winning the Nobel Prize. (Photocall)

I met Heaney in a bar one night that year and we fell into conversation. In the course of it I told him I'd met McGahern. He spoke very fondly of him. "John is a perfectionist," he said.

I wondered if I'd ever meet him again. I rang him sometime afterwards from Ballina, my home town, and another time from Enniscrone in County Sligo when I was on holiday there. He spoke very naturally to me on both occasions. It was like in 1990 when he refused to act superior to me. He still hadn't become "the writer."

I ran into him in the Westbury Hotel soon afterwards when I was on a night out with some journalistic colleagues. He was drinking there with John Banville. They were very different types of writers but good friends. Banville was once credited with opening the door to Europe for Irish writers. When he said this to McGahern, McGahern replied, "And I slammed it shut!"

This wasn't true. He was very popular in some European countries, especially France, as we saw. It showed how comfortable he was with Banville that he could put himself down like this. Banville experimented with different styles in his books. McGahern tended to stick to his comfort zone and finesse that. He was mindful of the old Yeatsian dictum, "Cobbler, mend thy last."

Banville chased more versatile markets, writing at times in an opaque manner that gave him more highbrow readership. McGahern talked in a highbrow manner when he was lecturing to university students but when he sat at his typewriter he reverted to a more down-home persona: a farmer coming in from milking the cows to write about other farmers milking other cows. Banville tended to begin his books on an elevated plateau. McGahern preferred to work up to one.

A humorous anecdote told of a conversation between the pair of them. Banville was agonising about a novel he was writing at the time. He said to McGahern, "I used the word 'lugubrious' twice in a paragraph. Was that a mistake?" McGahern is said to have replied in that unmistakable brogue, "You shouldn't even have used it wance!"[29] He tried not to use language that would make a reader have to consult a dictionary. Banville had no such compunctions.

Seeing them together reminded me of what Ernest Hemingway said to William Faulkner once: "Just because I don't use the ten dollar words doesn't mean I don't know them." Faulkner thought Hemingway occupied a narrow orbit in the same way Banville imagined McGahern did. Such a conception in no way deterred from their friendship.

I was wondering if I would go up to him. It was difficult because of the company he was in. There were others there as well. As the night drew to a close I intercepted him on his way to the Gents and we had a few words. After exchanging small talk he asked me if I was still writing. I told him I was embarking on a biography of Hemingway. The centenary of his birth was approaching. He didn't show too much interest in this save to wish me luck with it. He seemed to hold the view that Hemingway's embrace of machismo worked to the detriment of his more sensitive side.

I was also writing a book about the relationship between Brian and Brendan Behan at this time. I'd been working on it with Brian during the preceding year. I asked McGahern if I could mention him in it. He said I could. He didn't know Brendan well but was aware of his reputation. He'd died when he was writing *The Dark*. I wanted to draw a connection between the two of them *vis-à-vis* the problems they had with censorship and the church – in particular with John Charles McQuaid.

In my book I described them both as being "leaders of the banned" in the sixties, twin victims of a country where, as one writer put it, everyone was expected to wear bawneen jumpers, smoke pipes and write turgid poetry in Irish about fishermen. It was also the Ireland of Eamon de Valera. De Valera had famously described his vision of ideal Irish women as "comely maidens dancing at crossroads." A decade after McGahern's sacking, I wrote, "McQuaid would be gone, and De Valera's comely maidens turned into pillars of salt."[30]

We launched the book in McDaid's pub, the place McGahern hated, regarding it as the mecca of alcoholic writers who would have been better off working at their craft instead of bleating from bar stools about how badly Ireland had treated them. I wrote about Patrick Kavanagh in it as well. He'd had a long-running feud with Behan. The book was launched by Niall Toibin, another alcoholic of the time. Toibin had impersonated Behan in many one-man shows. He managed to get off the sauce and live a long life. For a while I considered writing a sequel to it called *The Brothers Joyce*. McGahern had been impressed by Stanislaus Joyce's book *My Brother's Keeper* when it came out in 1958.

I asked my publisher if he would "piggyback" a novel I wrote on the back of the Behan book. He agreed to this but told me "Novels don't sell unless you're well known." At that time I wasn't. He was right.

I sent McGahern the novel after it came out. He wrote back saying, "I liked this after some initial reluctance." In a letter I wrote to him later I said, "I know it has many flaws. Any good things probably come from you." I wanted it to be better to please him, like a pupil showing an essay to a teacher.

He was more forensic in his dissection of it on a later phone call, delivering his rapier thrusts with uncommon gentlemanliness as only he could. You couldn't be angry at him because you knew it wasn't personal. It came from his devotion to "The Work," a devotion that was almost religious. I knew I'd committed the crime he warned Paula Meehan against: premature publication. But he was too respectful to put it in such prosaic terms. I resolved to "fail better," as Samuel Beckett might have said, the next time – for his sake if not my own.

"I'm afraid I'm seldom kind when it comes to writing," he said, "It's too important."[31] That wasn't strictly speaking true. He was a painstaking judge but he always tried to look for the good parts in even poor writing in order to encourage burgeoning talent. He was less patient with established writers ploughing well-worn furrows.

Frank McCourt's Limerick memoir *Angela's Ashes* set the publishing world ablaze when it came out later that year. It sold astronomically on both sides of the Atlantic and made the previously unknown McCourt into an overnight sensation. He was lauded everywhere he went, though some people disparaged him for writing what became known as "Misery Lit."

This was an unfair estimation of the book. There was a lot of humour in it as well. McCourt was also very entertaining as an interviewee. McGahern liked it but felt here were unreal elements in it. Much of it didn't meet his stringent standards but he didn't begrudge McCourt the fame it brought him.[32] He likened the book to *The Playboy of the Western World* in its penchant for farcical scenarios but commended it for its emotion and humour.[33]

The year was also notable for a film version of McGahern's short story "Korea" directed by Cathal Black. It was only a few pages long but Black exploited its resonance to huge effect. It dealt with a man willing to sacrifice his son's life for money when he hears of a neighbour receiving a payout from the American government after his own son dies in the Korean war. It won Best Film at the Copenhagen Film Festival and was runner-up for the Audience Prize at the Seattle Film Festival. These were welcomed but it had only limited release in cinemas.

The film is strongly atmospheric with many haunting images, like the U.S flag draped over a coffin on a boat sailing across the lake where father and son have spent their lives fishing for eels. It's a tense and intense work with few concessions to commercialism. That confined it to the art-house circuit but it demands to be seen. It's a rare gem. The cast give it everything. Donal Donnelly and Andrew Scott ooze authenticity as father and son. Newcomer Fiona Molony also turned in a wonderful performance as Scott's girlfriend. The fact that a full length feature could be made from so few pages is a testament to the rich nature of McGahern's writing. So many more of his stories could – and should – have been treated likewise.

Nuala O'Faolain wrote a memoir later that year, the one that had her relationship with McGahern in it. He would have preferred if she didn't relate intimate details of this but he didn't ask her not to publish it. The only reason he read it was because her solicitor sent him a copy of it to vet. He remembered the relationship differently to the way she described it but he didn't care enough about this to change what she wrote.

O'Faolain was probably the model for the women in "Sierra Leone" and "My Love, My Umbrella" but he didn't speak personally about her to anyone. Having her do so about him no doubt removed whatever affection he ever had for her when they were seeing one another. This was a pity because they had a lot in common, not only the situation of having been rejected in love when they met but in their personalities and interests too. And they'd both had abusive fathers. O'Faolain spilt much ink on this subject elsewhere in her book. It became a best-seller but the passages dealing with McGahern did neither of them any favours.

Ireland's economy entered a boom decade in 1997. McGahern bemoaned the idolatry of consumerism. Prices went through the roof as Dublin became the style capital of Europe. The country in general had a renaissance of popularity. Visitors came to it from all corners of the globe to experience what became known as "the craic," i.e. Ireland's special form of mirth-making. McGahern stayed aloof from this as he'd always stayed aloof from such bouts of hysteria. Watching it he was reminded of someone who won the lottery and lost the run of themselves.

People wondered if he would write a book cantered around the Ireland of the Celtic Tiger but he was never the type of writer to ground himself in something so passing. As a writer in *Magill* magazine pointed out, his Tiger book was probably *The Pornographer*.[34]

Some people felt he was out of touch with modern Ireland. I asked him once if this bothered him. "There's nothing so out of fashion as yesterday's fashion," he said, "If the writing is any good it will last. That's all there is to it."[35]

He was never concerned about the subject matter of a book, only the way it was written: "You could get a book about failure that was a triumph, or you could have a boring book about success."[36]

Topics that were in the news bored him. He liked quoting a remark Dostoevsky made about the great earthquake of 1755 in Lisbon, which killed over 60,000 people. If he wrote about how the weather was that day, Dostoevsky said, he would be excoriated for his lack of humanity but after a hundred years the weather might be what was most remembered about it.[37]

McGahern felt the same about most events in history which people were supposed to feel profound about. It was difficult if you weren't there, be it a global catastrophe, a wonderful invention or anything else that changed the world. The writer in him saw detail, not largeness. If the shade was a more hospitable place for him than the sun, the ordinary was also more entrancing than the extraordinary, and the personal than the historical.

Ireland signed the Good Friday Agreement in 1998. Another line was drawn under the War of Independence. McGahern heaved a sigh of relief that the country looked set to finally shake off the shackles of violence. It's difficult to know what his father would have made of it. His Flying Column escapades were now thoroughly anachronistic as Ireland embraced a new pluralism, the shadow of the gunman hopefully gone forever from the national experience.

Adrian Hodges wrote the screenplay for a four-part TV series of *Amongst Women* later that year. This was a joint project between BBC Northern Ireland and Ireland's national broadcasting station, RTE. McGahern gave the project his backing but he didn't watch it. He'd never owned a television and he didn't plan to buy one now. When a book departed its author for another medium, he ceded control of it to that medium.[38] Tony Barry played Moran. He was a friend of McGahern's. He didn't take offence when McGahern told him he wouldn't be watching it.[39] The series was shot in a cavalry barracks in Castlebar, County Mayo.

Mary Keelan, his friend from the sixties, visited Ireland again in 1998. She sent him a postcard from Howth, the seaside village they'd both visited when she knew him in the sixties. She must have put her American address on it because he wrote back to her. The fact that she hadn't asked to meet him made him wonder if she wanted him to. There's no evidence of any further contact between them. He thought she might become a professor at some university but she didn't go quite that far, preferring to remain as a literary editor.

McGahern's brother Frankie died in October 1999. He was only 55. McGahern was sad but hardly surprised. Frankie had been an accident waiting to happen for many years now. He'd disobeyed his doctor's orders to cut down on his drinking after a stroke he'd suffered the previous year. He was also told to lose weight but he didn't do that either. McGahern felt guilty drinking with him anytime he called on him but he knew he would have drunk anyway, with or without him. He was as stubborn as his father when it came to things like that. He'd climbed the corporate ladder in England with some success but the instabilities he'd had in childhood lasted all through his life. McGahern was often uncomfortable in his presence. They were like chalk and cheese in temperament and had few shared interests. The age gap between them was too big to circumvent this.

Colm Toibin sent McGahern a copy of his novel *The Blackwater Lightship* in the same month. It had received glowing reviews and was shortlisted for the Booker Prize. In keeping with his reaction to the earlier books sent to him by Toibin – and indeed most other writers he knew – he maintained an attitude of caution in his comments on it. "I struggled with the opening," he wrote to Toibin, "but found the Wexford pages very fine."[40] Here again we see him carefully wording his praise. It's almost as if he's editing himself for fear of being quoted out of context.

The editor of a magazine called *The Phoenix* asked me to write a profile of Toibin apropos its shortlisting. When I was in his office talking to him about the piece he asked me if I was working on any books. I told him my biography of Hemingway was due out soon. You could have knocked me over with a feather when he said, "It's out already."

With that he took it down from a shelf. It was my first time seeing it. The publisher had sent out review copies before my promised author one. It was a sobering lesson to me about where writers stood in the pecking order of things. I rang my editor later that day to ask him what happened. He apologised. The following week I got six copies of the book. They'd been agreed on my contract. I sent one of them to McGahern. He said he was too busy to read it but would when he could.

By now he'd met Belinda McKeon, a young *Irish Times* reporter who would go on to become an exciting novelist. She'd been sent to interview him. As she sat down beside him to begin the interview she noticed his concentration drifting. He was so entranced eavesdropping on a couple who were arguing beside them that he asked her to delay the interview. It may have been raw material for his next novel. What was significant was that it mattered more to him at that moment than anything they might discuss themselves. Literature bowed to human interest.

McKeon became his friend afterwards. They wrote to one another often. Her boyfriend was from Leitrim. The two of them called in on McGahern any time they were down there. His hospitality, and that of Madeline, was always touching to them. The conversation flowed like the food and drink. Gossip abounded, McGahern's laughter cascading through the evening as mischievous anecdote followed mischievous anecdote.

"John would be in his element talking shop," she remembered, "talking scandal, talking books and plays and poets and priests." When she sought a referral from him for a post in an American university he was more than generous, giving her "the warmest recommendation possible."[41]

In May 2001 he went on a trip to Warsaw to promote *The Pornographer*. It had just been translated into Polish. A number of other writers were with him, including Cathal McCabe, a poet with a particular interest in the relationship between Ireland and Poland. Also on the trip where Harry Clifton and his wife Deirdre Madden. I'd been in the same class as Harry in UCD. We used to submit material to the "New Irish Writing" page of the *Irish Press* together. He went on to become one of Ireland's most respected poets.

McGahern enjoyed the trip. He hadn't been a fan of such junkets in earlier years. He was now more amenable to them, especially when they took place abroad. He allowed himself to forget his craft for a while. "I've learned to let my hair down," he joked, "or what's left of it!"

Madeline was on her way to join him in Colgate later that year when two hijacked planes of al-Queda struck the Twin Towers in New York. Her own one had to turn back to London. In the aftermath of the attacks he saw something that mesmerised him: two disabled motorised lawnmowers on a truck with flags attached to them. It's an image one imagines turning up in one of his novels.

America became gripped with a sense of patriotism in the months afterwards. It bordered on jingoism. He didn't agree with it. It reminded him of the fanaticism of his father, of the teacher in *The Rockingham Shoot*. So many people had died. Many more would in America's reprisals against al-Queda. Where was it all going to end?

On another occasion he saw a group of Americans banded together holding a Solidarity sign. He thought: Solidarity against what? His reaction was surprising. Americans had never seen anything like 9/11. Why did he deny them their experience of togetherness?

He started to think about mortality. "All our generation is in the waiting area now," he surmised at the beginning of 2002.[42] This was a prophetic pronouncement. The following month he was diagnosed with a cancerous tumour in the colon. He had an operation and chemotherapy.

The surgery was successful but a catheter was wrongly inserted afterwards which led to him developing trauma and septicaemia. He had to stay five weeks in hospital before the problem was solved. He did interviews for the book lying on the broad of his back "like a good courtesan."[43]

A BBC producer called Frances Byrnes went to Leitrim that year to make a documentary about him. It was going to be called *Another Country*. He didn't like programmes like this any more than he liked any publicity for his books, seeing them as necessary evils. He became even less enamoured of the project when he heard she was asking locals about him as background.

The tag of "Farmer John" never appealed to him. He imagined this was what was being sought here. He was at pains to point out to people that he was a writer who happened to live on a farm, not a farmer who happened to write. He disputed the notion that he dumbed himself down to people who weren't literary to ingratiate himself with them. He saw both sides of his character – the bookish and the earthy - as complementary rather than contradictory. Neither of them was more "him" than the other.

A university professor called Hermione Lee interviewed him at London's Southbank Centre in the middle of the year. She found him in jovial mood. He said he'd been told by somebody a short time before that he'd lived his life back to front. When he should have been enjoying himself in his youth he was full of violence and darkness and now, when he should have been saying his prayers, he was starting to enjoy himself.

His later years, he said, were "more rich and full than any others." This may have been due to the fact that his health situation meant he lived with the constant threat of them being taken away from him. To paraphrase the end of his story "Gold Watch", this was time that *did* have to run to a conclusion. Whether it was or not, he never let such concerns cut in on his hunger for life. "One of the more uncomfortable facts of growing old," he reflected, "is that while you are failing, everything around you becomes more interesting."[44]

He got a break from his chemotherapy at the end of 2002. He tried to write at this time but found it difficult. He even found it difficult to read. After half a century at the activity, he confessed, he still didn't understand why he did it. Maybe, he suggested, it was an attempt to recreate the world he lost when his mother died.[45]

Late Flowering

He had one last great novel left in him. *That They May Face the Rising Sun* was published in 2002. I reviewed it and he was as thankful as ever when he read the review. He was in America when it was printed so he didn't see it at the time. I sent a copy to Leitrim with a brief letter. He read it when he came home.

He was supposed to have a preview copy of the book sent to me for my review but he got too busy. I was relieved because of my dislike of proof copies. He apologised to me in a letter he sent in the March of that year.

"Dear Aubrey," he wrote in that spindly script of his, "Thank you for your very kind note, and your generous review of the novel. They rushed the novel out early, when I was still in the States, and I haven't had time to put any names down and came home to be caught up in the middle of publicity. I hope you are well, and with every other good wish, John."

By now a new McGahern novel, as his friend Kevin Reynolds pointed out, was almost like a national event.[1] "Of all the books I've written," he said, "This was the hardest. It was 1500 pages long at one stage."[2]

The title referred to a pagan custom of being buried facing the sun. Catholicism liked corpses facing churches instead.[3] McGahern doesn't ally himself to either camp. He's like a *seanchaí* relating tales of a section of society not usually presented to readers, a section rooted in the past and yet – like himself – intricately attuned to the present.

He described it as an "anti-novel." He didn't want to do something that would replicate previous work. It was more of a challenge to try and re-invent himself, to "raise the fences," as he put it. He wrote it for two or three hours a day, "with a lot of looking out the window in between."[4]

The experience of thirty years in Leitrim is crystallised in these pages. One might say it's taken him his whole life to write the book. His skill at creating scenarios has been purified even more than usual in a style that's both plain and profound. There are no frills, no excess words, no attempts

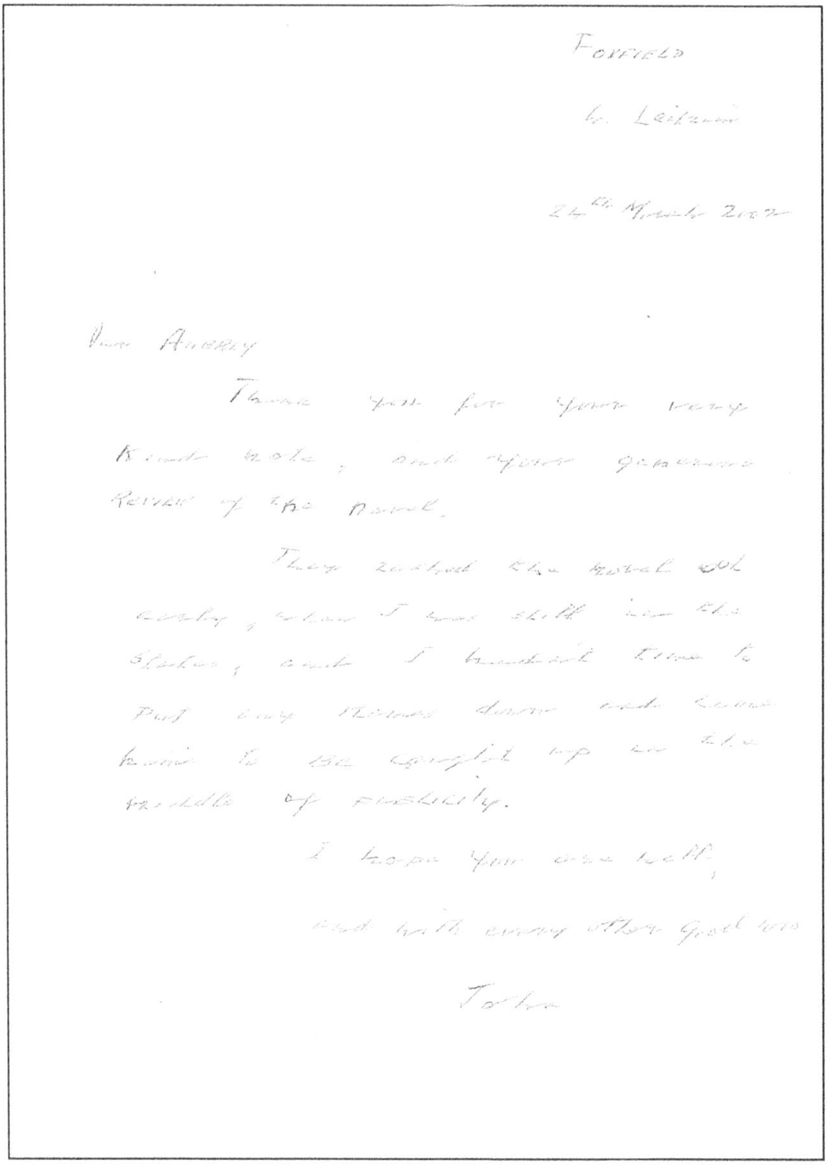

Foxfield
Co. Leitrim

22nd March 2002

Dear Audrey

Thank you for your very kind note, and your generous review of the novel.

They rushed the book out early, when I was still in the States, and I hadn't time to put any thoughts down and have been to be caught up in the middle of publicity.

I hope you are well, and with every other good wish

John

One of McGahern's letters to the author

to gild the lily. Freed from the constraints of telling a story he ends up telling many of them instead. Except they're not the usual kinds of stories. They're daily events given importance simply because he confers it on them.

We follow the characters from one summer to the next. It's a year in their lives but it could be twenty. They epitomise calmness. Nothing more than the flight of a flock of birds across the sky disturbs it. The passing of the seasons is like a metaphor for the transience of life itself.

The book doesn't bother itself much with plot. McGahern is more interested in showing life going on. The two main characters are Joe and Kate Ruttledge, a couple who've left London to live in Ireland. He's a writer from the area; she's Anglo-American. Already we can see the semi-autobiographical base of the book. It's furthered when we're made aware of the courtesies they extend to their neighbours. McGahern and Madeline were well-known for their hospitable natures. Anyone who ever visited them got a sympathetic ear.

Ruttledge is the "I" – or eye – of the novel, a kind of Greek chorus commenting on what he sees. Both he and Kate soak up the stories they hear like sponges.

All around them we see what Sydney Webb referred to as "the neutrality of gradualness." They interact with a neighbouring couple, Jamesie and Mary. Jamesie's brother Johnny dies in the course of the book. It's one of the few dramatic incidents in it.

Jamesie has lost faith but he still goes to Mass. Asked by Ruttledge why this is so he replies, "To look at girls."[5] McGahern identified with that. He thought Mass-going in Ireland often had more to do with socialising than spirituality: "It's a way of seeing the pretty girls on Sundays." When a neighbour asked him one day why he didn't attend Mass he said it was because he wasn't a believer. The neighbour said, "Ah sure none of us believes but its great *craic*. You see everyone on a Sunday!" When he analysed it, he didn't think he ever believed in the tenets of religion. He just feared a punitive deity. But religion had a benefit in that it articulated the mystery of life. "Otherwise there's just the pigs and the cows and the goats."[6]

Joe and Kate also interact with a character called Bill Evans who was taken from an orphanage as a boy and put to work as a skivvy. Another character, John Quinn, is an incorrigible womaniser. At one stage Kate says he looked at her as if she were an animal. Later in the novel he marries. It's a disaster – and a comedy. McGahern juxtaposes the two moods seamlessly.

There's also an IRA activist, Jimmy Joe McKiernan; an easy-going builder called Patrick Ryan; a kindly priest, Father Conroy; and Ruttledge's uncle, the colourful Shah, a millionaire who owns a garage and produces agricultural goods. The sale of his business to an associate he doesn't relate well to occupies much of the book. This isn't wildly exciting material but in McGahern's hands it becomes compulsive.

The Shah is based on McGahern's Uncle Pat. Like Quinn he's a larger than life character. He was called The Shah because of the secret sources he seemed to have for supplying petrol to his garage. Even during the shortage of the 1970s he was able to provide it – but only to his regulars. Others were left queueing interminably. A story McGahern liked to tell about him concerned a woman who pulled up at his garage one day and was given sixpence worth of petrol. He told her it would get her to the brow of the hill beside her. After that she'd have to "freewheel" home![7]

There's as much comedy as pathos in the book. At one point we're told a story about two public houses situated on opposite sides of the road in a nearby village. Each time a government changes, the proprietor supporting the 'in' party demands that the village's only phone box be moved to his side of the road. Such victories become huge within the context of local affairs.

McGahern is always at home in hermetically-sealed worlds like the one we get here. Unlike *Amongst Women*, here that world is expanded. If the family was a mini-republic in the earlier book, here the community by the lake performs that function. Gone is the nuclear family structure of *Amongst Women*. Joe and Kate are childless. The Shah is a bachelor. Different kinds of intimacies pertain than heretofore. Gone also is the religious domination of *Amongst Women*. Here the focus is on a secular universe surrounded by nature.[8] At times it becomes almost pantheistic.

With this autumnal novel McGahern returns to the land that spawned him. It becomes what Yoknapatawpha was to William Faulkner or Wessex to Thomas Hardy: a geographical conduit through which he can explore issues at the core of himself. It's McGahern's crowning achievement to date, even if on the surface it's one of his least ambitious undertakings. It flatters to deceive, using sleight of hand to immerse us in its web, the quaint snatches of conversation alchemising his lakeside retreat into a microcosm of Everyman's struggles.

Little things mean a lot in this neck of the woods. It seems rooted in some dimly suspended past. So much so that when something even vaguely contemporary intrudes – like, say, a discussion of the TV show "Blind Date" – the reader is thrown. McGahern hasn't so much removed himself from the real world as pinned a significantly minuscule portion of it down. He's analysed it microscopically, unleashing the subterranean tensions endemic in probably every parish in the country.

This is a book in which art has been distilled down to its very essence. McGahern's carefully crafted brushstrokes work in the same unadorned idiom he's made his own for many decades now. Images are heaped upon one another in incantatory fashion, creating a hypnotic effect.

He works hard to make the writing look easy. His rhythmic word painting teases out the pyrotechnics of cattle deals, Republican undercurrents, local rivalries, the warp and weft of rural felicities. Like the great Russian authors he admires and sometimes emulates, he poeticises daily events until they acquire the carapace of universality. More than once we're reminded of Chekhov's "magic lake."

The book grew out of the short story "Love of the World." In most of McGahern's work we see novels that were work-in-progress shrunk to the dimensions of short stories. Here a reverse pattern unfolded. It wasn't that he became long-winded. The leisurely language suited the mentality of his characters more than the "young men in a hurry" who'd peopled the earlier novels.

This is a disappearing Ireland but it still holds the mirror – or keyhole – up to it. People who would be minor characters with any other writer become central here. We're proffered word-painting of a high order. We get something from nothing over and over again with his vignettes.

McGahern was making a statement with the book, a statement that contemporary blandishments had little to offer him. The modern world conduced to homogeneousness in his view: "You see the same clothes in New York as in Mohill, and very often the same way of behaving."[9]

In *That They May Face the Rising Sun*, such a world hints with a whisper rather than resounding with a roar. The characters don't so much resist the advances of technology as remain immune to them. When telephone lines come in, or cable TV, the news is greeted nonchalantly. They would as well do without such conveniences.

They're more in tune with the absolutes of life and death. McGahern is graphic about the laying out of Johnny's body after he dies. When he writes about the removal of his watch one is reminded of the ending of "Gold Watch": "The only thing that remained on [him] was a large silver digital watch, the red numerals pulsing out the seconds like a mechanical heart, eerily alive in the stillness." His hairdresser remarks wryly, "He won't need that anymore."

McGahern was justifiably proud of what he achieved in these pages. If he couldn't have written *The Pornographer* without having first done *The Leavetaking*, as he said, I doubt he could have done this without having first written *Amongst Women*.

It was appreciated by anyone who loved good writing. McGahern won the Kerry Ingredients Irish Fiction Prize for it at the Listowel Writer's Week. He was in great spirits there despite his failing health. At one point between readings he put a book on his head as he clowned around with Anna Manahan and Ruth McCabe. He almost felt guilty accepting the 10,000 euro prize money, imagining most of the other shortlisted writers needed it more than he did. They probably did. But none of them had written a book of this calibre.

In the U.S. it was called *By the Lake*. Reviews on both sides of the Atlantic were ecstatic. "This is a novel," wrote Hilary Mantel in the *New York Review of Books*, "about a world the reader enters as an eavesdropper. The writing is so calm it seems like the text is listening to itself."[10]

"At last an Irish author," Seamus Deane wrote, "has awakened from the nightmare of history and given us a sense of liberation which is not dependent on flight or emigration or escape."[11]

"The literary editor of *Newsweek*," McGahern beamed, "told me he postponed reading the last twenty pages so that he could stay in the world by the lake. That meant a lot to me." He said these words not with big-headedness but rather the innocence of a child who's amazed he's found a niche in the upper echelons of *belles lettres*.

As I write, *That They May Face the Rising Sun* is about to be made into a film

Devastation

McGahern had a colonoscopy in early 2003. He was given the all-clear but before he left the hospital a radiologist who knew him decided to do a liver scan. He wasn't due to have one for another few months. It was done as a favour by the radiologist.

The scan showed cancer nodes which had remained hidden in his blood. That was why the colonoscopy hadn't picked them up. He was told there was only a 2% chance of this happening. The nodes were spread over various parts of his body. That made surgery not an option. Neither could they be killed off any other way. The bottom line was that there was no way to stop the cancer from spreading. All the doctors could do was stall its progress. The diagnosis was given to him in such a clear manner he didn't doubt it. A previous era may have sugar-coated his symptoms. The modern age believed in brutal honesty.

What a cruel irony that a man who tried to do him a favour ended up giving him the worst news imaginable. He would have been better off not knowing how ill he was considering so little could be done for him. Nothing was gained from the diagnosis except for giving him more time to come to terms with it.

Later conversations with doctors about his condition were more sophisticated. They discussed state-of-the-art treatments for cancer, state-of-the-art drugs. He tried to take in what they were saying but it proved to be beyond him. Then he thought: Why should he bother? What was going to happen was going to happen no matter how much he knew about it or not. "I'm a brilliant student," he said, sounding like a character from one of his books, "in a hopeless case."[1]

The man who wrote so intensely about his mother's cancer was strangely subdued regarding his own experience of the disease. The fact that he was going to die of it merited just a single line in a letter he wrote to his Colgate associate Janette Albrecht in May 2003. "My condition is terminal," he remarked baldly to her in the middle of the letter.[2] His stoicism reminds us of what Jamesie says in *That They May Face the Rising Sun*: "There's nothing right or wrong in this world, only what happens."

McGahern with the PEN A.T. Cross Award. (Photocall)

McGahern now became an unlikely ally for the church. The anti-clerical tide, he thought, had swung too far. Media gurus had become the new arbiters of morality, journalists and broadcasters sermonising from behind laptops in the same way priests used to from altars. At the Bath Literary Festival in 2003 he told of a priest friend of his that he'd met some time before dressed in plain clothes rather than his more usual black. He explained to McGahern that, because of the abuses, some of his friends had been assaulted when they dressed in their soutanes. He didn't want the same thing to happen to him.[3]

He didn't engage in grim forebodings about the future. "The amazing thing," he said, "is that any of us is here at all." He refused counselling on mortality with the characteristically blunt, "We bloom only once, and you'd want to be very foolish not to know that."⁴

What possible benefit could it have entailed? As someone who'd spent his life writing about mortality, who'd experienced it in all its horror at the age of ten, there was hardly anyone in the world in less need of it. Asked how he felt about dying he gave the kind of answer only McGahern would have been capable of: "The thing about death is that you only get one go at it!" ⁵

I interviewed him for the *Cork Examiner* at the beginning of 2004 because of his forthcoming 70th birthday. I hadn't known how ill he was at the time. I'd heard a rumour about his cancer but that was all. It was mainly with nonchalance I asked if he was concerned about having reached the Biblical span. "There's nothing you can do about ageing," he said, "Nobody pays too much heed to it down here."⁶

He'd received $125,000 for the prestigious American Lannan Award for fiction two months before. He took the news in his stride: "Literary prizes never improved the quality of the prose." The money was nice but it wasn't why he wrote. It kept the animals in "high style."⁷ In the old days the farming bolstered the books. Now it was the other way round.

It was a subject he never liked talking about. "Sometimes," he said, "my neighbours ask me if there's any money in writing the same way they might ask if there's any money in sheep. They seem mighty relieved to learn there isn't."⁸

I asked him how he felt about the fact that over a thousand people had attended a recent public interview he'd done with Myles Dungan. He signed so many books that when he finally got out of the venue to go to a restaurant where a meal had been booked for him, it was shut.

It wasn't always thus, he hastened to say. He related an anecdote about being in Sunderland once for a reading. Only one person showed up, a rather nervous-looking man: "There was a thunderstorm. I was worried about getting back to my hotel in Newcastle. I asked him if he'd prefer a reading or a pint. To my relief he opted for the pint."⁹

He said he'd enjoyed the evening immensely. The image of him as a recluse was ebbing. Dungan had interviewed him a number of times and found him great company, especially when he was being irreverent about other writers. He described him as being "bitchy but hilarious."¹⁰

As the interview drew to a close he read an excerpt from *The Pornographer* which caused the audience to erupt into laughter. It was a favourite passage of his, one in which he wrote about a visit of relations to a house where pleasantries are exchanged until the visitors leave. Afterwards the hosts descend into a litany of abuse towards their departed guests. It said a lot to him about the two-tiered nature of Irish life, the tendency to wear the mask of friendship to people when they were speaking to them and then tear them apart in their absence. Maybe it's the way things work in all societies. As the saying goes, hypocrisy is the lubricant that oils the wheels of social intercourse.

He asked me how my own writing was going. I'd just had a biography of Charles Bukowski published. I'd been telling him about it over the phone in recent months. I even sent him a cassette tape of a poetry reading Bukowski had done in Redondo Beach. It was a particularly riotous one where he'd told the audience, "I'll take you all on." Bukowski's readings had big fight atmospheres and this one more than most. It wouldn't have been McGahern's idea of a literary evening. Maybe it would have reminded him of the culture of McDaid's bar, of a time when the imprint of a pint of Guinness on copy was the mark of "true literature".

He didn't say whether he enjoyed the tape or not. I took his silence to suggest he hadn't. They were totally different kinds of people. I have no doubt he saw him as a vulgarian, though I knew he admired Bukowski's all-time favourite book, Louis-Ferdinand Celine's *Journey to the End of the Night*. A book I'd written on censorship evinced more interest from him. It was a subject closer to his heart. My area of scrutiny was cinema rather than literature. "It's a different world," he said, "but in ways we were all in the same boat."

He talked about Rilke's novel *The Notebooks of Malte Laurids Brigge*, the book he'd given to Nuala O'Faolain all those years ago. He'd mentioned it in the course of our 1990 conversation as well. It seemed to be imprinted on his brain. I'd dipped into it many times over the years upon his recommendation, finding something new in it each time.

He also talked about Alice McDermott's *Charming Billy* and Nathanael West's *Miss Lonelyhearts*. Did I like West's work? I had to admit ignorance on that score. What about Herman Melville? I said I loved *Moby Dick* but hadn't read anything else by him. He recommended *Billy Budd*. I said I'd seen the film with Terence Stamp. "Films don't usually bear much resemblance to books," he said, echoing his comment of a few moments before. I asked him how he felt about adaptations of his own works. "It's mainly television," he said, "I try not to get too involved. Directors don't like writers looking over their shoulders."

He mentioned some other writers he admired. I can't remember who they were apart from John Williams. He'd recommended Williams' 1965 book *Stoner* to me when I was trying to convert him to Bukowski. I tried to read it a few times but found my attention flagging. This despite the fine quality of the writing. I told him I admired Williams but he didn't keep me turning pages. I couldn't understand why he thought so much of the story of a university professor whose life left few imprints.

My views weren't shared by the reading public. Upon McGahern's recommendation the book went into a reprint with Faber and flew off the shelves. What was I missing? Williams impressed him as much as other writers he'd talked to me about in the past – Alastair McLeod, Michael McLaverty and others. The formalism of the writing echoed his own, though it lacked his eccentricity – the kick that made his sentences live. I also imagined the university setting would also have appealed to him. He hadn't written about his own experiences in universities.

Maybe that was why *Stoner* meant so much to him. Maybe it was the book he'd wanted to write but couldn't for one reason or another.

He didn't talk about his cancer, preferring to keep the conversation upbeat, but I detected a sadness in him, something that hadn't been there in any previous conversations I'd had with him. It underpinned everything we talked about.

I reminded him of our meeting in the North Star Hotel thirteen years before, about how he'd talked of his life as a writer, the nature of family, politics, exile – all the subjects that intrigued him. He was still intrigued by them. Maybe we never really changed, no matter how many years elapsed. Maybe we just shifted our priorities.

He talked about exile again. "I've always felt you could write just as badly in Ireland as anywhere else," he said. I suspected I was meant to

McGahern receiving the Irish PEN A.T. Cross award in 2003 (Photocall)

laugh at his joke but I couldn't for some reason. The remark didn't seem in character for him. How could I see John McGahern as ever writing badly anywhere?

Despite all his travels, he always preferred writing about Ireland: "I think one can pick up the nuances of one's own country easier than those of a different one. I don't think the writing would ring true." I asked him what drove him as a writer. He said his basic ambition was to disappear behind his words: "Flaubert put it best. The author should be like God – everywhere present but nowhere visible."[11]

How did he achieve such omnipresence? "By a sense of rhythm or tone more than anything else. That's a writer's stamp in the same way a splash of colour might be an artist's. If it's successful the reader gets to recognise it and look for it. In that way a writer will attract readers. But he also does it for himself. He finds the 'what' through the 'how.'"

That was his ambition with *That They May Face the Rising Sun*. "I wanted to see what would be left if I took the plot out of a book. Maybe it's a bit like going from representational painting to abstract. You hang the theme out to dry in a sense. It may not be to all people's tastes distilling the process down like that. If you're lucky you'll get purity."

He talked about his struggles with the book, how he worried about its formlessness at the beginning but later came to see this as its greatest strength. He said he thought it was his best book. "But maybe I thought that about the others when I'd done them too. You're closest to something when you've just finished it." When I asked him what he thought was its best quality he said, "Maybe the fact that it didn't call attention to itself." He said that had also been his ambition with his other books – as if I needed to be told.

A writer," he said, "is a man who puts down things other people mightn't think worth noticing – the sun setting on a lake, the configuration of the clouds, a tree blowing in the wind, the colour of the grass. Writing should give as much importance to the opening of a door as a big dramatic scene. Big scenes generally write themselves. I'm interested in what surrounds them, a primary central image in the mass of feeling, whether it's a razor blade or a can of Coca-Cola or someone peeling an orange. These are the envelopes I put the work into."[12]

Before we finished he told me he was working on a memoir. It would focus mainly on his early years. I was amazed. He'd been so protective of his life up to this, so threatened by anyone who tried to infiltrate it. Was he now going to blow his own cover? "I think it's time," he said.

Justine McCarthy, a journalist with the *Irish Independent*, interviewed him two months later. She knew more than me about the poor state of his health. Before the interview was printed he asked her if it would be possible to omit this topic from her piece. Not for reasons of privacy, he stressed, but in case it looked as if he was "courting sympathy."[13] She was happy to oblige such a dignified request.

He spent the next two years working on *Memoir*. His health was declining rapidly by now but he refused to give up on it, pushing himself to the limits to get it to ring true. Neil Belton, a former pupil of his at Belgrove, had become an editor at Faber. He said working on the book was the greatest experience of his life. He'd been in the school when McGahern was sacked so it was also a kind of revenge on that time for both of them – though McGahern never sought revenge.[14]

The book involved more research than he was accustomed to for a book. His sisters dredged up a vast trove of letters going back over the years to help him with his task. He had many of his own ones too. What his sisters added was a number written from his mother to his father. They gave him insights into the shifting parameters of their relationship.

Reading them made him more than aware how faulty his memory was. He learned, for instance, that the animals they owned were bought over a long period of time. He'd thought they all came with the farm after his mother died. He also thought her illness took place over the best part of a year. In reality it was only six weeks.[15]

Memoir presents us with the classic McGahern themes in high relief. The hatred of a father figure evident in so many of the novels and stories here becomes more strident than ever. His love for his mother, in contrast, is almost idolatrous.

As somebody who spent his life creating fiction it was a different kind of discipline to have to keep strictly to the facts. Did he find this difficult? "It was tricky. I was itching to alter material so that it conformed to a certain vision." But he resisted the temptation. "One was stuck with what happened."[16]

Autobiography was never going to be his favourite genre. The worst mistakes he made in his fiction, he confessed, was when he got too close to the world of facts. His work was poor when he drew from life or stuck close to the way things happened: "That's where the prose is dead."[17]

An even worse crime than factualising fiction was fictionalising fact. Once he decided to do the book he had to abide by a cardinal rule: Only tell what happened. Which meant avoiding any kind of embellishment.

That was easy when he wrote about his mother. He didn't have to exaggerate her to make the text dramatic. His love for her was so passionate, the drama created itself.

She's the votive lamp of the book, the gravitational force that drives it in a positive direction just as his father is the destructive one that pulls it down to its special hell.

"In the beginning was my mother," he writes.[18] With these words he leads us into the near-oedipal relationship with the woman who gave him his first exposure to emotion, security, religion.

He didn't just say he loved his mother; he said he was "in" love with her. This took filial bond to a different level.

When he writes about her, a different kind of person seems to appear behind the pen. There's affectionate writing about lovers threaded throughout his novels and stories but often it's truncated and/or short-lived. The love he shows for his mother is sustained and intense, even mystical. On the basis of *Memoir*, his relationship with her seems to be stronger than any other one he ever formed in his life. That isn't to say it was.

Undoubtedly he had great love for Madeline – this is evident in his letters – and for his sisters, but he didn't write about these people in such terms here. Neither does he write much about Anniki Laaksi in the book – less than five pages out of its 272 total. It virtually ignores his life from the mid-sixties to the mid-seventies, what we might call the "non-family years." Neither is there any mention of Mary Keelan or his love child.

Some of the most powerful writing he ever did documents the death of his mother and his reaction to it. In these pages we see the genesis of everything he wrote about death elsewhere, be it about his mother or characters

McGahern poured his heart onto the page in *Memoir*, particularly in the pages dealing with his mother (Photocall)

modelled on her. The passages about her death are even more poignant than they were in *The Leavetaking*, which is saying something. He can't come to terms with it, grudging himself every moment he spent away from her. "She was gone where I could not follow," he writes, "I would never lay eyes on her face again. The time I had spent in the flower garden by the lorry instead of going to her in the room came back to torture me."[19]

He was often told he resembled her in appearance. One writer believed his "courtly empathy" towards women came from her. "She certainly was a better person than I am," he confessed.[20]

He described *Memoir* as his posthumous Mass for her.[21] It was like an apology, sixty years delayed, for the actual one he'd promised her in1944 when he had visions of becoming a priest. Now in his "second priesthood" he could finally deliver on that.

The parts of it that concerned his father presented a different kind of challenge. In one of the earlier drafts he used fictional techniques to avoid doing so. In the end he scrapped these.[22]

His mother may be the heroine of the book but she dies early. The dead hand of his father, as Michael Harding wrote, is on "every piece of clothing, every farm implement, every teapot and oilcloth."[23]

If the pages dealing with his mother are cathartic, those featuring his father represent a different kind of exorcism. They fired his imagination with negative energy.

He was asked if he inherited anything from his father. "He liked to write," he said, "Maybe I got some of that from him." He was referring mainly to his letters. He couldn't have written fiction to save his life.

When I spoke to him in the interview I did for his seventieth birthday I mentioned that Charles Bukowski, like him, had a cruel father. He was aware of this but not of the fact that Bukowski used to raise toasts to him in perverse gratitude after his career took off. As was the case with McGahern, Bukowski's father fuelled his imagination. His hatred of him fed into some of his most powerful works. 'I owe it all to you, old man,' he would say jocosely as he guzzled his beer. McGahern wasn't quite so sardonic but the figure of Frank McGahern, the police sergeant who exerts such a dominant presence in everything from *The Dark* to *Amongst Women* in fictional form, birthed him much of his inspiration.

Did he write *Memoir* to get back at him for his cruelty? Some readers thought so. There's a joke about Ireland that goes, "Irish Alzheimer's is the disease where you forget everything but the grudges." That may be true of some writers but I doubt it was of McGahern. He never indulged bitter feelings, preferring to "move on," as the contemporary phrase goes. We saw this from his attitude to the brouhaha of the sixties that caused him to lose his job. He was similarly sanguine about his father. Writing about him helped him to tether his anger towards him rather than feed it.[24]

Such anger had been tethered in vicarious manners in much of the fiction he wrote up to this. Apart from Reegan in *The Dark* and Moran in *Amongst Women* there are many reincarnations of Frank McGahern in his fiction. "The Key," "The Stoat," "Coming Into His Kingdom," "Gold Watch,", "Korea," "Wheels," "Sierra Leone," and "Oldfashioned" all have father figures in them. He varies the characters slightly in these and other stories. In "Wheels," "Gold Watch" and Sierra Leone" they're small farmers. In "Coming into the Kingdom," "The Key," and "The Stoat" they're widowers.

"Wheels," "Gold Watch" and "Sierra Leone" all feature men who remarry after their wives die. In "Gold Watch" and "Sierra Leone" the son's relationship with the father is complicated by the son's involvement with a woman. McGahern seemed to enjoy teasing out the ramifications of these father-son tropes in all sorts of ways.

His father asked him once what his aim in writing was. He replied, "To write truly and well about fellows like yourself."[25] It's interesting that he didn't say, "About you."

It was a sore point between them ever since *The Barracks*. One of the reasons McGahern sent his father a copy of the book was to show him he wasn't afraid of him seeing himself in it. But he *was* in it, and in all the other writings mentioned above, however disguised he might have been. McGahern had an obsession with writing about him. He was able to develop him more as a character as the years went on. This reached its fictional apex in *Amongst Women* before reverting back to the factual in *Memoir*. Neither of these books could have been written while he was alive. His death freed McGahern's pen to develop new sides to him and to embellish already documented ones.

Memoir isn't a "key" to the themes dealt with in all his works up to this. McGahern often said, "Life is too thin for art." The prism of fiction for him was just that, a prism. As he said in another context, art was a form of "escaping into reality."[26]

He uses the book to show his father's truculence, his fragility, his manipulative sense, his charm, the way he could turn in micro-seconds from aggression to vulnerability depending on what he saw in a situation for himself. Fascinating and all as the characters based on him in the novels and stories were, the man himself comes across as more complex than any of them. From the early days of his marriage he was playing the martyr and so it continued through Susan's death, his widowhood, his second marriage, the growing independence of McGahern and his daughters, the rebelliousness of Frankie and finally his declining health.

McGahern said the writing of the book didn't help him to understand him any better than he had when he was growing up. That's probably because he was too close to the events he transcribes. For the reader he falls into an understandable pattern. Though he may appear to have had many contradictions in him, the main one was the way he pushed people away from him and then tried to draw them back. "He would never let go of a relationship," McGahern maintained, "no matter how bad it was."[27]

There's only one instance in the book where McGahern is proud of him. It's when he wants to bring him to a football match after Mass as a boy. A Canon wants him to attend a Catechism class instead. He pulls McGahern's ear when he tries to run from the church. His father tells him to let go but he refuses. He then pulls the Canon's ear. It was one of the few times in his life he challenged a church figure. Anger caused him to do so. If it happened more often, McGahern's relationship to him could have been so much better.

As well as being a haunting evocation of his parents and family, *Memoir* shone in its descriptions of places. Michael Harding, a fellow Leitrim man, said McGahern imbued the landscape with a stillness that was almost sacramental: "The lane up the road, the white thorn bush, the wild flower in the field, the sound of a spade hitting a rock - all these graph out a presence of things that resonate for the reader with the barely audible music of transcendence."[28] Harding believed the "old" Leitrim died with McGahern. After he was gone it was replaced with cranes on the streets, flowing concrete and bulldozers "shifting the banks of the Shannon, which had remained still for centuries."[29]

Liam Kelly said he'd be forever linked with the landscape of Leitrim and Roscommon just as Yeats is with Sligo or Kavanagh with Monaghan.[30] It was one of the qualities he most admired in the writings of William Trevor. Michael McLaverty had it too. Jamesie said in *That They May Face the Rising Sun*, "I may not have travelled far but I know the whole world." The remark applied to McGahern as well. Leitrim was that world for him, the fields and lanes of his youth captured 101 different ways as he threaded them through these pages. Place names were hugely important to him. He missed them in the works of other writers, like Beckett, for instance.[31]

The book was launched in the Long Room of Trinity College Library. McGahern's sisters Rosaleen and Monica were there. Both of them were enthralled with it. Said Rosaleen, "It's very accurate but some of it I would rather not remember. It brought back many things I'd forgotten, like when my mother was ill John used to get up every morning at six and light the fire and we'd mix her powder with water for her." She now believed that was morphine. Monica said the book made her both laugh and cry: "At times I wished it was fiction." She loved her brother and was proud of him. For her it was even more powerful than his novels.[32]

The cover had a sepia photograph of McGahern and three of his sisters in childhood. All of them are gazing bewildered at the camera. They had every right to do so when you consider the horrors inflicted upon them by their father. "One of my sisters was twice in a catatonic state after a beating," McGahern said, "She turned blue. It took five or six hours before she could stand up."[33]

That was all in the past. He wanted to let it go. What was important now was to see how the book would be received, what readers it would find.

It was generously reviewed. Many people were shocked by it; many more enthralled by the beauty of the writing. Seamus Deane said it was "a millimetre away from perfection."[34] The *Observer* described McGahern as the greatest living Irish writer.[35]

It was re-titled *All Will Be Well* in the U.S. That sounds optimistic but the phrase represents false hope in the book. It's used sardonically in the chapter where McGahern's mother is dying of cancer in hospital but doesn't know it. She writes to her husband, "I am feeling very well...I place my trust in God, knowing all will be well."[36] The phrase is also used sardonically in T.S. Eliot's *Four Quartets*. In *The Pornographer* it refers to an unwanted child.[37]

Memoir, like *Amongst Women* and *That They May Face the Rising Sun*, sold well in the U.S. McGahern wasn't able to promote it over there because of his poor health but he did some group interviews for it in Ireland. A descendent of the Moroney family, having read about his reminiscences of being at their estate in his childhood, turned up at one of them. After it was over she presented him with a book taken from her library. How long had it been since he borrowed the last one? More years ago than he wanted to remember. Was it sixty? He jokingly asked her when she wanted it back. She informed him that this one he could keep.

Philip King produced a documentary about McGahern for television in 2005. Despite his recent reservations about Frances Byrnes, he willingly submitted to this. It was called *John McGahern – A Private World*.

It was directed by Pat Collins. Collins had a history of making quality-studded documentaries set in rural areas. He was a great fan of McGahern's writing. The earthiness of it spoke to him.

"I don't like the notion of a countryside kept pristine for the holiday home-owners who visit once a year," he said. There was no fear of that with McGahern.

McGahern with Olive Braiden and Mary Cloake on the way to an Arts Council meeting in 2003. (Photocall)

His friend Emer O'Kelly, like many other people, was surprised he allowed the outside world into his home for the film, surprised he opened his doors for "the evening sun to gleam through."[38] Had his poor health something to do with it? Was it his swansong? These were the thoughts in many people's minds.

Collins captured the minimalism of his life. His house looked monastic. The walls were bare, the furniture as spare as his prose. He was obviously unwell but his mind was as sharp as ever. His comments were like a distillation of all the interviews he'd given over the years.

"The familiar," he said at one stage, "is always more interesting than what's exotic or strange. You need to have a good boring life in which nothing much happens except what's going on in your head."

He liked *A Private World* apart from the footage of him in Japan that appeared towards the end of it. He couldn't see the point of this. It was taken in the Kyoto Gardens during a promotional visit to the country.

He gave another reading of *Memoir* in The South Bank in London. Tony Whelan attended it. He hadn't seen him since his appearance at the launch of his *Collected Stories* in 1992. He thought he looked well but he knew how ill he was. He was surprised to see Madeline with him as she didn't usually attend the readings.

The next time he met him was at Carrick-on-Shannon. They went for a drink in a hotel. He was wearing a cap to hide the baldness that had been caused by his chemotherapy. Madeline was there again. Whelan didn't remember much about the meeting. They talked only of trivial things. McGahern said he didn't like the new supermarket that had just opened in the town. He was also shocked at the price of a drink. After their meeting drew to a close, McGahern walked Whelan to the car park. Then he drove off.[39] Whelan wondered if he would ever see him again. For the first time in years he wasn't envious of him. He may not have been famous but at least he had his health. McGahern hadn't..

He was given new hope that August when stem cell treatment was mixed with his chemotherapy. It increased his discomfort but offered a chance of killing off the rogue cells. He didn't show much interest in this, being all too well aware it was, at best, going to be little more than an exercise in containment. He referred to it disparagingly as "the monkey gland" treatment. It resulted in the reduction in the size of four of the lesions and the disappearance of the other three.

Surgery was now considered but he had little interest in this either, pointing out that disappearance wasn't the same as eradication. Where had the cells gone, he wondered? If they hid in his blood at the onset of his disease, surely they could do so again.

In the same month a woman drove her car into the lake beside his house. She did so deliberately. He was desperately clinging on to a life she was willing to end by her own hand. But he sympathised with her. She was a local woman. A police helicopter located her car under the water. They dragged "the car and the poor woman" to the shore.[40]

He finally received his teacher's pension that year. The timing was choice. It was a decade overdue and he had one foot in the grave. Maybe Beckett could have written a good play about the situation.

As well as struggling with the chemotherapy he came down with a bout of food poisoning in early 2006.

No matter how sick or tired he was he continued doing readings and signings. He even attended Arts Council meetings. He didn't want pity or talk about his condition.

He was now working on a reprint of his *Collected Stories* anthology which had appeared in 1992. The new book was called *Creatures of the Earth*. It contained a story of that name as well as another new one, "Love of the Earth," and a story many consider to be his all time best, "The Country

Funeral." These three stories close the book with a powerful flourish.

This last one, dealing with three brothers who travel from Dublin to the country for the funeral of their uncle, was both moving and funny by turns. It was the kind of story only McGahern could have written. He'd watched these kinds of people in all their moods and colours over the years and he captures them here to a t. The story is almost of novella length. It was subsequently issued by Faber in a separate volume of its own. Like all his work it's characterised by a disarming simplicity in the narration.

Emer O'Kelly reviewed the book in the *Irish Independent*. She was always eloquent about him and she didn't disappoint here. "McGahern," she said, "writes of a world where the tiger's roar of prosperity is shrill and nervous, pierced through with the memory of love stilled by hardship and kindness, trampled by privation and fear." In his work, she wrote, "There's a sense of life unlived, our passage on earth a stopped watch that forces the ending into our sights almost before we've begun." [41]

He didn't fear death. In one of the last interviews he gave he spoke of his childhood fascination with the attitude towards it that he saw in the country of his youth. If someone was dangerously ill, people accepted whatever transpired: "One way or another it will be the will of God." If the person died, all attention turned towards their wake. These were as much social occasions as anything else in McGahern's memory. Maybe it was always thus in Ireland. Joyce once called funerals "funferalls."

McGahern remembered the hive of activity that took place in the house of a dead person, mourners arriving with bottles of whiskey or poteen, their conversation becoming more animated the more they drank. At times it seemed as if the dead person was almost forgotten. They discussed "the price of cattle, the unsuitability of the weather for cutting turf, the most recent football match."

Afterwards the eulogies would begin. "He was a *dacent* man, God rest him. One of the auld sort." A rosary would be said. Then people would touch the corpse lightly. It was thought they'd be haunted by the dead person from the hereafter if they didn't.

Though McGahern had fond memories of such rituals, they were counterbalanced by the other side of religion – the fearful one. He often spoke of the horror he had of parish missions, of the fire-and-brimstone priests who officiated at them. Of one priest it was said, "He'd make the hair stand on your head even if you were bald." [42]

Sex was the usual theme of the sermons. As McGahern recalled, "It was thought a greater crime to make love to someone than to kill them." The sermons lingered "maddeningly" in his head: "It was no wonder I entered the confession box trembling."[43]

His father shared his horror of such men. "They only make the pious more insufferable," he said, "and the sinner more despairing. Trying to get people to change their lives by ranting and raving is about as sensible as trying to cut turf with a razor blade." [44] It was one of the few things the two of them agreed on.

Not everyone was threatened by the mission priests. Some people laughed them off with comments like, "Sure they're the only entertainment we get in chapel all year." In a way they were preferable to the intellectual types who analysed how many angels could dance on the head of a pin. Of one of this breed it was said, "He was so wishy-washy he was worse than watery tea." [44]

Such reflections are scattered pell-mell through McGahern's writings and discourses. They form a central part of his outlook on life. Now, however, he wasn't thinking of them as themes for his work. Death was too close for that. He was in the eye of the storm, in the same position his mother was sixty years before, a victim of the same disease. Would he be able to deal with it as bravely as she did?

He didn't have her faith to console him. There was no God to bribe now with promises of ordination Masses. Heaven wasn't in the clouds anymore. If it was anywhere it was inside his books. These had taken him on an adventure from puberty to the present but now that was ending.

Shortly before he died he was invited to speak at Belgrove School, the location of his sacking. He declined, saying he would have felt like "an old ghost" rattling around its corridors.[45]

He knew his time was short. He sold his cattle and planned his funeral.

The King is Dead

McGahern died on March 30, 2006. I was shocked when I heard the news even though his appearance in *A Private World* painted a clear picture of how ill he was. I should have realised it was his way of saying goodbye to us all.

There were tributes from around the world. In Ireland the great and the good lined up to pay homage to him. Friends, colleagues, fans of his work and life, neighbours, anyone who'd known him, however briefly, testified to the fact that he left a mark on them. Madeline was dignified in her grief, his sisters similarly so.

"The king is dead," Jennifer Johnston wrote, "Dear John, may your coffin be covered with wild orchids and windflower."[1] Alastair McLeod said, "No one will have his literary fingerprints." John Spain described him as being "ferocious in his depiction of the truth." The "small world" he featured in his work, wrote Spain, became through the spiritual force of his writing, "transformed into an Everywhere."[2] Emer O'Kelly said his lyricism was "a soaring bird, its flight always circumscribed by the angry stoicism that gave it birth."[3]

Declan Kiberd saw him differently, describing him as being similar to a Renaissance painter who did the same painting over and over again until he got it right.[4] After being taught by him at Belgrove he went on to become a professor of Anglo-Irish literature at University College, Dublin. "He was gentle and rather old-fashioned in his politeness," he said, but at the same time he had "a good-humoured mischievousness."[5]

Joe Kennedy berated himself for not keeping in touch with him at the end. They used to speak on the phone every Christmas but he failed to ring him on the last one. "We never expect sudden changes," Kennedy wrote in his obituary of him, "no matter what the portents. We feel life will continue to drift onwards. The bad weather will go away, grass growth will start up in the fields, lie will be renewed in the hedgerows. But sometimes this doesn't happen. We realise too late we've missed things through carelessness."[6]

Justine McCarthy alluded to his lack of faith when she said he had "no expectation of linking hands with his beloved mother to stroll down the lanes of eternity together" but, like many another, she felt he achieved a different kind of immortality through his work.[7]

Despite being a non-believer he asked for a Catholic funeral. Religion had brought as many ecstasies as agonies to his life. Indeed, the combination of both led to the richness of his prose. It would have been an impossible request to honour in a previous era but we were living in a different Ireland now. Its pluralism, combined with a church reeling from all the scandals, saw to that.

His body left the Mater hospital at 7 a.m. on March 31, travelling west in a hearse followed by a dozen cars. It was a sunny morning. The cortege stopped at the N4 diner in Mullingar. People sipped tea as trucks roared by outside. After a brief time there the journey continued. As the cortege reached Connacht, small knots of people came out of their doors. They bowed their heads, blessing themselves as the hearse passed by. They were not, as one writer put it, "the literati or the glitterati."[8] They were farmers and shopkeepers and mechanics in their overalls, the kind of people McGahern featured in his books, people who may never have read a book in their lives, not even his ones.

Soon their numbers grew. By the time the cortege reached Leitrim there were hundreds of people lining the streets of Mohill, Fenagh and Bal-

McGahern's widow Madeline in an emotional moment at his funeral with his sisters Rosaleen and Monica (Photocall)

linamore. People who knew him – and even those who didn't – came out of their houses to pay their respects.

His funeral Mass was concelebrated by no less than eight priests. "Not bad for a non-believer," Tony Whelan noted.[9] One of them was his cousin Liam Kelly. He mentioned Marcel Proust in his sermon. It was perhaps the first time the author had been quoted in an Irish Church.

Fr. Kelly was the main celebrant. "It was here," he said in his homily, "that John learned to serve Mass. It was here he had his first brush with authority when he was denounced from the altar for rattling his beads loudly as a boy. He had other brushes with authority later on but he never held a grudge or a trace of bitterness. He was too big for that."[10]

He was buried beside his mother. It was 62 years since she'd died. The letters "N.T.," standing for "National Teacher," were put on her headstone. It was suggested they should have been put on his one too.[11] It was one of the many things they shared, albeit for such a brief time. Both of them had, as they say, chalk in the blood.

There were no orations at the graveside. This was as he wanted it. A decade of the rosary was said. By now the sun had disappeared. The sky was a slate grey. Afterwards came the dull sound of clods of earth thumping down on the coffin. A gentle rain hinted. A farmer was back in the soil from which he'd sprung.

After Philip Larkin attended the funeral of his friend Barbara Pym he said, "I could almost imagine her writing about it." People might have thought the same of McGahern. In his stories he'd written about so many country funerals – including the one of that name - with their sacrosanct rituals: the prayers, the exchange of sympathies, the treasured memories. There would be no shortage of these for him.

A man once seen as an apostate had now attained the aura of an icon. A graveside mourner wrote, "It was heartwarming to witness the manner in which the Catholic Church responded to this unbeliever's death. The breadth and generosity of its comforting embrace contrasted favourably with those grim days when neither unbaptised child nor suicide victim was allowed a funeral or a Christian burial."[12]

Mary McAleese, Ireland's president, was probably the most high profile figure in attendance. Like many other heads of state she admired his writing. She said it often "pitched him into a place of some discomfort, not only for himself but for the reader also." Despite that – or because of it – it was "outstanding."[13]

Seamus Heaney was there too. Like McGahern he'd dug with his pen. Now a different type of excavation was going on, a more basic one. The death of a naturalist.

Heaney might have been thinking of the words McGahern said to him at Strand Road in 1976 when he was moving into his new house: "You've bought your coffin." Such words could also have been said to McGahern himself in 1971 when he moved back to Leitrim. He'd bought his coffin too.

Heaney liked the funeral for its plainness. It befitted its subject. There was "no music, no addresses by friends or writers. The coffin [was] carried down the aisle the same as at the funeral last week and last year and last century, the rosary said at the graveside and then local men shovelling in the mould."[14]

He saw McGahern as being on a "secret errand" with his writing: "He was strict in judgement, sympathetic in his understanding, courageous in the face of personal difficulties and always capable of merriment and grace."[15] Heaney liked the incantatory quality of his work, what he called "the melancholy of his music." Cadence, he thought, was as important to it as its content, maybe even moreso.[16]

Liam Kelly commended him for his generosity of spirit in coming back to the country that had disowned him. This is true but he returned to Ireland not only because he was free of bitterness but because he depended on its landscapes – and heartscapes – for his inspiration. Other countries failed to light his fire with the same intensity. "All good writing is local," he said, "and I think nearly all bad writing is national."[17]

His miniaturist style, documenting a country that was morphing before his eyes, was fondly remembered. Roger Boylan said, "The Ireland John McGahern was born into was an impoverished, backward, near-theocracy lit by candle and heated by peat fire. The Ireland he died in 71 years later was a dynamic modern nation boasting the second highest per capita income in the European Union."[18]

Melvyn Bragg put it best of all. "He ended where he began," he wrote, "rooted in Leitrim where he's buried beside his mother, the teacher who walked beside him all his life. Their two names share a modest headstone."[19]

Aftermath

McGahern's reputation rose after his death. People came to regard him as a national treasure, a man whose humility camouflaged a supreme talent. He rarely if ever wrote a bad sentence. He created imagery that resonated with a subdued profundity.

The interview he'd done with Joe Kennedy in 1965 now appeared for the first time. It was over forty years since it had been conducted. At last he was allowed speak about the injustices perpetrated on him – but only from the grave.

An article in *Magill* magazine in 2006 pointed out that though McGahern may have looked like a remnant of picture postcard Ireland, though he may have carried the image of a schoolteacher wearing a tweed jacket with worn elbows, "the sort of jacket worn by a man leaning up against a closed gate," he was quintessentially modern in his writing.[1]

He created his sentences, as one commentator put it, until they rang out loud and clear, "like a tuning fork striking against the chest."[2]

He said to John Banville once, "There's verse and there's prose. Poetry can happen in either."[3] Most people would agree that he could be said to have written poetry all his life, albeit in prose form.

His life wasn't as perfect as his work. Whose is? Nobody is immune from criticism. There were those who castigated him for failing to acknowledge the child he had by Joan Kelly. Anniki Laaksi also came out of the closet after he died, giving a tell-all interview to the *Daily Mail* in which she said some corrosive things about him. She accused him of being self-obsessed, tight with money and prone to telling lies. She said he was much happier to have been a figure of scandal in the 1960s than he admitted.

One had to suspect an element of sour grapes in her "revelations." He hadn't spoken to her since they broke up in 1969. She said she didn't know he'd become such a successful writer in the meantime. This is hard to believe in a world of mass communication – even if, like her, one was a

A seat erected in McGahern's memory in Leitrim (Kenneth Allen)

recluse in a distant country.

More worryingly, she claimed he married her not so much from love as the knowledge that such a marriage (in a registry office) would accentuate his notoriety. And, by extension, the loss of his job. This was headline-grabbing material but was it true? When she added that he was looking for "a surrogate mother" in their relationship, her allegations became even more suspect.[4] It seemed that she more than McGahern was attracted to the limelight.

Her words fly in the face of everything we know about him as a man and a writer. Because of their unhappiness together in London after he lost his job and the troubled way their relationship ended soon afterwards, one is tempted to accuse her of having a "creative memory".

She would have been aware that he had a long and happy marriage with another woman. That led to a perception in many people's minds that she was the problem. Such a perception could have made her defensive. Those who live with people before they become famous sometimes attest to a kind of superior knowledge of them, an "ownership" of their fame. They may feel resentful that they weren't a part of it.

Was her interview an attempt to hitch herself vicariously onto his wagon? His career went on in leaps and bounds after they split up; hers didn't. She had a prolific output of directorial work but it didn't catapult her onto the world's stage as his did.

She never talked about him when he was alive and thus able to counter her claims. Corpses can't speak. She was opportunistic in selling her story to a national newspaper after he died. Her slurs left a sour aftertaste to the tributes paid to him by most others who knew him. If he was as interested in publicity as she made out, why would he have run from it when it was offered to him? He didn't know that his books would make him economically comfortable. The years following his sacking were characterised by financial hardship and repeated uncertainty on the employment front. Only in recent years had he become economically comfortable.

Her views didn't have any long term impact on his reputation. After she gave her interview she disappeared again, becoming as invisible after it as she'd been before. McGahern continued to be honoured.

In 2007 a summer school in Leitrim was founded in his memory. I wrote a remembrance piece for him in the Yearbook of 2008 put out by the NUIG in Galway. It was one of a number of these volumes published annually. I thought it was important to stress his humility in the piece. I quoted him as saying, "It's a brutal idea to expect somebody to be interested in something you wrote merely because you wrote it."[5] The following year saw the publication of Colm Toibin's novel *Brooklyn*. It was a deceptively simple story about a young girl travelling from Ireland to New York in the 1950s. What a shame McGahern didn't live to see it. It's Toibin's McGahern novel. He emulates his hero in the writing of it. The influence is more apparent in some chapters than others. McGahern wouldn't have begrudged it to him. Imitation is the sincerest form of flattery.

In 2009 Niall Walsh, the Ballinamore pathologist with whom McGahern was friendly, found seventy letters he'd written him stuffed in an envelope at the back of a drawer. He had no memory of having put them there but was chuffed to find them. How were there so many? "I never wrote a letter to him," he said, "that I didn't get a reply to." He kindly donated them to the NUIG.

Eamon Maher, an academic with a deep interest in McGahern's work, wrote a book about his relationship to Catholicism in 2011. He'd done a previous book about his literary style in 2003. Also that year there was a radio programme called *Liveline* in which the presenter interviewed a number of McGahern's past pupils from Belgrove.

Some of them criticised his teaching. They abjured what they called the "canonisation" of him that seemed to be prevalent since his death. Some of them said he was violent in the classroom. He wasn't slow to give them a "box," one of them said. Another claimed he "ate away at your confidence." A third even described him as "dangerous." There were some fond tributes but most of those interviewed felt he was in the wrong job.[6]

McGahern might well have agreed with that last estimation of him. He was unhappy during these years and it probably reflected itself in his lack of patience if the children misbehaved. They were no doubt tougher than ones he would have encountered if he'd been teaching in a country school in his home county.

A balance to the discussion was struck by Eamon Maher. He said McGahern never claimed to be perfect and neither would he have wanted to be put on a pedestal. It was a pity the emphasis of the programme leant so much on the negative side. How had Declan Kiberd not seen that side of him? Or Neil Belton? A teacher can't hide his bad behaviour. If it's indulged in it's there for all to see.

One of his pupils, Clem Loscher, recalled him looking out the window a lot of the time. "The pupils were unruly," he said, "and he was having trouble with the principal." One imagines his mind was often elsewhere. He may have been contemplating his next story or novel – or an exit strategy from a job he came to despise the longer it went on.

Denis Sampson, a writer who'd become friendly with him in the late seventies, published a book about his literary apprenticeship, *Becoming a Novelist*, in 2012. Years earlier he'd done the first serious study of his writing in his book *Outstaring Nature's Eye*. Many other books about his writing followed afterwards.

Madeline sold the Foxfield house in 2013. Its spartan nature suited her time with McGahern. By now she'd been seven years without him. Living alone wasn't advisable in a deserted location, especially with rural crimes on the rise.

In the ensuing years there were a number of books written about his work. University studies of it also appeared. So did many articles in scholarly magazines. There were also some personal memories in various publications.

Leitrim people spoke about how personable he was, how he merged so much into the community in which he lived. Some residents of towns like Mohill and Ballinamore spoke of how he would suddenly appear in front of them and stop to talk with them about anything and everything. The only subject he was evasive about was his books. These were off-limits.

In 2016, the tenth anniversary of his death, a Culture Week was devoted to him in Athboy, the town where he'd lived in Drogheda before moving to Dublin to teach.

Faber published his letters in 2021. This was a treasure trove that shone a light into almost every aspect of his life. It was edited by Frank Shovlin. He immersed himself assiduously in the material, creating a mosaic around each communication that brought McGahern's personality alive. They

An aerial view of the McGahern Museum. (Keith Nolan)

helped me enormously in my efforts to join the dots on his life in this book. They were as beneficial to me as the letters McGahern's sisters gave him to help him write *Memoir*.

They were compiled from various archivists and collectors on both sides of the Atlantic. Some of them had already appeared in books like John Killen's *Dear Mr McLaverty*, Sophie Hillan King's *In Quiet Places*, and in donations like those of Niall Walsh to the NUIG. These were only a tiny fraction of the Faber book. It ran to over 800 pages and proved to be an Aladdin's cave of riches.

Shovlin's notes, contextualising the letters, are sometimes longer than the letters themselves. They form a picture not only of McGahern's life but of his personality too, in all its humour and old world decency. No matter how many frustrations he underwent, he always negotiated them with good grace. When submitting work, or trying to arrange rendezvous with a colleague or friend, a frequent comment is, "I wouldn't mind at all if it doesn't suit." Maybe that was his secret right through his life. He never minded at all.

"I don't like writing letters," he said in 1960.[7] It was difficult to believe that from the hundreds of them that appeared in this book, ranging from 1943 to four days before he died. The only fault in it is that it doesn't show any examples of his handwriting.

This was annoying to some people. John Montague was a case in point.

At the end of 1961 McGahern submitted part of *The Barracks* to him for inclusion in *The Dolmen*, a magazine Montague was editing at the time. He included a cover letter written by hand as his typewriter was broken. He wrote back to say that his handwriting was dreadful. "You also write on both sides of light paper," he added, "thus ensuring that the script on one side is blotted out by the other."[8] I experienced the same difficulty myself when I received letters from him. His script sloped towards the right. Each word seemed to be carved by a pen that looked as if it was about to run out of ink.

His books continue to be reprinted. They're as true to the bittersweet beauty of life as everything else about this simple man with the wispy voice and the crooked smile.

The Cootehall barracks closed in 2012. A former cell that was there is now a unisex toilet. The upstairs room where the young McGahern slept with his father is a working hub for computers. The family living room is a museum housing exhibits relating to his life.

The Aughawillan school is a holiday home, the Rockingham estate the Lough Key Forest Park.

Notes

Early Years

1. John McGahern, *Memoir*, (London: Faber & Faber, 2005), 51.
2. Cliodhna Ní Anluain, ed., *Reading the Future* (Dublin: Lilliput Press, 2000), 141.
3. *Journal of the Short Story in English*, 41, Autumn 2003.
4. *Irish Independent*, August 27, 2005.
5. *In Dublin*, September 1985.
6. Ní Anluain, ed., *Reading the Future*, 140.
7. *Guardian*, April 8, 2006.
8. *Sunday Independent*, April 23, 2006.
9. *Journal of the Short Story in English*, 41, Autumn 2003.
10. *Irish Times*, March 21, 2006.
11. McGahern, *Memoir*, 226.
12. *Observer*, August 28, 2005.
13. *Ibid.*
14. McGahern, *Memoir*, 226.
15. *Journal of the Short Story in English*, 41, Autumn 2003.
16. *Ibid.*

Breaking Away From Home

1. John McGahern, *Love of the World*: Essays (London: Faber & Faber, 2009), 87.
2. *Evening Press*, April 30, 1990.
3. Marcel Proust, *On Reading* (London: Souvenir Press, 1972), 3.
4. Feheny, Matthew J., ed., *A Time of Grace: School Memories* (Dublin: Veritas, 1996), 135.
5. McGahern, *Memoir*, 270.
6. *John McGahern at the NUI*, Seamus O'Grady, 2007, National Uni-

versity of Ireland, Galway.
7. *Books Ireland*, February 2002.
8. *Journal of the Short Story in English*, 41, Autumn 2003.
9. *Ibid.*
10. *Ibid.*
11. Denis Sampson, *Young John McGahern: Becoming a Novelist* (New York: Oxford University Press, 2012), 23.
12. Julie Carlson, *Banned in Ireland: Censorship and the Irish Writer* (London: Routledge, 1990) 63.
13. Ní Anluain, *Reading the Future*, 142.
14. *Journal of the Short Story in English*, 41, Autumn 2003.
15. *Ibid.*
16. McGahern, *Memoir*, 212.
17. *Ibid.*, 247.
18. John Kenny, ed., *John McGahern Yearbook*, Volume 2, 2009, 28.
19. Tony Whelan, *The Last Chapter* (Leicester: Matador, 2010), 127.
20. *Irish Times*, April 3, 1991.
21. McGahern, *Memoir*.
22. Special Collections: John McGahern, NUIG.
23. Daniel Murphy, ed., *Education and the Arts: A Research Report* (School of Education, Trinity College Dublin), 138.
24. Carlson, *Banned in Ireland*, 63.
25. John Kenny, ed., *John McGahern Yearbook*, Volume 1, 126.

Two Lives

1. *Irish Independent*, April 1, 2006.
2. Interview with the author.
3. John McGahern, *The Leavetaking* (London: Faber & Faber, 1974), 155.
4. *Irish Times*, March 31, 2006.
5. *Ibid.*
6. Zeljka Doljanin and Máire Doyle, eds., *John McGahern: Authority and Vision* (Manchester University Press, 2017), 217.
7. *Leitrim's Annual County Magazine*, Number 30, 1998.
8. *Sunday Independent*, December 30, 2001.
9. *Irish Times*, October 26, 1999.
10. *Hot Press*, September 17, 1990.
11. McGahern, *Memoir*, 243.
12. Eamon Maher, *John McGahern: From the Local to the Universal* (Dublin: Liffey Press, 2003), 156-7.

13. McGahern, *High Ground*, 149.
14. McGahern, *Memoir*, 241-2.
15. *Journal of the Short Story in English*, 41, Autumn 2003.
16. *Ibid*.
17. John Kenny, ed., *John McGahern Yearbook* Volume 3, 2010, 15.
18. *Culture in Dublin*, January 1991.
19. McGahern, *Memoir*, 240.

First Strides in Publishing

1. John Killen, ed., *Dear Mr McLaverty: The Literary Correspondence of John McGahern and Michael McLaverty*, 1959-1980 (Belfast: Linen Hall Library, 2006), 18.
2. *Irish Times*, April 1, 2006.
3. Killen, ed., *Dear Mr McLaverty*, 21.
4. Veronica Jane O'Meara, ed., *P.S...Of Course: Patrick Swift 1927-1983* (Oysterhaven, Cork: Garden Books, 1993), 150.
5. *Journal of the Short Story in English*, Autumn 2003.
6. Whelan, *The Last Chapter*, 139-40.
7. John McGahern, *High Ground* (London: Faber & Faber, 1986), 87.
8. Killen, ed., *Dear Mr McLaverty*, 25.
9. *Journal of the Short Story in English*, Autumn 2003.
10. Frank Shovlin, ed., *The Letters of John McGahern* (London: Faber & Faber, 2021), 44.
11. Killen, ed., *Dear Mr McLaverty*, 24.
12. Shovlin, ed., *The Letters of John McGahern*, 57.

On the Up and Up

1. *Irish Times*, April 1, 2006.
2. Nuala O'Faolain, *Are You Somebody?* (Dublin: New Island, 1996), 90.
3. *Irish Times*, April 1, 2006.
4. O'Faolain, *Are You Somebody?*, 90.
5. *Ibid*.
6. Shovlin, ed., *The Letters of John McGahern*, 62.
7. Killen, ed., *Dear Mr McLaverty*, 26-7.
8. Brien Friel Papers, National Library of Ireland.
9. *Irish Independent*, April 1, 2006.
10. John McGahern, *The Barracks* (London: Faber & Faber, 1963), 7.
11. *Irish Times*, March 31, 2006.

12. *Ibid.*
13. *Sunday Independent*, April 2, 2006.
14. *Kenyon Review*, Summer 1964.
15. McGahern, *Memoir*, 243.
16. *Journal of the Short Story in English*, Autumn 2003.
17. *Ibid.*
18. Carlson, *Banned in Ireland*, 56.
19. *Irish Independent*, August 27, 2005.
20. Killen, ed., *Dear Mr McLaverty*, 30.
21. *Ibid.*, 30-1.
22. Michael McLaverty, *Collected Short Stories* (Dublin: Poolbeg, 1978), 7.

Romantic Entanglements

1. Shovlin, ed., *The Letters of John McGahern*, 97.
2. Killen, ed., *Dear Mr McLaverty*, 32.
3. Eamon Maher, *The Church and its Spire: John McGahern and the Catholic Question* (Dublin: Columba Press, 2011), 206.
4. Eibhear Walshe, *Kate O'Brien: A Writer's Life* (Dublin: Irish Academic Press, 2006), 146.
5. John McGahern, *That They May Face the Rising Sun* (London: Faber & Faber, 2003), 213.
6. Shovlin, ed., *The Letters of John McGahern*, 111.
7. *Ibid.*, 116.
8. *Ibid.*, 125.
9. McGahern, *Memoir*, 246.
10. *Daily Mail*, May 27, 2006.
11. Carty, *Intimacy with Strangers*, 35.
12. Shovlin, ed., *The Letters of John McGahern*, 121.
13. Doljanin and Doyle, eds., *Authority and Vision*, 192-4.
14. Whelan, *The Last Chapter*, 163-5.
15. *Daily Mail*, May 27, 2006.
16. *Ibid.*
17. *Ibid.*
18. McGahern, *High Ground*, 106.
19. McGahern, *Memoir*, 247.
20. *Daily Mail*, May 27, 2006.
21. Doljanin and Doyle, eds, *Authority and Vision*, 200.
22. *Daily Mail*, May 27, 2006.
23. *Ibid.*
24. McGahern, *That They May Face the Rising Sun*, 20.

Notoriety

1. Kenny, ed. *The John McGahern Yearbook*, Volume 3, 37.
2. Sophie Hillan King, ed., *In Quiet Places: The Uncollected Stories, Letters and Critical Prose of Michael McLaverty* (Dublin: Poolbeg, 1989), 217.
3. McGahern, *Memoir*, 188.
4. Kenny, ed, *The John McGahern Yearbook*, Volume 3, 37.
5. Dermot Keogh, *Twentieth Century Ireland: Nation and State* (Dublin: Gill & Macmillan, 1994), 257.
6. Tony Faber, *Faber & Faber: The Untold Story* (London: Faber & Faber, 2019), 272-3.
7. *Ibid.*, 275.
8. *Ibid.*, 273.
9. *Irish Studies Review*, March 19, 2011.
10. Diarmuid Ferriter, *Occasions of Sin: Sex and Society in Modern Ireland* (London: Profile Books, 2009), 209.
11. *Rattlebag*, RTE, October 18, 2002.
12. John McGahern Special Collections, National University of Ireland, Galway.
13. Carlson, *Banned in Ireland*, 62.
14. *Irish Independent*, February 20, 2015.
15. *The Writing Life*, March 24, 2015.
16. John McGahern Special Collections, NUIG.
17. Carlson, *Banned in Ireland*, 59.
18. *Irish Independent*, February 20, 2015.
19. John Cooney, *John Charles McQuaid: Ruler of Catholic Ireland* (Dublin: O'Brien Press, 1999), 277.
20. *Ibid.*, 277-8.
21. *Ibid.*, 369-70.
22. John Kenny, ed., *The John McGahern Yearbook*, Volume 4 (Galway: NUIG, 2011), 63.
23. Cooney, *John Charles McQuaid*, 285-7.
24. *Sunday Independent*, April 6, 2006.
25. Ní Anluain, ed., *Reading the Future*, 145.
26. *States of Mind*, RTE, July 18, 1979.
27. John McGahern, *The Pornographer* (London: Quartet, 1980), 343-4.
28. Doljanin and Doyle, eds, *Authority and Vision*, 202-3.
29. Carty, *Intimacy with Strangers*, 36.
30. Carlson, *Banned in Ireland*, 61.
31. *Irish Times*, March 31, 2006.

32. Keogh, *Twentieth Century Ireland*, 257.
33. John McGahern, *Amongst Women* (London: Faber & Faber, 1990), 4.
34. *Irish Independent*, May 18, 2013.
35. Killen, ed., *Dear Mr McLaverty*, 43.
36. *Ibid.*
37. Hillan King, ed., *In Quiet Places*, 4.
38. Carlson, *Banned in Ireland*, 55.
39. Ní Anluain, ed., *Reading the Future*, 144.
40. Carlson, *Banned in Ireland*, 62.
41. *Studies*, Spring 2001.
42. Mary Kenny, *Goodbye to Catholic Ireland* (London: Sinclair-Stevenson, 1997), 264-6.
43. McGahern, *The Leavetaking*, 157.
44. Tom Inglis, *Moral Monopoly: The Rise and Fall of the Catholic Church in Ireland* (Dublin: Gill & Macmillan, 1987), 246.
45. Keogh, *Twentieth Century Ireland*, 258.
46. *The Writing Life*, March 24, 2015.
47. He once said he saw *The Dark* primarily as a religious book.
48. Aubrey Malone, ed., *Talk Nation* (Dublin: Currach Press, 2004), 150.
49. *Irish Quarterly*, Spring 2001.
50. Carlson, *Banned in Ireland*, 66.

Exile

1. King, ed., *In Quiet Places*, 45.
2. *Leitrim Annual County Magazine*, 30, 1998.
3. Killen, ed., *Dear Mr McLaverty*, 46.
4. Shovlin, ed., *The Letters of John McGahern*, 203.
5. Killen, ed., *Dear Mr McLaverty*, 46.
6. *Irish Times*, March 31, 2006.
7. Richard Murphy, *The Kick: A Memoir* (London: Granada, 2002), 258.
8. *Ibid.*, 258-9.
9. Shovlin, ed., *The Letters of John McGahern*, 258.
10. *Sunday Independent*, December 30, 2001.
11. *Daily Mail*, May 27, 2006.
12. *Irish Times*, March 31, 2006.

Emerging from Writer's Block

1. Shovlin, ed., *The Letters of John McGahern*, 257.
2. Originally called Madison University, it was re-named in 1890 as a result of the financial injections of the toothpaste magnate, William Colgate.
3. Shovlin, ed., *The Letters of John McGahern*, 98.
4. *Irish Times*, July 23, 1994.
5. Aubrey Malone, ed., *The Mammoth Book of Irish Humour* (London: Constable, 2012), 400.
6. Shovlin, ed., *The Letters of John McGahern*, 285.
7. John McGahern, *Nightlines* (London: Granada, 1973), 73.
8. *Journal of the Short Story in English*, Autumn 2003.
9. McGahern, *Nightlines*, 82.
10. *Ibid.*
11. *Journal of the Short Story in English*, Autumn 2003.
12. *Irish Times*, October 24, 1970.
13. Shovlin, ed., *The Letters of John McGahern*, 720.
14. *Ibid.*, 224.
15. Murphy, *The Kick*, 294.
16. *Leitrim Annual County Magazine*, 30, 1998.
17. Maher, *From the Local to the Universal*, 156.
18. Murphy, *The Kick*, 280.
19. Malone, ed., *Talk Nation*, 100.
20. Kenny, ed., *The John McGahern Yearbook*, Volume 4, 73.
21. Murphy, *The Kick*, 262.
22. *Ibid.*

Back to Leitrim

1. *Irish Independent*, August 27, 2005.
2. *Ibid.*, April 1, 2006.
3. McGahern, *Memoir*, 205.
4. *Books Ireland*, February 2002.
5. Doolan to McGahern, September 28, 1972, BBC Written Archives Centre.
6. McGahern to Capon, June 22, 1971, BBC Written Archives Centre.
7. *Irish Independent*, March 16, 1963.
8. Ní Anluain, ed., *Reading the Future*, 153.
9. This exchange is repeated in the story "Gold Watch."

10. McGahern, *The Leavetaking*, 9.
11. *Canadian Journal of Irish Studies*, December 1981.
12. Shovlin, ed., *The Letters of John McGahern*, 375.
13. *Irish Times*, January 4, 1975.
14. Shovlin, ed., *The Letters of John McGahern*, 388n.
15. Doljanin and Doyle, eds, *Authority and Vision*, 201.
16. Carty, *Intimacy with Strangers*, 37.
17. Inglis, *Moral Monopoly*, 223.
18. *Irish Times*, January 3, 1976.
19. John Doyle, *A Great Feast of Light* (London: Aurum Press, 2007), 281.
20. Dennis O'Driscoll, *Stepping Stones: Interviews with Seamus Heaney* (London: Faber & Faber, 2008), 228.
21. Shovlin, ed, *The Letters of John McGahern*, 384.
22. *Film Directions*, Volume 1, Number 2, 1978.
23. Shovlin, ed., *The Letters of John McGahern*, 411.
24. *Ibid.*, 403.
25. Carty, *Intimacy with Strangers*, 35.
26. *Magill*, October 1987.
27. *London Review of Books*, January 2022.
28. Malone, *The Mammoth Book of Irish Humour*, 18.
29. Kenny, ed., *The John McGahern Yearbook*, Volume 2, 99.
30. Kenny, ed., *The John McGahern Yearbook*, Volume 4, 103.
31. Carty, *Intimacy with Strangers*, 35.
32. Kenny, ed., *The John McGahern Yearbook*, Volume 1, 14.
33. *Irish Times*, March 31, 2006.
34. He often liked to say, "Art is prayer."

Change of Direction

1. *Irish Times*, June 17, 1978.
2. *In Dublin*, September 1985.
3. *Ibid.*
4. *Observer*, January 6, 2002.
5. Shovlin, ed., *The Letters of John McGahern*, 491.
6. McGahern, *The Pornographer*, 56.
7. *Ibid.*, 63.
8. *Ibid.*, 99.
9. *Ibid.*, 97.
10. *Ibid.*, 79.
11. *Ibid.*, 128.

12. *Ibid.*, 107.
13. *Ibid.*, 226-7.
14. *Ibid.*, 136.
15. *Canadian Journal of Irish Studies*, July 1985.
16. Kenny, ed., *The John McGahern Yearbook*, Volume 3, 21.
17. McGahern, *The Pornographer*, 13.
18. *Ibid.*, 11.
19. *Times Literary Supplement*, November 27, 1970.
20. Maher, *From the Local to the Universal*, 43.
21. *Journal of the Short Story in English*, Autumn 2003.
22. *Irish Independent*, October 13, 1979.
23. McGahern, *The Pornographer*, 21.
24. *Irish Times*, April 8, 2006.
25. Shovlin, ed, *The Letters of John McGahern*, 459.
26. Maher, *From the Local to the Universal*, 41.
27. McGahern, *The Pornographer*, 25.
28. *Irish Independent*, April 1, 2006.
29. John Updike, *Hugging the Shore: Essays and Criticism* (London: Penguin, 1984), 391.
30. McGahern, *The Pornographer*, 214.
31. Updike, *Hugging the Shore*, 390.
32. McGahern, *Getting Through*, 72.
33. *Ibid.*, 75.
34. Doljanin and Doyle, eds, *Authority and Vision*, 201.
35. McGahern, *The Pornographer*, 236-7.
36. McGahern, *That They May Face the Rising Sun*, 52-3.

New Decade

1. Shovlin, ed., *The Letters of John McGahern*, 514.
2. Tom Corkery, *Tom Corkery's Dublin* (Dublin: Anvil Boks, 1980), 125.
3. *Ibid.*, 11.
4. *Sunday Independent*, January 4, 1981.
5. Shovlin, ed., *The Letters of John McGahern*, 539.
6. *Irish Times*, September 11, 2008.
7. McGahern, *The Leavetaking*, frontispiece.
8. Rudiger Imhof, *Irish Novelists After 1945* (Dublin: Wolfhound Press, 2002), 220.
9. Shovlin, ed, *The Letters of John McGahern*, 559.
10. Tom Inglis, *Truth, Power and Lies* (Dublin: UCD Press, 2003), 570-1.

11. *Irish Times*, March 31, 2006.
12. Shovlin, ed., *The Letters of John McGahern*, 496.
13. *Ibid.*, 570.

Farmer John

1. *Irish Times*, January 7, 2005.
2. *The Writing Life*, 24 March, 2015
3. *Irish Times*, April 5, 2021.
4. Aubrey Malone, ed., *Don't Quote Me on That* (Dublin: Currach Press, 2008), 71.
5. *Magill*, October 1987.
6. *Ibid.*
7. *Ibid.*
8. McGahern, *Memoir*, 167-8.
9. *Magill*, October 1987.
10. Carty, *Intimacy with Strangers*, 33.
11. *Ibid.*, 32.
12. *Irish Times*, September 9, 1987.
13. *Magill*, October 1987.
14. Louise Fuller, *Irish Catholicism Since 1950: The Undoing of a Culture* (Dublin: Gill & Macmillan, 2002), 17.
15. Doljanin and Doyle, eds., *Authority and Vision*, 187.
16. *Ibid.*, 186.
17. *Ibid.*, 188.
18. *Irish Independent*, August 27, 2005.
19. Ní Anluain, ed., *Reading the Future*, 138.
20. He generally preferred to let readers interpret his work than be asked to do so himself.
21. Doljanin and Doyle, eds, *Authority and Vision*, 186-8. 22. *Journal of the Short Story in English*, Autumn 2006.

Moran and His World

1. *Canadian Journal of Irish Studies*, July 1991.
2. Liam Harte and Michael Parker, eds., *Contemporary Irish Fiction: Themes, Tropes, Theories* (London: Palgrave, 2000), 71.
3. *Canadian Journal of Irish Studies*, July 1991.
4. *Magill*, October 1987.
5. Ní Anluain, ed., *Reading the Future*, 149-150.
6. As well as having the obvious religious overtone, it carried the

suggestion that women had been very much the centre of his world all his life.
7. *Books Ireland*, February 2002.
8. Maher, *The Church and its Spire*, 128.
9. "I'd won it at four o'clock" he told a journalist in *Woman's Way* in 1992, "There were two judges for me and two judges for the eventual winner. The chairman sided with me. Then they argued for an hour and a half and it went to the other writer."
10. *Irish Independent*, October 23, 1993.
11. Kenny, ed., *The John McGahern Yearbook*, Volume 1, 91.
12. *Irish Independent*, August 27, 2005.
13. *Evening Press*, April 30, 1990.
14. *Hot Press*, July 17, 1990.
15. *Ibid.*
16. *Ibid.*
17. *Ibid.*
18. *Evening Press*, April 30, 1990.
19. *Hot Press*, July 17, 1990.
20. *Evening Press*, April 30, 1990.
21. James Whyte, *Strategies of Transcendence: History, Myth and Ritual in the Fiction of John McGahern* (New York: Edwin Mellen Press, 2000), 136.
22. *Evening Press*, April 30, 1990.
23. *Ibid.*
24. *Ibid.*
25. *Ibid.*
26. *Ibid.*
27. *Ibid.*
28. *Ibid.*
29. *Ibid.*
30. *Ibid.*
31. *Hot Press*, July 17, 1990.
32. *Ibid.*
33. *Ibid.*
34. *Ibid.*
35. *Ibid.*
36. *Ibid.*
37. Kenny, ed., *The John McGahern Yearbook*, Volume 4, 126.
38. *Ibid.*, 122.
39. *Ibid.*
40. Shovlin, ed. *The Letters of John McGahern*, 635.

From Page to Stage

1. Maher, *The Church and its Spire*, 129-30.
2. Van Der Ziel, ed., *John McGahern: The Rockingham Shoot and other Dramatic Writings* (London: Faber & Faber, 2019), 255-56n.
3. Kenny, ed., *The John McGahern Yearbook*, Volume 2, 83.
4. Kilroy letter to McGahern, August 24, 1988, NUIG.
5. *Irish Independent*, October 17, 1991.
6. Krino, Number 13, 1992.
7. Kenny, ed., *The John McGahern Yearbook*, Volume 2, 90.
8. Shovlin, ed., *The Letters of John McGahern*, 646.
9. *Irish Times*, October 28, 1991.
10. Kenny, ed., *The John McGahern Yearbook*, Volume 2, 87.
11. Penelope Fitzgerald, *House of Air: Selected Writings* (London: Harper Perennial, 2005), 405.
12. *Ibid.*, 404.
13. McGahern, *High Ground*, 88.
14. *Ibid.*, 57.
15. Whelan, *The Last Chapter*, 181-3.
16. Doljanin and Doyle, eds., *Authority and Vision*, 210.
17. *Sunday Independent*, December 30, 2001.
18. Kenny, ed., *The John McGahern Yearbook*, Volume 2, 111.
19. Kenny, ed. *The John McGahern Yearbook*, Volume 4, 97.
20. *Sunday Independent*, March 23, 1992.
21. *Irish Times*, March 31, 2006.
22. *Journal of the Short Story in English*, Autumn 2003.
23. *Irish Times*, October 26, 1999.
24. Sampson, *Young John McGahern*, 105.
25. *Sunday Independent*, April 6, 2006.
26. Murphy, *The Kick*, 377.
27. Shovlin, ed, *The Letters of John McGahern*, 692.
28. Colm Toibin, *Bad Blood: A Walk Along the Irish Border* (London: Vintage, 1994), 80.
29. Aubrey Malone, *Losers* (Cheshire: Penniless Press, 2020), 154.
30. Aubrey Malone, *The Brothers Behan* (Dublin: Ashfield Press, 1998), 225-6.
31. Shovlin, ed., *The Letters of John McGahern*, 788.
32. McGahern, *Love of the World*, 396.
33. *Le Monde*, September 5, 1997.
34. *Magill* Annual, 2002.
35. *Cork Examiner*, January 17, 2004.

36. Ní Anluain, ed. *Reading the Future*, 139.
37. *Ibid.*, 155.
38. As an avid filmgoer he was well aware that cinema and television were primarily visual mediums no matter how much lip service was paid to scriptwriters.
39. *Rattlebag*, RTE, October 18, 2002.
40. Shovlin, ed., *The Letters of John McGahern*, 721-2.
41. *Irish Times*, March 31, 2006.
42. Shovlin, ed., *The Letters of John McGahern*, 741. 43. *Ibid.*, 747.
44. Maher, *From the Local to the Universal*, 160. 45. *Sunday Independent*, December 30, 2001.

Late Flowering

1. Kenny, ed., *The John McGahern Yearbook*, Volume 2, 99.
2. *Books Ireland*, February 2002.
3. *Irish Times*, March 31, 2006.
4. *Observer*, August 28, 2005.
5. McGahern, *That They May Face the Rising Sun*, 2.
6. *Magill*, October 1987.
7. *Irish Independent*, March 18, 2013.
8. Kenny, ed., *The John McGahern Yearbook*, Volume 3, 21-3.
9. *Irish Independent*, August 27, 2005.
10. *New York Review of Books*, May 23, 2002.
11. *Guardian*, January 12, 2002.

Devastation

1. *Irish Times*, March 31, 2006.
2. Shovlin, ed., *The Letters of John McGahern*, 765.
3. *Poetry Ireland News*, September/October, 2007.
4. *Irish Times*, March 31, 2006.
5. *Poetry Ireland News*, September/October, 2007.
6. *Cork Examiner*, January 17, 2004.
7. *Irish Times*, June 13, 2002.
8. *Cork Examiner*, January 17, 2004.
9. *Ibid.*
10. *Irish Independent*, September 19, 2021.
11. *Cork Examiner*, January 17, 2004. See also *The Letters of Gustave Flaubert, 1830-1857*, ed. Francis Steegmuller (New York: Harvard University Press, 1981), 173.

12. *Ibid.*
13. *Irish Independent*, March 31, 2006.
14. *Irish Times*, March 31, 2006.
15. *Journal of the Short Story in English*, Autumn 2003.
16. *Observer*, August 28, 2005.
17. *Irish Times*, April 8, 2006.
18. McGahern, *Memoir*, 203.
19. *Ibid.*, 129.
20. *Irish Independent*, August 27, 2005.
21. *Ibid.*
22. *Irish Times*, September 23, 2006.
23. *Ibid.*
24. *Boston Review*, January 1, 2007.
25. McGahern, *Memoir*, 263.
26. Maher, *From the Local to the Universal*, 147.
27. *Observer*, August 28, 2005.
28. *Leitrim Observer*, May 29, 2012.
29. *Irish Times*, September 23, 2006.
30. Kenny, ed., *The John McGahern Yearbook*, Volume 1, 101.
31. Denis Sampson, *Outstaring Nature's Eye: The Fiction of John McGahern* (Dublin: Lilliput Press, 1993), 19.
32. *Irish Independent*, September 13, 2005.
33. *Ibid.*, August 27, 2005.
34. *Sunday Tribune*, May 6, 1990.
35. *Irish Independent*, August 27, 2005.
36. McGahern, *Memoir*, 77.
37. McGahern, *The Pornographer*, 216.
38. *Sunday Independent*, April 2, 2006.
39. Whelan, *The Last Chapter*, 200.
40. Shovlin, ed., *The Letters of John McGahern*, 791.
41. *Irish Independent*, January 28, 2007.
42. *The Word*, June 2006.
43. *Ibid.*
44. *Ibid.*
45. *Sunday Independent*, April 6, 2006.

The King is Dead

1. *Irish Times*, March 31, 2006.
2. *Irish Independent*, March 31, 2006.
3. *Sunday Independent*, April 6, 2006

4. *Boston Review*, January 1, 2007.
5. *Irish Times*, March 22, 2006.
6. *Irish Independent*, April 1, 2006.
7. *Ibid.*, March 31, 2006.
8. *Sunday Independent*, April 2, 2006
9. Whelan, *The Last Chapter*, 202.
10. *Sunday Independent*, April 2, 2006.
11. He would hardly have appreciated this. His pedagogical strengths showed themselves best with third level students.
12. *Irish Times*, March 28, 2007.
13. *Irish Independent*, March 31, 2006.
14. O'Driscoll, *Stepping Stones*, 473.
15. *Irish Independent*, March 31, 2006.
16. O'Driscoll, Stepping Stones, 251.
17. Kenny, ed., *The John McGahern Yearbook*, Volume 1, 102.
18. *Boston Review*, January 1, 2007.
19. Doljanin and Doyle, eds, *Authority and Vision*, 194.

Aftermath

1. *Magill*, December 27, 2006.
2. *Ibid*.
3. *Harvard Crimson*, February 26, 2010.
4. *Daily Mail*, May 27, 2006.
5. He'd also said this to Richard Murphy in Cleggan.
6. *Liveline*, RTE, April 5, 2011.
7. Shovlin, ed., *The Letters of John McGahern*, 32.
8. John Montague Papers, University of Victoria.

Bibliography

Carlson, Julia. *Banned in Ireland*: *Censorship and the Irish Writer*. London: Routledge, 1990.

Carty, Ciaran. *Intimacy with Strangers*: *A Life of Brief Encounters*. Dublin: Lilliput Press, 2013.

Cooney, John. *John Charles McQuaid: Ruler of Catholic Ireland*. Dublin: O'Brien Press, 1999.

Doljanin, Zelijka, and Márie Doyle, eds., John McGahern: *Authority and Vision*. Manchester: Manchester University Press, 2017.

Fitzgerald, Penelope. *House of Air: Selected Writings*. London: Harper Perennial, 2005.

Genet, Jacqueline, and Wynne Hellegouarc'h. *Irish Writers and their Creative Process*. Gerrards Cross: Colin Smythe, 1996.

Harte, Liam, and Michael Parker, eds., *Contemporary Irish Fiction: Themes, Tropes, Theories*. London: Palgrave, 2000.

Hone, Joseph, ed. *John Butler Yeats: Letters to his Son W.B. Yeats and Others, 1869-1922*. London: Faber, 1944.

Imhof, Rudiger. *Irish Novelists After 1945*. Dublin: Wolfhound Press, 2002.

Inglis, Tom. *Moral Monopoly: The Rise and Fall of the Catholic Church in Ireland*. Dublin: Gill & Macmillan, 1987.

Kenny, John, ed., *The John McGahern Yearbook Volume 3*. Galway: NUIG, 2010.

Kenny, Mary. *Goodbye to Catholic Ireland*. London: Sinclair-Stevenson, 1997.

Keogh, Dermot. *Twentieth Century Ireland: Nation and State*. Dublin: Gill & Macmillan, 1994.

Killen, John, ed. *Dear Mr. McLaverty: The Literary Correspondence of John McGahern and Michael McLaverty, 1959-1980*. Belfast: Linen Hall Library 2006.

King, Sophia Hillan. *In Quiet Places: The Uncollected Stories, Letters and Critical Prose of Michael McLaverty*. Dublin: Poolbeg Press. 1989.

Lennon, Peter. *Foreign Correspondent: Paris in the Sixties*. London: Picador, 1994.

MacLeod, Alastair. *As Birds Bring Forth the Sun and other stories*. Ontario: McClelland & Stewart, 1992.

Maher, Eamon. *From the Local to the Universal*. Dublin: Liffey Press, 2003.
- *The Church and its Spire: John McGahern and the Catholic Question*. Dublin: Columba Press, 2011.

McGahern, John. *The Barracks*. London: Faber & Faber, 1963.
- *The Dark*. London: Panther, 1967.
- *Nightlines*. London: Granada, 1973.
- *The Leavetaking*. London: Faber & Faber, 1974.
- *Getting Through*. London: Faber & Faber, 1978.
- *The Pornographer*. London: Quartet: 1980.
- *High Ground*. London: Faber & Faber, 1986.
- *Amongst Women*. London: Faber & Faber, 1990.
- *The Collected Stories*. London: Faber & Faber, 1992.
- *Creatures of the Earth: New and Selected Stories*. London: Faber & Faber, 1992.
- *That They May Face the Rising Sun*. London: Faber & Faber, 2003.
- *Memoir*, London: Faber & Faber, 2003.

Murphy, Richard. *The Kick*: A *Memoir*. London: Granta, 2002.

Ní, Anluain, Cliodhna. *Reading the Future*: *Irish Writers in Conversation with Mike Murphy*. Dublin: Lilliput Press, 2000.

O'Driscoll, Dennis. *Stepping Stones: Interviews with Seamus Heaney*. London: Faber, 2008.

O'Fáolain, Nuala. *Are You Somebody?* Dublin: New Island, 1996.

Reid, Forrest. Brian Westby. Virginia: Valancout Books, 2013.

Sampson, Denis. *Young John McGahern: Becoming a Novelist*. Oxford: Oxford University Press, 2012.
- *Outstaring Nature's Eye*: The Fiction of John McGahern. Dublin: Lilliput Press, 1993.

Shovlin, Frank, ed. *The Letters of John McGahern*. London: Faber, 2021.

Toibin, Colm. *The Night of the Generals: Selected Journalism, 1980-1990*. Dublin: Raven Arts Press, 1990.

Updike, John. *Hugging the Shore: Essays and Criticism*. London: Penguin, 1984.

Van Der Ziel, Stanley, ed., *Love of the World*: *Essays*. Faber, 2009.
- *The Rockingham Shoot and other dramatic writings*. London: Faber, 2018.

Whelan, Tony. *The Last Chapter*: A *Memoir*. Leicester: Matador, 2010.

Williams, John. *Stoner*. London: Vintage, 2012.

Index

Note: Bold script indicates photograph of subject

Abbey Theatre 41, 102, 149, 151
Abelard-Schuman 48
Ackerley, Joe 80-1
AE Award 48-9
Albrecht, Janette 173-4
"All Sorts of Impossible Things" 112
All Will Be Well 184
"Along the Edges" 148
Amongst Women (novel) 7-8, 9, 78, 129, 133-43, 170, 171, 181, 182, 184
Amongst Women (TV production) 163
Angel 123
Angela's Ashes 161
"Another Country" 165
Arts Council, The 59, 96, 130, 186
Atlantic Monthly 94, 112

Balzac, Honoré de 43, 105
"Bank Holiday" 39, 125-6
Banville, John 159, 193
Barracks, The (dramatization) 102
Barracks, The (novel) 46-8, 53-5, 70, 79, 84, 94, 134, 182, 198
"Bank Holiday" 39, 148
Barrie and Rockliff 48
Barry, Tony 163
"Bat, The" 24, 25
Bath Literary Festival 174
Beatles, The 57
Beckett, Samuel 24, 35, 40, 41, 61, 77-8, 84, 96, 139, 160, 183
Becoming a Novelist 196
"Beginning of an Idea, The" 112
Behan, Brendan 36-7, 159-60
Behan, Brian 159-60

Belgrove National School 32, **33**, 34-5, 43, 74, 106, 123, 130, 179, 188, 189, 195-6
Bell, The 35-6
Belton, Neil 179, 196
Best, George 64
Billy Budd 176
Black, Cathal 105-6, 161
Blackboard Jungle, The 41
Blackwater Lightship, The 163
"Blind Date" 170
Boland, Eavan 54
"Bomb Box" 91
Booker Prize, The 104, 138
"Books at Bedtime" 139
Books Ireland 96
Boylan, Roger 192
Boys Town 41
Bragg, Melvyn 64, 192
Braiden, Olive **184**
Brando, Marlon 41
Breen, Margaret 54, 60, 96
Broderick, John 59, 78
Brooklyn 1195
Browne, Noel 75
Bukowski, Charles 176, 181
Burgess, Anthony 133
By the Lake 172
Byatt, Antonia 138
Byrne, Gay 81
Byrnes, Frances 165, 184

Callan, Tom 10
Camus, Albert 118, 123
Capon, Susanna 102

217

Carton, Fr 74-5
Casey, Bishop Eamonn 155
Casque d'Or 41
Celine, Louis-Ferdinand 176
Charming Billy 176
Chekhov, Anton 56, 109, 171
Chesterton, G.K. 144
Chicago Review, The 60
Choice, The 43
Cleary, Fr Michael 156
Clifton, Harry
Cloake, Mary **185**
Colgan, Michael 150-1
Colgate University 91-3, 101-2, 120, 165, 173
Collected Stories 152, 186
Collins, Pat 184-5
"Coming Into His Kingdom" 182
Cooney, John 75-6
Copenhagen Film Festival 161
Cork Examiner 175
Corish, Brendan 77
Corkery, Daniel 43
"Coronation Street" 122
Council of Civil Liberties, The 78
"Country Funeral, The" 187
Creatures of the Earth 186-7
Cronin, Anthony 38
"Crossing the Line" 124, 125, 152

Dahl, Roald 119
Daily Mail, The 193
Dali, Salvador 61
Dark, The 46, 58, 59, 64-6, 68, 69-83, 94, 96, 107, 114, 116, 117, 119, 120, 123, 126, 134, 137, 150, 152, 160, 181, 182
Davison, Peter 94
"Day in the Life of Ivan Illych, A" 43, 126
De Sautoy, Peter 47
De Valera, Eamon 75, 78, 96, 105, 160
De Vere White, Terence 104, 105
"The Dead" 43, 126
Dead as Doornails 38
Dean, James 41, 93
Dean, Joan 153
Deane, Seamus 107, 172, 184
Dear Mr McLaverty 197
Delahaye, Alan 119, 123

Deschamps, Maguy, 130
Dolan, Pat 76
Dolmen, The 198
Donnelly, Donal 161
Donoghue, Denis 107, 137
Doolan, Lelia 102
"Doorways" 119, 148
Dostoevsky, Fyodor 43, 126, 162
Doyle, Roddy 71
Doyle, Tony 139
Dubliners 94, 102
Duffy, Joe 156
Duffy, Paddy 32
Dungan, Myles 175
Dunne, Lee 78
Dylan, Bob 82

Easy Rider 92
Eblana Bookshop 40
Eliot, T.S. 46, 184
Ellis, John 125, 141
"Encounter, An" 94
End or the Beginning of Love, The 38, 43, 45, 46-7, 48, 54
"Epic" 127
Eucharistic Congress, The 11
Evening Herald 81
Evening Press 139
"Faith, Hope and Charity" 112
Family Protection Act 112
Faulkner, William 109, 159, 170
Field Day 49-51
Fitzgerald, F. Scott 40
Fitzgerald, Penelope 152
Flaubert, Gustave 58, 153, 178
Flynn, Eileen 123, 125
Ford, Richard 40, 153
Four Quartets, The 184
Fox, Eileen 81
Friel, Brian 53, 79, 104, 105, 149-51

Gate Theatre 41, 150
Gebler, Carlo 123
Getting Through (short story collection) 112, 119, 126
Getting Through (short story) 112
Gilligan, Patrick 127
Goad, Rosemary 157
"Gold Watch" 65, 99, 126, 146, 166,

218

171, 182
Golding, William 48
Good Friday Agreement, The 162-3
Gordon, Donald 101
Grey, Zane 19
Great Gatsby, The 40
Great Wave, The 52
Green, Madeline (See Madeline McGahern)
Gregory, Patrick 65, 88, 99
Grene, Nicholas 151

Haley, Bill 41
Hamilton, Phyllis 156
Hanson, Barry 104
Harding, Michael 181, 183
Hardy, Thomas 170
Haughey, Charles 42, 117, **138**, 139
Hayes, Joanne 125, 149
Heaney, Marie 157, **158**
Heaney, Seamus 56, 80, 105, 107, 110, 136, 157, **158**
Heather Blazing, The 154
Hemingway, Ernest 40, 107, 136-7, 159, 164
Hennessy Awards, The 105
Hickey, Kieran 130
High Ground 125
Hitchcock, Alfred 117
Hodges, Adrian 163
Hogan, Bosco 130
Hogan, Des 106
Holt, Eddie 118
Homer 127
Hot Press, The 147
House of Bernardo Alba, The 41
Hughes, Ted 99
Hynes, Garry 151-2

Iliad, The 127
In Quiet Places 197
Inglis, Tom 125
Ionesco, Eugene 61
Irish Independent 71, 151, 178, 187
Irish Press 36, 50, 71, 97, 105, 164
Irish National Teacher's Organisation (INTO) 74, 152, 157
Irish Times 71, 104, 112-3, 124, 125, 151, 164

Ivy Leaf Ballroom **28**, 41, 101
John McGahern – A Private World 184-5, 189
John McGahern Museum, The **22**, **44**
Johnston, Jennifer 189
Johnston, Fred 106
Jordan, Michael 130, 141
Jordan, Neil **106**, 107, 112-3, 123, 130-1
Jordan, Tom 35, 1211
Journey to the End of the Night 176
Joy, Neill 120
Joyce, James 24, 35, 43, 52, 54, 56, 82-3, 84, 91, 94, 96, 102, 106, 126, 131, 187
Joyce, Stanislaus 160
Julius Caesar 41
Kafka, Franz 58, 60
Karikoski, Eeva 61
Kavanagh, Katherine 56
Kavanagh, Patrick 35-7, 39, 40, 45, 56, 125, 127, 141, 160, 183
Keelan, Mary 57-8, 59, 60, 62, 163, 180
Keeler, Christine 57
Kehoe's bar 37
Kelleher, Mícheál 74
Kelly, Joan 50, 113-4, 115, 121, 193
Kelly, Joseph 50, 113-4, 121
Kelly, Fr Liam 98, 183, 191, 192
Kennedy, Joe 32, 53, 81, 101, 118, 189, 193
Kennedy, John F. 58
Kenyon Review, The 54
"Key, The" 95-6, 182
Kiberd, Declan 34-5, 110, 189, 196
Kiely, Benedict 40-1, 65
Kierkegaard, Soren 35
Kiernan, Francis 112, 120, 126
Killen, John 197
Kilroy, Julia 136
Kilroy, Tom 136, 150, 151
King, Philip 184
King, Sophie Hillan 197
Knopf, Alfred A. 78
Korea (film) 161
"Korea" (short story) 95-6, 182

Laaksi, Anniki 61-8, 77-8, 86-9, 97, 98, 180, 193-5

219

Lady Chatterley's Lover 24, 57, 71
Lannan Award 175
Larkin, Philip 57, 126, 144, 145, 191
Last Tango in Paris 117
"Late Late Show, The" 81
"Lavin" 94, 124
Lavin, Mary 43, 52
Lawrence, D.H. 24, 71
Leavetaking, The (adaptation) 123
Leavetaking, The (novel) 7, 34, 82, 103-4, 105, 115, 117, 123, 134, 137, 148, 171, 181
Lee, Hermione 165
Lehane, Kevin 51, 121-2
Leitrim Observer 110
Lemass, Sean 57, 58
Lenihan, Brian 82
Lennon, Peter 61, 78
Leonard, Hugh 91, 102
Leventhal, Con 77
"Like All Other Men" 124, 125, 148
"Liveline" 195-6
London Evening Standard 123
Lorca, Federico Garcia 41
Loscher, Clem 196
Love in Winter 117-8
"Love of the World" 171, 187
Lovett, Ann 124, 125

Macaulay Fellowship Award 59
MacBride, Maud Gonne 58
Mackle, Joanna 53
MacNamara Brinsley 79
Madden, Deirdre 164
Magill 128, 162, 193
Maher, Eamon 195-6
Manahan, Anna 172
Manchester Guardian 61
Manila Rope, The 67, 68, 117
Mann, Thomas 35, 99
Mansfield, Jayne 86
Mantel, Hilary 172
Marcus, David, 80-1
McAleese, Mary 191
McCabe, Cathal 164
McCabe, Eugene 70-1
McCabe, Ruth 172
McCarthy, Justine 178-9, 190
McCarthy, Vera 79-80

McCourt, Frank 161
McCullers, Carson 109
McDaid's bar **36**, 38-9, 43, 160, 176
McDermott, Alice 176
McDermott, Philip 81, 126
McGahern, Breege 11, 16, 26, 29, 30, 45, 53, 64, 65, 89, 136
McGahern, Dympna 11, 15, 28, 31, 53, 60, 89, 136
McGahern, Frank 11-12, 15-18, 25-31, 44-5, 55-6, 65, 70, 78-9, 96, 97-9, 101, 103, 112, 163, 181-3
McGahern, Frankie 11, 15, 17, 28, 31, 44-5, 89, 112, 121, 136, 140, 163, 182-3
McGahern, Madeline 10, 87-90, 93, 96-7, 98-9, 101, 103-4, 105, 107-8, 110-1, 117, 124, 153, 165, 169, 180, 186, **190**, 196
McGahern, Margaret 11, 16, 30, 31, 45, 89, 136
McGahern, Monica 11, 30, 31, 45, 89, 136, 183-4, **190**
McGahern, Rosaleen 11, 26, 29, 30, 45, 64, 65, 69, 89, 136, 183-4, **190**
McGahern, Susan 11-12, 14-16, 136, 142, 166, 179-81, 182, 191
McGarry, Emmet 101
McHugh, Roger 74
McIniff, Eddie 18
McKeon, Belinda 164
McLaverty, Michael 36, 38, 43, 47-8, 50, 53, 56, 58, 70, **80**, 84-5, 126, 131-2, 154, 177, 183
McLeod, Alastair 131-2, 177, 189
McManus, Pat 170
McManus, Susan (See Susan McGahern)
McQuaid, John Charles 61, 75-6, 78, 90, 94, 113, 160
McShara, Agnes 25, 26, 27-8, 29, 30, 31, 65, 112, 124, 136, 142
McShara, Tommy 26, 28
Medicin de Campagne, Le 43
Meehan, Paula 130-1, 160
Melville, Herman 35, 176
Memoir 11, 28, 39, 179-84, 185-6, 197
Meri, Veijo 67, 117
Metamorphosis 58, 60
Mikowski, Sylvie 131

Miss Lonelyhearts 92, 176
Moby Dick 176
Moloney, Fiona 161
Monsieur Hulot's Holiday 41
Monteith, Charles 48-9, 50, 53, 56, 64-5, 69-70, 71, 94, 96, 101, 104, 123, 126, 157
Montague, John 153, 197-8
Montgomery, James 71
Moore, Brian 54
Moroney, Andy 19-21, 141-2
Moroney, Willie 19-21, 141-2
Muldoon, Paul 109-10
Munro, Alice 40
Murphy, Annie 155
Murphy, Richard 57, 65, 99-100
"My Love, My Umbrella" 95, 117, 146, 148, 161

"New Irish Writing" 105, 106-7, 164
New York Review of Books 118, 172
New Yorker, The 53, 112, 120, 124, 125, 126
Newcastle University 104-5
Newsweek 172
Ní Dhuibhne, Eilis 147-8
Night in Tunisia 106, 131
Nightlines 93-4, 96
Niven, David 120
Niven, Primula 120
Nobel Prize 157
Notebooks of Malte Laurid Briggs, The 40, 176

O'Briain, Professor 77
O'Brien, Con 30, 89
O'Brien, Edna 71 78
O'Brien, Flann 38
O'Brien, Kate 59
Observer, The 151, 184
O'Céileachair, Donncha 35, 43, 47, 56
O'Connor, Frank 35, 40, 53, 96
O'Criomhthain, Tomás 41
O'Faolain, Nuala 50-2, 58, 61, 131, 161-2, 176
O'Faoláin, Seán 35-6, 40, 96, 106, 113
O'Flaherty, Liam 24
O'Hehir, Eanna 24
O'Kelly, Emer 152, 185, 187, 189

Old Man and the Sea, The 136-7
"Oldfashioned" 152, 182
O'Malley, Ernie 41, 153
On Another Man's Wound 41
On the Waterfront 41
O'Regan, Michael 125
O'Súilleabháin, Seán 30
O'Toole, Fintan 53
O'Toole, Joe 157
Outsider, The 118, 123
Outstaring Nature's Eye 196

"Peaches" 146
Pearse, Padraig 129
Peig 118
Phoenix, The 164
Pinter, Harold 126
Plath, Sylvia 99
Playboy of the Western World, The 96, 161
Poolbeg Press 81, 126
Pope John Paul II 156
Pornographer, The 114-9, 126, 137, 148, 162, 164, 171, 175, 184
Possession 138
Pound, Ezra 46
Power, Tyrone 120
Power of Darkness, The 102, 149-52
"Prelude" 40
Profumo, John 57
Proust, Marcel 20, 24, 58, 153, 191
Pym, Barbara 191

Quinn, Colleen 102, 128

Reading in the Dark 107
Rebel Without a Cause 41
"Recruiting Officer, The" 91, 95
Reid, Forrest 35
Renoir, Jean 41
Reynolds, Albert 57
Reynolds, Kevin 167
Rilke, Rainer Maria 35, 40, 176
Robinson, Mary 147
"Rock Around the Clock" 41
"Rockingham Shoot, The" 129-30, 165
Rooney, Mickey 41
Rowe, Marsha 133
Rules of the Game, The 41
Rupert Bear 43

221

Rushe, Desmond   151
Ryan, Bishop Thomas   81-2

St. Patrick's Training College   **23**, 24-5, 27-9, 34, 85, 107, 130, 140-1, 153
Sampson, Denis   196
Scoil Eoin Baiste (See Belgrove National School)
Scott, Andrew   161
Seattle Film Festival   161`
Shakespeare, William   19-20, 21, 41
Share, Bernard   96
Sheehan, Ronan   106
Sheridan, John D.   55
Sheridan, Peter   106
Shovlin, Frank   10, 196-7
"Sierra Leone"   112, 161, 182
Sillitoe, Alan   105
"Sisters, The"   102
Smyth, Brendan   155
South, The   133, 154
Spain, John   189
Spock, Benjamin   93
Stamp, Terence   176
Stephen D   91
"Stoat, The"   182
Stoner   176-7
"Strandhill, The Sea"   53
Streetcar Named Desire, A   41
Sunday Independent   122
Sunday World   156
"Swallows" (dramatization)   104, 130
"Swallows" (short story)   104
Swift, Jonathan   123
Swift, Jimmy   37-8, 53, 113, 121
Swift, Patrick   38, 45
Swift, Tony   37

Tailor and Ansty, The   94
That They May Face the Rising Sun   24, 59, 68, 119, 167-72, 174, 178, 183, 184
Tidey, Don   123
Tóibín, Colm   113, 133, **134**, 153, 154-5, 157-8, 163-4, 195
Toibin, Niall   160
Tolstoy, Leo   102, 149-52
Tom Corkery's Dublin   121-2
Tracy, Spencer   41
Truth, Power and Lies   125

Ulysses   54, 82-3
Updike, John   118-9, 137

Valley of the Squinting Windows   79

Waiting for Godot   24
Walking Along the Border   133
Walsh, Caroline   44, 124, 125
Walsh, Niall   104, 195
Warrenpoint   137
Weevil, Assia   99
West, Nathanael   92, 176
Westby Brian   35
Wheels (film)   106
"Wheels" (short story)   95, 105-106, 182
Whelan, Tony   26, 46-7, 64, 110, 152-3, 186, 191
Williams, John   176-7
Williams, Nigel   138-9
"Wine Breath, The"   112
Woodworth, Paddy   151, 152
Woof, Robert   112
Wright, David   38
Writer's Co-Op, The   106-7

X magazine   38, 45-6, 48

Yeats, W.B.   35, 40, 58, 96, 99, 106, 144, 183

Printed and bound by CPI Group (UK) Ltd, Croydon, CR0 4YY
22/04/2026
02094789-0001